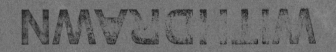

Many Wives, Many Powers

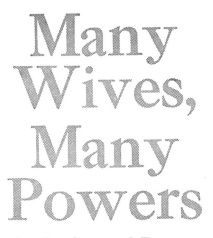

Many Wives, Many Powers

Authority and Power in Polygynous Families

Remi Clignet

Northwestern University Press · Evanston · 1970

Remi Clignet is Associate Professor of Sociology at Northwestern University and coauthor of *The Fortunate Few*.

To Robert LeVine

Les maris sans reproche sont durs à supporter. Ils tyranni-
sent leur femme avec la meilleure conscience du monde. Le mien
est parfois si délibérément méchant que j'en viens à regretter
sa fidélité. S'il avait une maitresse, nous serions deux à le supporter. Tant de choses que je n'ose lui dire, elle les lui dirait
peut-être.

It is difficult to live with faultless husbands. They are likely
to tyrannize their wives with the best conscience in the world.
My own husband is sometimes so nasty that I regret his faith-
fulness. Had he a mistress, there would be two of us to support
his crankiness. She would let him have it with things that I
dare not tell him.

COURRIER DU COEUR, Elle, September 14, 1967

Les hommes y ont plusieurs femmes et en ont d'autant plus
grand nombre qu'ils sont en meilleure réputation de vaillance.
C'est une beauté remarquable en leurs mariages que la même
jalousie que nos femmes ont pour nous empêcher de l'amitié et
de la bienveillance, d'autres femmes, les leurs, l'ont toute pa-
reille pour leur acquérir. Etant plus soigneuses de l'honneur de
leur mari que de toute autre chose, elles cherchent et mettent
toute leur sollicitude à avoir le plus de compagnes qu'elles peu-
vent, d'autant que c'est un temoignage de la vertu de leur mari.

[In these countries] men have more than one wife and the
number of these wives varies with their station in life. It is
quite remarkable that, whereas our wives are keen to prevent
us from acquiring the friendship and the favors of other
women, their wives are anxious to enable them to acquire such
favors and friendships. These women place the honor of their
husbands above anything else and seek to have as many co-
wives as possible, for this testifies to the good reputation of
their husbands.

MONTAIGNE, Les Essais

Table of Contents

List of Tables

List of Figures

Foreword

The idea for this book grew from what was originally an afterthought. In 1960 I was the head of a psychological institute attached to the Ivory Coast government, and I was asked, in this capacity, to make a variety of predictions concerning the educational or occupational behavior of people who were being differently exposed to modernizing forces. However unreliable they may be, such predictions require preliminary assumptions and the testing of some basic propositions concerning the modes of response of traditional African organizations to the numerous challenges of urbanization and industrialization.

We decided, accordingly, to examine the direction and size of differences in the patterns of familial relations prevailing among households with distinct cultural backgrounds and which have been differentially exposed to various forms of social change. This strategy assumes that an evaluation of academic or occupational behavior remains fruitless without an initial assessment of the impact of modernization on family groups. Indeed, familial arrangements constitute the most significant determinants of individual behavior patterns in traditional Africa.[1]

The success of our enterprise depended on being able to

1. See D. Paulme, "Structures traditionnelles en Afrique noire," *Cahiers d'études africaines*, I (1960), 15–27.

overcome two basic problems. First, there are eighty ethnic groups which live in the Ivory Coast and it is obviously impossible to examine how each of these peoples has coped with the forces of economic, social, and political development. Nevertheless, from the assumption that familial arrangements constitute the most significant determinants of individual behavior patterns, we can infer that variations in these arrangements should constitute reasonable criteria for choosing a sample. Familial groups differ with regard to their rules of residence, of division of labor, and of descent. In the Ivory Coast, rules of residence and of division of labor vary both within a given ethnic group and between different groups. In contrast, the geographic distribution of types of descent is more clearly patterned: on the whole, matrilineal peoples occupy the eastern sections of the country, whereas patrilineal ethnic groups are most numerous in the west. Accordingly it was deemed appropriate to compare families with matrilineal and patrilineal types of descent.

The second problem concerns the nature of the strategy most appropriate to an investigation of the potential contrasts in the patterns of family relations prevailing among two peoples with differing types of descent. Our concern was to test the variability of such patterns throughout social space, and it was consequently necessary to interview a large number of individuals. But should we interview males or females? The range of status of African males is rather wide and depends upon a large number of factors. In contrast, variations in the domestic positions of African women are narrower and should probably reflect more closely the dominant structural properties of the different types of familial organization. It was deemed appropriate, therefore to interview the spouses of monogamous males and the senior co-wives of polygynist individuals.

Having resolved these two problems, we were in a better position to restate the main purpose of our investigation. What are the results of comparing urban and rural families characterized by matrilineal or patrilineal types of descent? In other words, given the similarities and differences in the perceptions of their family life by the married women of the two peoples compared, does urbanization lead to an accentuation of the contrasts, or is it instead associated with an erosion of these cleavages and with the corollary emergence of a common style of urban family life? Thus, the chief purpose of the study was to establish the form and the extent of both the convergences and divergences of the adaptation processes of familial groups and actors faced with new environments.

The main results of this survey have been published elsewhere.[2] On the whole, there was a high degree of agreement between hypotheses and concrete observations. Yet it remained obvious that the similarities and differences observed were not always entirely in conformity with our expectations. Up until 1965, I was tempted to believe that discrepancies along these lines resulted from the presence in the various subsamples of a relatively large number of polygynous families—and I must add that all the friendly colleagues who had enough patience to follow the progress of the analysis shared this temptation.

In 1965, however, I started—for some odd reason—to suspect that this explanation was not satisfactory. First, it was still necessary to determine why plural marriage acted as an intervening variable only in selected areas of behavior and interaction and to identify the mechanisms accounting for the differential impact of polygynous arrangements. Second, and most important, I suddenly realized that this explanation presupposed that the consequences attached to plural marriage are universal. Indeed, we are accustomed to contrast monogamy and polygyny as if there is little variability in the internal organization of these two institutions and as if there is no overlap in the distribution of the patterns of interaction prevailing within these two types of familial groups.

2. See Remi Clignet, "Type of Descent, Environmental Change and Child-Rearing Practices," in *The City in Modern Africa*, ed. H. Miner (New York: Praeger, 1967), chap. 10.

xvii

This book intends to demonstrate that these two hypotheses are problematic and suggests that the significance of plural marriage varies with the nature of the cultural and geographic environments in which polygynous families are found. In short, comparisons between monogamous and polygynous arrangements or only between polygynous arrangements rest upon a certain number of conditions which are explored here. To be sure, this exploration is not complete. As is too often the case, a controlled comparison enables the researcher to tame certain demons, but it also opens up a full Pandora's box of other still uncontrolled problems and unsolved propositions.

Thus, this book, by the very nature of the study, constitutes an invitation for further research. All the hypotheses, propositions, and treatments presented here were developed *after* the completion of the fieldwork, in contrast with the basic requirements of a sound methodology. As a result, there are obvious limitations in the research design and in the strategy that I have used. Yet, to a certain extent, it can be argued that these weaknesses reinforce the validity of the argument and that the unintended nature of the whole investigation makes it more challenging.

The completion of this work is the result of the generosity of the Program of African Studies and the Council of Intersocietal Studies, at Northwestern University, and the National Institute of Mental Health, which have financed the gathering of additional information and the completion of necessary analyses.

Nevertheless, if *l' argent est le nerf de la guerre,* as we say in French, it is not the brain of it, and the completion of this analysis also owes much to the intellectual generosity of Professors Howard Becker, Ronald Cohen, Lloyd Fallers, Jenny Ross Hill, Robert LeVine, Robert Mitchell, and George Spindler, who have been kind enough to read various forms of the initial manuscript and to help me clarify issues, problems, and propositions. Similarly, some of the analyses presented here are the results of conversations held during a seminar at

Northwestern University on problems of African families, and they reflect suggestions made by Miss Norma Perchonok and Mrs. Rae Blumberg. Lastly, I would never have gotten through the maze of statistical analysis without the assistance of Mrs. Joyce Sween, Larry Felt, and Don Morrison, who have tamed for me the respectable animal we call a computer. The weaknesses which remain are obviously mine and not theirs.

I remain, of course, indebted to the persons who made possible the initial fieldwork and particularly to Son Excellence Mr. Alcide Kacou, Minister of Public Works, who financed the original research and helped me to obtain the indispensable clearances from various Ministerial Departments.

Finally, I must thank my wife who is kind enough to believe that my interest in polygyny has remained solely intellectual.

Many Wives, Many Powers

CHAPTER 1

An Introduction to Polygyny

Polygyny is a stimulating concept. Depending on our sex and also on our morality, we dream of exotic islands where Don Juan loses his mask of tragic villain and acquires all the attributes of a respectable hero. Conversely, polygyny also conjures up visions of mysterious and desolate continents where surreptitious and sinful traffic forces women into a desperate condition. Our fantasies are so powerful that they superimpose intense colors on our views of the "primitive" world: our vision is rosy when we associate this world with images of pleasurable innocence; dark, when we see in it sin and brutal, ruthless instinct.

But is polygyny a museum artifact, a form of household to be found only in books relating our most remote history or that of societies which still have not been admitted to the delights of civilization?

Beliefs such as these, prevalent in all Western cultures, elicit only amusement from Africans, whose polygynous practices this book will examine. To Africans generally, our marriage practices are not necessarily distinctive: they argue that remarriage subsequent to a divorce is merely another form of polygyny, one less desirable because it imposes on Westerners succession and discontinuity in married life. In addition, Africans maintain that polygyny is a ubiquitous practice which, when suppressed, becomes clandestine and therefore more dangerous. In support of this contention they contrast the role and status of a co-wife with that of a concubine or a mistress. They are as concerned as Westerners about morality, and they affirm with us—but for other reasons—that it is declining.

It is nevertheless true that polygyny tends to be viewed by Western cultures as an instrument for the merciless domination of women by men, and as a socially accepted search for an ever more demanding virility—a search that is allegedly a property of many noncomplex societies and which declines as social and economic development takes place.

Much too often, however, this social and economic development is equated with a weakening of traditional determinants of individual behavior, as if these two forces were absolutely and definitely mutually exclusive. Indeed, there is a deep-rooted belief in the universality of the push-and-pull principle. Certainly modernization requires that individuals become more mobile, it assumes greater mobility and individualization of rights in economic resources—factors which at first glance do not appear compatible with polygyny.[1] The emergence of nuclear monogamous families is said to be a correlate of modern industrial social systems. But what precisely is the nature of this correlation? How rapidly does the "fit" between the development of industrial systems and the reorganization of familial structures occur?

So far as Africa is concerned, it might also be said that modernization requires a certain mobilization of individual resources and energies by central governments, and that this mobilization is made possible by stressing original African values and norms. Since polygyny belongs to the cultural heritage of the African past, it becomes necessary for Africans to decide whether to accept the past indiscriminately or to differentiate between the wheat and the chaff of this historical

1. On this point, see W. Goode, *The Family* (Englewood Cliffs, N.J.: Prentice-Hall, 1964), pp. 103–17.

4

legacy. But how? And by what criteria? Most African governments, so far, have recognized the conservative nature of civil laws whose primary purpose is to sanction the present organization of a social system; they probably fear that any legal innovation in this area is likely to be poorly implemented and might ultimately lead to the dislocation of an already too frail authority-system. After all, it is often claimed that the political control exerted upon familial behavior is necessarily limited in both extent and intensity. A few governments are willing to stake their authority on this issue and have promulgated laws forbidding plural marriage on the assumption that this institution hinders modernization and that forced nuclearization of the family is a prerequisite to any process of industrialization.[2]

But what if their endeavor fails? What if such a policy rests upon a set of unwarranted beliefs that confuse cause and effect? Although the emergence of the nuclear family is deemed to be coterminous with economic development, the one is not necessarily the cause of the other. This does not mean that we want to advocate polygyny. However, implementation of the programs of social and economic planning which we are so keen to export to African countries should, perhaps, be more considerate of familial institutions and, most specifically, of circumstances surrounding polygyny. Perhaps, also, we should attempt to make a more just assessment of the conditions under which familial institutions conflict with the processes of modernization. Yet even if polygyny really constitutes nothing more than another landmark of the African past, irrevocably doomed to disappear, this should not deter us from recording its complexities.

Nonetheless, this brief introduction to polygyny is not only a plea designed to celebrate or criticize the dominant features

2. To my knowledge, there are only three countries which have taken such a stand: Tunisia, Ivory Coast, and Guinea. For the reasons underlying the decision of the Ivory Coast in this regard, see *Fraternité*, no. 286 (October, 1964).

of an exotic and increasingly obsolete institution, nor is it only an invitation to improve our social planning policies toward developing nations. Our interest is scholarly, as well. Any discussion of polygyny evokes, implicitly or explicity, an assessment of the universality of the nuclear family.[3] Up to now, the inadequate character of our methodology, the looseness of our theoretical framework, and the variety of our ideologies have prevented us from determining accurately the variability of the boundaries and functions of this particular group.

The Theoretical Issues Involved in the Study

The concept of the nuclear family refers to the social system constituted by the three following positions: husband-father, wife-mother, and offspring-sibling (if minor and unmarried). Yet, we are not sure whether the properties of this system are independent of the number of incumbents in each one of these positions. Some scholars assume that nuclear families are universal, that they perform identical functions everywhere, and that their boundaries are constant. These scholars expect, accordingly, that the most salient features of nuclear families will be apparent even in the context of polygynous cultures and, within such cultures, in the context of polygynous households. Other scholars challenge this view as atomistic and argue that the polygynous nature of a culture or a household erodes the main characteristics of the nuclear family. Both views are nevertheless problematic, and to decide that families are only nuclear when they are monogamous requires an examination of the consequences attached to the contrast between monogamy and polygyny.

But how should we conduct this comparison? The units

3. For a general discussion of the universality of the nuclear family, see G. P. Murdock, *Social Structure* (New York: Macmillan, 1949), who argues in favor of the universality of this institution, and M. Levy and L. Fallers, "The Family: Some Comparative Considerations," *American Anthropologist*, LXI (1953), 647–51, who are against this view.

compared must be typical, and their relationships with the environment in which they operate must be systematically controlled. To be sure, the roles characteristic of nuclear families—father-husband, wife-mother and offspring-sibling—are found in all human societies. Nevertheless, the individualization and the specificity of these roles depend upon the connections between the family which defines them and the rest of the society in which this family participates. The centrifugal forces which accompany specialization and differentiation must always be compensated by centripetal principles which insure a maximal amount of permanence and stability in interpersonal relations. In the family, as in any other social system, the perception and management of the differences between *you* and *I* are contingent upon the perception and management of togetherness, of our *We*-feelings. Forms of differential sociability and sociability in depth are closely interlocked.[4] Thus, the content, form, and intensity of the reciprocal obligations among familial actors are not independent of the functions and boundaries of the family group; they are, in fact, influenced by the corresponding content, form and intensity of the reciprocal obligations between the family group as a unit and its social environment. Thus, a comparison of monogamy and polygyny involves an examination of both the variability of the roles found in these distinctive family types and the circumstances surrounding the emergence of these institutions. In other words, a comparison of monogamy and polygyny may be undertaken at two levels: on the one hand, we may examine monogamous and polygynous cultures; on the other, we may investigate the similarities and differences between monogamous and polygynous families within cultures which allow plural marriage.

In the present study we have adopted the second strategy. Indeed, we believe that cross-cultural comparisons of familial roles along these lines initially demand the assessment of: (1)

4. See G. Gurvitch, *Vocation actuelle de la sociologie* (Paris: Presses Universitaires de France, 1957), pp. 143–78.

The universality of the contrast between monogamous and polygynous households. This contrast should be constant in size and direction in a variety of societal contexts. (2) The uniform nature of polygynous familial institutions. Their functioning should present regularities across a variety of peoples with differing principles of social organization. (3) The homogeneity of polygynous cultures. Whereas monogamous cultures do not include legitimate polygynous households, polygynous cultures contain a certain number of monogamous families, whose position we must ascertain.

The Dimensions of the Study

The distinction between monogamy and polygyny is significant only insofar as it is accompanied by a differentiation in the patterns of behavior characteristic of the familial actors. We have previously argued that centripetal and centrifugal forces operating within the family must be kept in balance. In turn, this balance is influenced by the power structures prevailing in the family and in the largest system of which it is a part. We have noted that the relevant stereotypes depict polygyny as insuring a merciless domination of women by men. We will therefore evaluate the validity of the distinction thus established between monogamy and polygyny by comparing the domestic power structure of these two types of familial unit.

Yet, domestic power structure comprises three concepts which must be distinguished from one another: deference, authority, and power. Deference may be defined as the ritual expression of unequal relationships.[5] As such it is clear-cut, standardized, and public. The relationship between deference and power must still be ascertained; does a person who behaves deferentially toward another individual necessarily occupy an inferior social position? In other words, is there a consistent association between deference and power? If so, is

5. See W. Stephens, *The Family in Cross Cultural Perspectives* (New York: Holt, Rinehart and Winston, 1963), chaps. 6 and 7.

it positive or negative? This facet of the family scene might be appropriately compared with a stage situation. The deference displayed on stage by a given actor does not tell us much about his status offstage. We might, likewise, be tempted to argue that the power structure of a theater company is dominated by the actors who are most visible and are receiving cheers and boos directly from the audience. Yet their acting is dependent upon assistance from the director, the stage manager, and the stage hands. What, then, is the most significant locale in which to analyze the power structure of this company: onstage or backstage? Similarly, we may sometimes confuse public and private manifestations of power within the familial scene, especially when we deal with a culture alien to our own. Indeed, appearances are frequently misleading. In our culture, we know that the romantic image of medieval ladies does not tell us much about the demands they could impose upon their husbands. Similarly, we know that African co-wives are uniformly deferential to their polygynous husbands, but can we infer from this that the domestic power structure of a polygynous family is characterized by an unequivocal domination of women by men, and that such a pattern is significantly different from that prevailing among monogamous families and cultures? We should not forget that there is a considerable amount of variance in the intensity and the direction of deference displayed by the members of monogamous families, and that therefore the degree of contrast between polygyny and monogamy along these lines is not necessarily constant.

It is important to differentiate between power and authority. To be sure, both are attributes of social relationships rather than personal characteristics. A first distinction between these two dimensions concerns the degree to which they are institutionalized and given the stamp of legitimacy.[6] The concept of authority emphasizes the legitimized processes by which decisions concerning familial actors are carried out,

6. See Paul Bohannan, *Social Anthropology* (New York: Holt, Rinehart and Winston, 1963), pp. 267–68.

while the concept of power stresses the uncertainty surrounding the concrete exercise of decision-making processes, legitimated or not. Thus, the power of a person is defined as his or her ability to direct and exploit the behavior of significant other peoples and is, accordingly, influenced by their uncertainty regarding his or her relevant behavior.[7] The more this individual is vested with exclusive control over the resources necessary to satisfy the needs and aspirations of others, the greater his power becomes, since the dependence of the others on him is maximal.[8] This power, and reciprocally this dependence, are in turn determined by the social circumstances which surround the establishment of their mutual relationship. An examination of the domestic power and authority held by an individual requires an examination of the discrepancies between the models of familial interaction prevailing in his social environment and the perceptions of the relevant familial actors about the actual nature of such interaction.

A second distinction between power and authority refers to the right to take initiatives in familial relations and to the right to challenge such initiatives. While authority pertains to legitimate initiatives, power is concerned with the degree to which these initiatives are challenged.

In any analysis of familial relationships, one of the most important tasks is to determine the conditions which make power and authority coterminous or, alternatively, to assess the factors which lead to a significant differentiation between these two dimensions. There is scarcely any doubt that subordination of children to parents is characteristic of all societies. In this instance power and authority coincide absolutely. Socialization of the oncoming generation—a prerequisite to the

---

7. On the definition of power, see R. Dahl, "The Concept of Power," *Behavioral Science*, II (1957), 201–15; and M. Crozier, *The Bureaucratic Phenomenon* (Chicago: University of Chicago Press, 1964), pp. 157–59.

8. On the relationship between power and dependence, see R. Emerson, "Power-Dependence Relation," *American Sociological Review*, XXVII (1962), 31–41.

survival of any society—can only be insured by a limited group of people. The group most apt to perform this function is the family.[9] Therefore, the power exerted by parents over their offspring is legitimized. The power of parents is additionally reinforced by their ability to use available resources as rewards and consequently as instruments of social control over the behavior of their offspring. However, the degree to which the authority and power of each parent over each child coincides is highly variable, depending on the form and intensity of the relationships established between the parents themselves.[10]

It is therefore necessary to explore the universal and specific determinants of differentiation in the roles of conjugal partners. We know that the actual discrepancy between the relative power and authority exerted by each partner varies specifically with each one of the functions performed by the family group.[11] We know that this discrepancy is a function of the social characteristics of this group: thus, in the United States, both the degree and direction of divergence between the power and the authority held by a father-husband are influenced by the urban or rural residence of the nuclear family and also by the style of life prevalent in the social class to which the family belongs.[12] We also know that this discordance varies with the

9. On this point, see M. Zelditch, "Role Differentiation in the Nuclear Family: A Comparative Study," in *Family, Socialization and Interaction Process*, ed. Talcott Parsons and Robert F. Bales (Glencoe, Ill.: Free Press, 1955), pp. 307–52.

10. See *ibid.* on the distinction between instrumental and expressive roles.

11. Such variations are indirectly suggested in P. G. Herbst, "Conceptual Framework for Studying the Family," in *Social Structure and Personality in a City*, ed. O. A. Olsen and J. B. Rosemond (London: Routledge and Kegan Paul, 1954), pp. 125–37. The differentiation of regions of activities implies variations in the distribution of authority among familial actors and hence variation in the distribution of instrumental and expressive roles; see also M. Freilich, "The Natural Triad in Kinship and Complex Systems," *American Sociological Review*, XXIX (1964), 529–40.

12. See, for instance, R. Middleton and J. Putney, "Dominance in Decisions in the Family: Race and Class Differences," *American Journal of*

11

direction and intensity of the differences in characteristics of origin of the marital partners. For example, the matrifocal character of the Negro family is partly explainable in terms of the high proportion of Negro women who work.[13]

A more difficult task remains: to determine the universality of the forces that account for this potential discordance. For example, in traditional societies it is often argued that the discrepancy between the relative authority and power of the husband-father and the wife-mother only reflects distinctions and cleavages in the roles of husband and wife's brother. To this extent, descent lines are deemed to be a more powerful discriminant of domestic power structures than sex lines.[14] As suggested, most current stereotypes emphasize, similarly, a sharp contrast in the actual organization of domestic power structures of monogamous and polygynous families. In contrast with what happens in monogamous families, the power and authority in polygynous families are supposed to coincide and to be held by the husband-father. The present study intends to examine the validity of this view and to demonstrate that the contrast between monogamy and polygyny requires many qualifications. We will initially suggest that the authority and power vested in individual familial actors vary according to areas of behavior. Second, we will demonstrate that factors which lead to discrepancies in the distribution of domestic power and authority differ widely, less between monogamous and polygynous families than between cultures.

Sociology, LXV (1960), 605–9; David M. Heer, "Dominance and the Working Wife," *Social Forces*, XXXV (1956), 341–47; and E. Bott, *Family and Social Network* (London: Tavistock Institute, 1957), pp. 52–61, 92–96.

13. On this point, see F. Henriques, *Family and Color in Jamaica* (London: Eyre and Spottiswoode, 1953); M. J. and F. S. Herskovits, *Trinidad Village* (New York: Knopf, 1947); and R. T. Smith, *The Negro Family in British Guiana* (London: Routledge and Kegan Paul, 1956).

14. On this point, see M. Zelditch, "Cross-cultural Analysis of Family Structure," in *Handbook of Marriage and the Family*, ed. Harold Christensen (Chicago: Rand McNally, 1964), pp. 462–99.

A Brief Review of Our Strategy

Stereotypes tend to represent polygyny as an attribute of non-complex and ahistorical societies. Yet such societies are not uniform in their political, social, and economic organization, and their differences in these areas are paralleled by variations in the distribution of plural marriage. We intend to demonstrate here that variations in the nature and number of functions ascribed to plural marriage lead to disparities not only in the distribution of polygyny among a variety of cultures but also in the organization of the corresponding familial institutions. Further, since none of the African noncomplex societies has remained entirely free of colonial influences, we will examine how the functions, the diffusion and the organization of polygynous families are affected by social change.

In short, Chapter 2 is devoted to an examination of the distribution of polygyny in Africa and to an analysis of the differing social forces and individual motivations associated with the emergence of such families. This will enable us in Chapter 3 to make some assumptions about the variability in direction and size of the contrasts between monogamy and polygyny and about the variance to be found in the organization of differing types of polygynous families. There are two possible strategies that could be used to test the validity of our assumptions. The first consists of examining the functioning of polygynous families from a variety of cultural and geographic contexts. The presence of a random sample of cultures should enable us to eliminate circumstances which are irrelevant to the purpose of our study and to isolate factors accounting for the emergence of similarities and contrasts between the monogamous and polygynous families observed. The second strategy is an application of the method of concomitant variations and involves examining a limited number of peoples who present both certain identical traits and certain systematic differences in their general outlook. We have adopted here the

13

second strategy and will compare the functioning of monogamous and polygnous families derived from two ethnic groups
of the Ivory Coast: the Abouré and the Bété. We should be
aware, however, of the limitations of this approach. Methods
of concomitant variations facilitate the isolation of conditions
necessary for the emergence of the phenomenon under study,
but do not necessarily lead to an identification of those conditions which are both *necessary* and *sufficient.*

With this caveat in mind, we will analyze in Chapter 4 the
political, economic, and familial organizations of the two peoples being compared as well as the circumstances underlying
their participation in urban structures. This should enable us
to specify the conditions under which our hypotheses concerning the variability of the domestic power structures of monogamous and polygynous families can be tested.

After briefly sketching in Chapter 5 our measurements of
power and authority, we will demonstrate that, disregarding
ethnicity, polygynous and monogamous families are very similar to each other. Does this mean, then, that we should dismiss
altogether the distinction between single and plural marriage
on the grounds that it is not conducive to a differentiation of
the behavior patterns of the relevant categories of family
members?

This question will lead us to examine more thoroughly the
patterns of familial interaction prevailing among the two peoples, and in Chapter 6 we will see not only that there are
differences in the general domestic power structures of Abouré
and Bété families but also that the size and direction of the
contrasts between monogamy and polygyny within each of
these peoples are dissimilar.

Yet, to assess the differences between Abouré and Bété in
this regard does not tell us anything about the origin of such
differences. We must therefore attempt to break down the
concepts of culture and social organization and examine the
degree to which differences in certain selected forms of social
participation exert uniform effects on the organization of mon-

14

ogamous and polygynous families. Thus, we will investigate the impact that variations in the functionality and the economic autonomy of single spouses and senior co-wives have on the position they hold in their affinal group. Similarly, we will explore the consequences that differences in the social backgrounds of these women have on their patterns of interaction within familial institutions. This is the theme of Chapter 7.

Such an approach tends, however, to be static, and it disregards the effects of an ever changing social environment. In Chapter 8, we will determine whether the contrasts between monogamous and polygynous families with differing cultural environments are changed by urbanization and socioeconomic differentiation. We will demonstrate that the significance of the contrast between various types of marriage seems to be greater in an urban and socially differentiated environment than in rural and socially uniform areas.

Having, up to this point, considered only one variable at a time in our equations, we will undertake in Chapter 9 a discriminant function analysis of the behavioral patterns and attitudes investigated and measure the explanatory power of each of the factors that we deem able to affect the contrasts between the types of families. We will be able then to confront again the questions we addressed ourselves to at the outset of this introduction: What is the meaning of the distinction between monogamy and polygyny? Under what conditions is this distinction associated with an unequivocal differentiation of the behavior patterns and attitudes of the relevant types of familial actors? Under what conditions can we say either that there is one source or that there are many sources of power in families with more than one wife?

CHAPTER 2

Determinants of African Polygyny

In our introduction we argued that extant distinctions between monogamy and polygyny require the dominant traits of polygynous cultures to be alike. In this chapter, our purpose is to demonstrate that such requirements are not fulfilled and that there are variations in (1) the distribution of plural marriage among African cultures, (2) the principles underlying the recruitment of additional co-wives, (3) the social, economic, and political characteristics of African societies which practice plural marriage, and (4) the individual motivations which underlie this particular form of familial arrangement. In a last section, we will show how social change affects these various dimensions.

The Distribution of Polygyny in Africa

The distribution of polygyny in a given population presents two characteristics relevant to our analysis: its incidence and its intensity.[1] *Incidence* is measured by the number of married

---

1. On this point, see Vernon Dorjahn, "The Factor of Polygamy in African Demography," in *Continuity and Change in African Cultures*, ed. M. Herskovits and W. Bascom (Chicago: University of Chicago Press, 1959), pp. 87–112.

women per hundred married males or, alternatively, by the number of males married to more than one wife. For the first measure to be useful, however, the communities investigated should be demographically stable. This first indicator of incidence is misleading in urban centers, where the relative excess of men over women and the uneven incidence of singles among the male and female segments of the population prevents distributions of married men and women from being really matched. *Intensity,* on the other hand, refers to the number of married women per hundred polygynous men or, alternatively, to the number of polygynous males with more than two wives.

An examination of the Human Relations Area Files gives us a first approximation of the significance of plural marriage in Africa.[2] Approximately three-fourths of the 136 peoples included in these files are characterized by general polygyny—that is, by both an incidence of polygynous families in excess of 20 per cent, and an absence of special restrictions on the recruitment of additional co-wives. Of the entire world sample, Africa has the lowest percentage of monogamous cultures; Hence, we can see the importance of an analysis of the dominant behavior patterns in African polygynous institutions.

For all sub-Saharan countries, the mean number of wives per hundred married males is 150, but the variance is extremely large.[3] Maximal ratios are found in Ghana and Sierra Leone, and the lowest percentages in the southeastern parts of the continent. Intensity has an equally large variance and ranges from a minimal level of 201 for Bechuanaland to a maximal value of 325 for Sierra Leone, as shown in Table 1.

More important, these two dimensions have remained stable throughout time. The figures obtained from adjacent territories at different points in time are comparable. In the specific

2. For all criteria used in the first section of this chapter, see G. F. Murdock, *World Ethnographic Sample*, as quoted in *Readings in Cross Cultural Methodology*, ed. F. Moore (New Haven: Human Relations Area Files Press, 1961), pp. 193–216.

3. *Ibid.*

Table 1

Incidence and Intensity of Polygyny in Selected African Countries

Countries	Date	Married Women per 100 Married Men	Married Women per 100 Polygynous Men
Basutoland	1936	114	218
Bechuanaland	1946	112	201
Swasiland	1936	168	307
South Africa	1921	112	216
Northern Rhodesia	1947	122	211
Tanganyika	1934	117	219
Kenya	1951	236	283
Sudan	1945	199	253
Congo	1947–48	131–44	224–73
Portuguese Guinea	1950	159	245
French Equatorial Africa	1952	145	?
French Cameroon	1942	152	?
Togo	1931	131–57	?
Upper Volta	1951	190	233
Nigeria	1950	155	237
Gold Coast	1909–39	190–218	?
	1945	160	252
Sierra Leone	1945	304	325
Gambia	1951	184	276

Derived from Vernon Dorjahn, *The Demographic Aspects of African Polygyny* (Ph.D. diss., Northwestern University, 1954), pp. 134–36.

case of the former Gold Coast, the incidence of polygyny has apparently increased throughout time.

Finally, Table 1 indicates that there is no clear-cut relationship between incidence and intensity of polygyny. It would be tempting to assume *a priori* that the number of women per polygynous family declines as the institution spreads among a greater variety of social levels.[4] This is obviously not the case.

4. On this point, see Vernon Dorjahn, "The Demographic Aspects of African Polygyny" (Ph.D. diss., Northwestern University, 1954), chap. 1. In

Principles of Recruitment of Co-wives

Both the incidence and the intensity of plural marriage should reflect the principles underlying the recruitment of additional co-wives. Polygyny should be more frequent wherever there are few boundaries in the definition of the field of eligible additional spouses. Thus, in some societies, polygyny is at least partially due to *levirate,* or "inheritance of widows"—that is, the transmission to the inheritor of all the rights that the deceased testator had in his wife or wives. In contrast, the field of eligible co-wives may be narrowly defined; in some societies, for example, *sororal polygyny,* in which a man marries two or more sisters, is the only form of plural marriage socially allowed. This type of plural marriage tends to prevent the multiplication of polygynous arrangements. It also tends to erase the incompatibilities between the functions of polygyny, more specifically, the division of the loyalties of each co-wife between her affinal group and her family of origin. The common background of co-wives, as it exists in this case, should help to lower potential tensions between familial actors. This leads us to predict that variations in the number and the form of restrictions imposed on plural marriage will be accompanied by similar variations in the types of relationships prevailing both within and between polygynous families.

Only 8 per cent of the African societies included in the Human Relations Area Files practice sororal polygyny exclusively and they are concentrated in the cluster of Bantu subcultures.[5]

---

fact, it has been demonstrated that there was a positive relationship ($r = .85$) between incidence and intensity of plural marriage among the twenty-six districts of the Congo. See W. Brass *et al.*, eds., *The Demography of Tropical Africa* (Princeton: Princeton University Press, 1968), p. 215.

5. Twenty-two out of forty Bantu cultures are characterized by general polygyny; in the southern cluster of these people, five out of ten cultures indulge in sororal polygyny.

Characteristics of Polygynous Societies

Since the incidence and intensity of polygyny are higher in some parts of Africa than in others, it is necessary to determine whether African cultures that are characterized by similar distributions of plural marriage also present certain common traits in their economic, political, and social organizations. The absence of such regularities should lead us to suspect that variations in type of marriage reflect a number of factors, and that, accordingly, the organization of polygynous families is not stable throughout time or space. Conversely, the identification of certain recurrent patterns in the distributions of plural marriage across African cultures would not necessarily exclude the possibility of observing marked disparities in the functioning of these families.

Interestingly enough, although monogamous families are characteristic of modern, highly industrialized nations, they also tend to be frequently found in African social systems whose subsistence patterns are predominantly gathering and hunting. In these societies, the proportion of resources available to an individual declines as the population density increases.[6] Associated with a high density, polygyny would lead to starvation. On the other hand, general polygyny tends to prevail in societies where subsistence is based upon the cultivation of roots and tubers and upon arboriculture. This type of economic organization encourages the maintenance of large-

6. See M. Zelditch, Jr., "Cross-cultural Analysis of Family Structures," in *Handbook of Marriage and the Family*, ed. Harold Christensen (Chicago: Rand McNally, 1964), pp. 462–99. For a more exhaustive discussion of the correlates of marriage type, see M. Osmond, "Correlates of Types of Marriage," *Social Forces*, XLIV, (1965), 8–16, who demonstrates on a worldwide basis that the relationship between monogamy and societal complexity is curvilinear in nature; see also J. Sawyer and R. LeVine, "Cultural Dimensions: Factor Analysis of the *World Ethnographic Sample*," American Anthropologist, LXVIII, (1966), 708–31. It is quite clear that the correlations between polygyny and other variables remain quite low when the investigation deals with a world-wide sample.

sized households and also constitutes a necessary condition to the emergence of any form of social differentiation. It is to this point that we will turn our attention first.

The existence of politically or socially stratified divisions in the population, associated with the transmission of land or other resources, which ensures that a man's children will remain grouped around his own place of residence, favors the emergence of polygynous households. In fact, the relationship between the incidence of polygyny and social stratification is curvilinear in nature. Rare among societies characterized by a lack of social stratification or, alternatively, by a large number of social levels, plural marriage is most frequent among societies divided into age grades or in which a hereditary aristocracy is separated from the bulk of the population (Table 2).

A stabilized mode of agricultural production, however, is not only conducive to the emergence of certain forms of social

Table 2

Relationship between Social Stratification and Marriage Practices Among Selected African Cultures (Percentages)

Type of Stratification	Monogamy	Limited Polygyny [a]	General Polygyny [a]
Complex stratification	22	8	17
Hereditary aristocracy	0	25	27
Wealth distinction	11	8	10
Age grades	11	13	14
No social stratification	56	42	28
Unascertained	0	4	4
Total	100	100	100
N	9	24	103

Computed from G. F. Murdock, *World Ethnographic Sample.* The Horn, Ethiopia, and Moslem Sudan have been added to African samples.
[a] Limited polygyny means that the incidence is below 20 per cent, whereas general polygyny refers to all societies where this threshold is exceeded. Variations in the form of polygyny have been disregarded.

21

stratification, but it also tends to encourage the maintenance of large households and to accentuate the division of labor among individual actors of the family group. In contrast to monogamous cultures, polygynous social systems are characterized by principles of division of labor leading women to carry out a substantial part of the agricultural activities of the household (Table 3). In effect, the incidence of polygyny is positively related to the productive value of the female mem-

Table 3

Relationship Between Division of Agricultural Labor and Plural Marriage (Percentages)

Division of Labor in Agricultural Work	Monogamy	Limited Polygyny	General Polygyny
Division of labor equal along sex lines	11	50	49
Female share of the work greater	0	12	21
Male share of the work greater	56	4	20
No agricultural activity	33	17	8
Work performed by slaves	0	0	1
Not ascertained	0	17	1
Total	100	100	100
N	9	24	103

bers of a group. It might have been assumed that plural marriage would decline with the development of cash economies and that successful individuals would be anxious to invest their surpluses of cash income in assets more readily negotiable than women, but this does not appear to have happened. In societies where subsistence depends upon agricultural production and where such production depends heavily on the manpower available, particularly so on the productive value of women, each family group tends to use its surplus income to increase its labor force—and, more specifically, the number of its polygynous units as well as the number of its co-wives. In short, polygyny is most tenacious in cultures where economic rights to women can be acquired and have a high significance.[7]

The productive value of a woman in turn influences the brideprice, that is, the goods and services which either the bridegroom or his family must pay to the bride's family as a compensation for the emotional, social, and economic loss resulting from her marriage. Since polygyny is most frequent among cultures which invest high values in their female members, it is not surprising that the institution of brideprice is more often found in polygynous than in monogamous African societies.[8]

Finally, the incidence of plural marriage depends on the rules of residence followed by each culture. Where 84 per cent of African peoples with widespread polygyny are patrilocal, this is true of only two-thirds of the societies with a limited rate of polygyny, and of 54 per cent of the cultures which practice monogamy. Influenced by the productive value of women, polygyny is also associated with a predominance of male orientations because patrilocal rules of residence tend to reinforce the loyalties and obligations of a husband toward his own family.

Having determined some relationships between the incidence of polygyny and some features most typical of the African cultures under study, it would be useful to examine the extent to which these features are associated with one or another form of polygyny. Unfortunately, the number of African cultures practicing sororal polygyny is too small to enable us to do so. Analysis of a world-wide sample of matrilineal

7. Paul Bohannan, *Social Anthropology* (New York: Holt, Rinehart and Winston, 1963), p. 109.

8. Of African monogamous societies, 22 per cent are characterized by an absence of any significant matrimonial compensation in marriage. This percentage drops to 16.6 among cultures with a limited incidence of polygyny. Regardless of the form of polygyny that they practice, none of the remaining societies presents this feature.

descent groups, however, has led to the assumption that so-roral polygyny is most likely to be found in societies with matrilocal residence combined with a weak descent group that is not permanently attached to stable, scarce cultivation sites. Under these circumstances, ties between sisters and their offspring are easily maintained, the interests of co-resident husbands are more easily harmonized, and the commitment of these husbands to their respective conjugal groups is increased.[9]

Thus far, we have determined the limits within which the incidence and the intensity of plural marriage vary. We have also examined those traits in the economic and social organization of a given culture which tend to facilitate or impede plural marriage. More specifically, we have isolated two functions of polygyny. On the one hand, plural marriage is associated with social differentiation and makes significant distinctions between certain categories of "have" and "have not" of the particular ethnic groups investigated. On the other hand, this institution may also constitute a basic mechanism indispensable for economic survival. In the first context, additional co-wives are mainly liabilities, but in the second they are additional assets. It remains of course to determine the extent to which these two types are mutually exclusive.

However, the most necessary condition to the emergence of polygynous families in a given society is, of course, an imbalance in its sex ratio; it may be said that polygyny constitutes a most rational solution to the problem of absorbing an actual surplus of females. Our initial task, therefore, is to assess the sex ratio of the populations of African countries.

A high sex ratio may result from an insufficient gross or net reproduction rate;[10] it may reflect discrepancies in the distribu-

9. See K. Gough, "Preferential Marriage Forms," in *Matrilineal Kinship*, ed. D. Schneider and K. Gough (Berkeley: University of California Press, 1961), pp. 623–24.

10. For definitions of these terms, see Robert Winch, *The Modern Family* (New York: Holt, Rinehart and Winston, 1964), pp. 186–87. These

tion of mortality rates by sex at various points in the age pyramid. For example, male fetuses may be more vulnerable to miscarriage than female; or males may be more susceptible to death in childhood or in early or late adulthood. As a matter of fact, the sparse information available on these points in various parts of the world leads us to believe that miscarriage occurs less frequently to male than to female fetuses. While it is a fact that the number of male children born is consistently greater than the number of female births, this unbalanced character of the sex ratio tends to disappear later on since male children are inclined to be more vulnerable to fatal diseases than females.[11] In addition, the hunting, military, and commercial enterprises of males also increase their exposure to death. To rebut this, many scientists argue that only women are involved in the most hazardous of all activities—child-bearing—and that this offsets any increased male exposure to death.[12]

Data available on the over-all population of African countries indicate that the sex ratio tends to be roughly equal (Table 4). For the Gold Coast, Table 4 establishes that, between the turn of the century and 1948, while polygyny increased slightly, the rate of female births declined. In short, plural marriage cannot be explained by disparities in the natural distribution of male and female populations. Such disparities, however, might still be the product of cultural or social factors. For example, massive urbanization of males of a given rural society will skew the distribution of that segment of the population which remains at home. Migrations facilitate polygyny, not only for the stable male elements of the rural society but also for the mobile members of the population who, with an increased cash income, are able to support

---

rates answer the question of how many female children the average woman in a hypothetical cohort of females will bear.

11. On this point, see Dorjahn, *Demographic Aspects of African Polygyny*, pp. 310–70.

12. See Bohannan, *Social Anthropology*, p. 109.

25

Table 4

Sex Ratio in Selected African Countries

Country	Date	Number of F per 100 M
Southern Rhodesia	1948	101.0
Tanganyika	1948	108.4
Kenya	1948	102.6
Uganda	1948	100.0
Portuguese Guinea	1950	103.0
French Equatorial Africa	1948	104.0
Ruanda Urundi	1951	114.4
Gold Coast	1891	118.0
Gold Coast	1948	98.0

Derived from Dorjahn, *The Demographic Aspects of African Polygyny*, p. 267.

two households and two wives—one in the city and one in the village of origin.[13]

If male migrations can facilitate polygyny, so also can female migration, most especially the importing of marriageable women. For example, in a tribal or inter-village war, the women of a weaker society may be captured and taken home by victorious males, who thus artificially augment the female population of their own village. On the other hand, marked inequalities in the amount of brideprice required by neighboring societies may foster variations in the number of eligible women available to men in both groups. The males of the wealthier society will be able to invade the field of potential brides of the poorer society. Similarly, the differential rates of mobility of African males and females are also likely to affect the sex ratio of the marriageable populations derived from distinctive subparts of a given territory or region. For example, the adult population of Upper Volta probably comprises a larger proportion of women than the eastern zones of the

13. Africans are not the only ones to follow this practice. The film *The Captain's Paradise* explains the *de facto* polygyny of some sailors and the difficulties which result from this state of affairs.

Ivory Coast, which attract a considerable number of male migrants. The influence of such factors on polygyny depends, however, on the degree of ethnocentrism prevalent in the societies in question. The extent of this ethnocentrism varies naturally with the various patterns of interaction investigated. Evidence concerning patterns of interethnic marriage and the distribution of the relevant motivations remains unfortunately scarce. In Dakar, it has been established that in 1954 the incidence of interethnic marriages increased with socioeconomic status and, more important, was higher among polygynous than monogamous families.[14] It is difficult, however, to derive long-term generalizations from this evidence, which is limited both in time and space.

It might be interesting to speculate that polygyny reflects a difference in the incidence of marriage for each sex. A large percentage of celibate males certainly increases the number of available marriageable women and thus increases polygyny. But it has been authoritatively estimated that the proportion of adult single males in African populations does not exceed 28 per cent, while that of unmarried adult females is still lower (22 per cent).[15] Neither the low percentage among males nor the limited difference in the occurrence of male and female celibacy can account for polygynous marriages.

A more satisfactory explanation lies in the age characteristics of conjugal partners. An excess of marriageable women can be the result of the difference in mean age at first marriage in both sexes, as well as of the specific mean ages of the people who marry. Assuming that (1) the incidence of singles is equally low among both sexes, (2) there is little variation in the average age at marriage of male and female populations, and (3) the size of various age groups is equally uneven for the two sexes, it is possible to evaluate the surplus

14. See P. Mercier, "Un essai d'enquête par questionnaires," in *Social Implications of Industrialization and Urbanization in Africa South of the Sahara* (Paris: UNESCO, 1955), p. 553.
15. See Dorjahn, *Demographic Aspects of African Polygyny*, pp. 269–309.

of marriageable women. Thus, Dorjahn has established that if, for example, the first-marriage age of women is 16 and that of men 25, there will be a surplus of 26 per cent of marriageable women. If the first-marriage age of women is 24 and that of men 33, there will be a 33 per cent surplus of marriageable females. Yet inequalities in the number of marriageable men and women may also result from differences in the relative number and duration of their respective matrimonial experiences. The imposition of differing limitations upon male and female divorcees or widows concerning their remarriage is likely to affect the over-all number of potential partners.[16]

In summary, inequalities in the distribution of polygyny throughout Africa mainly reflect the variety of cultural norms pertaining to age at marriage and to the respective matrimonial experiences of male and female actors.

Polygyny and Individual Motivations

African informants frequently indicate that polygyny constitutes the most efficacious way of maintaining a high birth rate in their societies. This proposition has been critically examined by various observers and social scientists; but the discussion has sometimes been obscured by religious and political considerations which generally lead to formal condemnation of plural marriage. Thus the belief that modernization of a country necessitates a constant increase of population is often accompanied by the opinion that modernization is incompatible with the maintenance of polygynous families. The organization of such families, it is deemed, does not meet the require-

16. *Ibid.*, p. 299; the additional comments presented here result from private communications with R. Cohen. In this context, we must note a highly significant correlation ($r = .80$) among Congo districts between number of married women per 100 married men and difference in mean age at marriage between the sexes. There is, alternatively, a negative correlation ($r = -.45$) between this indicator of polygyny and the proportion of widowed and divorced among women fifteen to forty-five years old. See Brass *et al.*, *Demography of Tropical Africa*, pp. 220–21.

ments of an industrial system and also has negative effects on the desired growth of the population. It is possible to demonstrate, for example, that fertility of monogamously married women is one-third higher than that of women in polygynous families.[17]

Sterility of his senior co-wife often leads a man to acquire an additional wife. This necessarily affects the distribution of children born in polygynous households. Further, since polygyny presupposes a certain order in sexual relationships between a man and his spouses, it can be argued that the frequency of sexual intercourse per woman decreases, leading to a corresponding decline of fertility.[18] In addition, all African societies are subject to various sexual taboos; and it is obvious that such taboos are more likely to be enforced with greater frequency and for longer periods of time by women who are polygynously married. Given the fact that there is a significant relationship between polygyny and the severity of post-partum taboos, the nature of this relationship remains to be explored. It might be argued that the severity of this taboo leads married males to contract plural marriage. Alternatively, however, plural marriage may lead to the formulation of universal prescriptions regarding the appropriate behavior of new mothers.

The effects of all these factors are convergent and account for the lower number of children born to polygynous wives. Perceived by all Africans as the most effective way to insure a numerous posterity, is polygyny nevertheless destined to main-

17. For a general discussion of the factors affecting fertility, see J. Blake and K. Davis, "Social Structure and Fertility, an Analytic Framework," *Economic Development and Cultural Change*, IV (1956), 211–14. More specifically on the problem of fertility and plural marriage, see J. Whiting, "Effects of Climate on Certain Cultural Practices," in *Explorations in Cultural Anthropology*, ed. W. Goodenough (New York: McGraw-Hill, 1964), pp. 511ff.

18. See H. V. Muhsam, "Fertility of Polygynous Marriages," *Population Studies*, X (1956), 3–16. Yet distinctions should be made between senior and junior co-wives in this respect, and it is, for example, necessary to control the ages of the women analyzed.

tain fertility below a certain threshold? A proper answer to this question depends on the level of analysis selected. A decline in the number of children born of a given category of women does not necessarily imply a corresponding decline in the number of children of a male individual. In fact, a decline in fertility may be compensated for by an increase in the number of potentially child-bearing women.

A second justification of polygyny offered by Africans concerns the complexity of female roles in the society. The obligations of a woman to her husband and his family do not cancel her duties to the members of her own family. For example, in many African cultures a married woman is required to visit her kin group at regular intervals and on special occasions, such as funerals. These prescribed absences lead to the often-voiced complaint of African husbands that to have one wife is to have none, intimating that wives spend more time in their households of origin than in their own.[19] Furthermore, this situation might impose on husbands the performance of domestic chores, such as cooking and fetching water and wood, which are considered female tasks and therefore incompatible with male dignity. Regardless of these strains, females are expected to fill plural roles and, as in many societies, the significance of a wife for the hearth can be contrasted with the importance of a wife for the heart.

Besides economic and symbolic properties attached to female roles, Africans cite other social and psychological factors which influence the size of a family group. If there is no difference between having only one wife and having none, as African husbands say, then males with two wives only are not much better off. The positive effects of an additional wife are too often mitigated by the husband's obligation to mediate in the conflicts and jealousies which arise between the women.

19. As quoted by A. Kobben, "Le Planteur noir," *Études éburnéennes*, V (Abidjan: Centre IFAN, 1956), 128. See also Serere proverb, quoted by Vincent Monteil, *L'Islam noir* (Paris: Le Seuil, 1964): "With one wife, a man has only one eye."

Since three is conducive to the formation of coalitions, four is generally considered the optimal number of co-wives for a man to have.[20]

Social Change and Polygyny

Having established that, on the whole, both the incidence and intensity of polygyny have not varied throughout time, can we then infer that there has been no alteration in the motivations which support it? Let us examine the effects of social change.

Social change implies differential access of the male population to modern residential, educational, and occupational structures and is accompanied by a modification of the criteria on which the social hierarchy is based. Education, occupation, and experience in urban centers increasingly differentiate the positions occupied by males within the social structure. Yet changes in the degree of social stratification and in the routes leading to higher status do not necessarily imply corresponding shifts in the symbolic qualities attached to the various positions in the status system. Indeed, with one notable exception, many observers of the contemporary African scene agree that the incidence of polygyny in cities tends to increase with the length of time spent there and with the higher levels of occupation achieved.[21]

20. See Gaston Joseph, "La Condition de la femme en Côte d'Ivoire," *Bulletin de la Societe d'Anthropologie de Paris*, 1913, p. 595.

21. For a discussion of the diffusion of polygyny in Senegalese urban areas, see, for instance, L. Masse, "Preliminary Results of Demographic Surveys in the Urban Centers of Senegal," in *Social Implications of Industrialization and Urbanization in Africa South of the Sahara*, pp. 523–35. See also P. Mercier, "Étude du marriage et enquête urbaine," *Cahiers d'études africaines*, I (1960), 28–43. See also L. Thore, "Monogamie et polygamie en Afrique noire," *Revue de l'action populaire*, 1964, pp. 807–21. For the diffusion of polygyny in Belgian Congo, see P. Clement, "Social Patterns of Urban Life," in *Social Implications of Industrialization and Urbanization in Africa*, pp. 393–469. For Dahomey, see C. Tardits, *Les nouvelles generations africaines entre leurs traditions et l'occident* (Paris: Mouton, 1958), pp. 47–49 and 63–65. For English-speaking Africa, see K. Little, "Some Patterns of

Social change implies a restructuring of ideology. The persistence of polygyny has been reinforced by the diffusion of Islam, which on this very point converged with the principles of social organization prevalent in traditional African cultures. It should be pointed out, however, that Islamic teaching is not always equated with male domination over women. Koranic laws provide a legal status for women which is often refused them by traditional African customs.[22] Likewise, in spite of its missionary success, Catholicism has failed to eliminate this type of family deemed incompatible with Christian principles.

Even though, during most of the colonial period, efforts of the Christian missionaries to end polygyny have been supported by administrative authority, the institution has survived. In French territories few women have taken advantage of the right to protest their traditional matrimonial status. Theoretically, French citizenship was reserved to African individuals who were monogamously married. Yet this provision has too often conflicted with other sections of the law which accorded citizenship to the most educated and most economically successfully segments of the population, within which many polygynists were to be found. In addition, in the early 1950's the French government decided to extend to African workers in both public and private sectors certain fringe benefits already existing in metropolitan France, among which was an allotment of money to individuals with many children. The

---

Marriage and Domesticity in West Africa," *Sociological Review*, VII (1959), 72–73. For Sierra Leone, see D. Gamble, "Family Organization in New Towns in Sierra Leone," in *Urbanization in African Social Change*, Proceedings of the Inaugural Seminar in the Centre of African Studies (Edinburgh: University of Edinburgh, 1963), pp. 75–84. Against these views, see M. Banton, *A Study of Tribal Life in Freetown* (London: Oxford University Press, 1957), pp. 207ff. See also M. Bird, "Urbanization, Family, and Marriage in Western Nigeria," in *Urbanization in African Social Change*, pp. 59–74.

22. On this point, see Monteil, *L'Islam noir*, pp. 50–51.

purpose of the decision was both to stimulate a natural increase in the population and to satisfy the demands of local politicians and union leaders to be treated as "Black Frenchmen." This lagniappe had the unexpected effect of reinforcing polygyny among the already privileged wage-earners in urban areas. Introduction of this legislation in Africa is an illustration of the inconsistencies which characterize a colonial policy based on "assimilationist" principles that appear to favor at the same time both the emergence of new patterns of action and the persistence of traditional ways of life.[23]

Of all manifestations of social change, schooling of the female population is the only one which has had a negative effect on polygyny and has, thus, tended to contribute to the disruption of the over-all functioning of traditional family structures. Not only have educated women refused to belong to polygynous families, even as senior co-wives, but they have frequently been in a position to force males to change their domestic attitudes and behavior. For example, educated women have repudiated mealtime etiquette which obliges them to eat, in another room, leftovers from meals taken by men. They have challenged the principle on which the payment of a brideprice is based, and they have become increasingly eager to marry mates of their own choosing.[24] Hence, there is a certain amount of ambivalence on the part of both males and older females toward educated women. Male domination is too ancient a phenomenon to be easily eroded, and elder women tend to perceive formal education as a devious way of dissociating oneself from traditional duties. The first generation of educated women is therefore necessarily marginal, and many of them seem doomed to remain single or to marry at a late age.

23. On the general effects of laws on changes in familial organization, see T. Baker and M. Bird, "Urbanization and the Position of Women," *Sociological Review*, VII (1959), 110ff.

24. For a description of the African educated woman, see D. Desanti, "Quand l'africain revient d'Europe," in *Le Dossier Afrique* (Verviers: Marabout Universite, 1962), pp. 156–63.

Summary and Conclusions

In a polygynous culture, co-wives may be perceived as direct (through their work) and indirect (through their offspring) sources of increased income and prestige. In other words, the functions ascribed to polygyny may be instrumental in character. Yet, although they augment the family's social and economic resources, additional co-wives are also a privilege reserved to individuals who initially hold higher than average positions. In other words, the functions ascribed to plural marriage may also be symbolic and closely related to social differentiation.

The recruitment of co-wives, the size of the surplus of marriageable women, the instrumental or symbolic nature of polygyny, and the variety of motivations experienced by individual actors—all these factors should affect the functioning of polygynous families and introduce variations both within and among distinctive cultures in the style of interaction of a senior co-wife with her husband, her family of origin, the other spouses of her husband, and her own children. The next chapter is devoted to an examination of the hypotheses which may be developed along these lines.

CHAPTER 3

Many Wives, Many Powers: A Theoretical Framework

Most polygynous societies present certain common organizational features. Polygyny does not necessarily imply sexual promiscuity or inequality.[1] Wives in such societies have equal rights in certain areas which extend beyond the field of sexual relations; rights and obligations regarding the preparation of meals and other domestic functions are carefully defined and guarantee a certain amount of equality. Co-wives are set up in separate establishments, which enables them to enjoy a relative autonomy with respect to one another, and to their husband. The senior co-wife is nevertheless given special powers and privileges: among many peoples she distributes the work load among other co-wives, divides all monetary rewards accorded to them by the husband, and is usually consulted by the head of the household whenever he wishes to take an additional spouse. It can thus be concluded that the rigid institutionalization of interrelationships among the main actors of the family scene helps to prevent conflict.

1. W. Stephen, *The Family in Cross Cultural Perspective* (New York: Holt, Rinehart and Winston, 1963), pp. 49–69; see also Paul Bohannan, *Social Anthropology* (New York: Holt, Rinehart and Winston, 1963), pp. 105–12.

Two principles which underlie individual interrelationships in Africa and in most of the so-called primitive societies are evident in the organization of polygynous families: subordination of women to men, and subordination of the youngest elements of the society to the senior age groups. Yet, although the system of allocation of authority within an organization exerts a decisive influence on the behavior patterns of individual members, it always presents internal strains which must withstand the challenges of those members. There are, accordingly, differences in the degree to which the system is concretely enforced, and the relative amount of authority a senior co-wife is able to impose on the newest brides of her husband varies markedly between societies and within each society. The sentiments displayed among these co-wives differ accordingly. It is not unusual that "in a well-organized conjugal group, the women usually take turns working on the land while one of them remains at home to cook and tend the children."[2] Conversely, however, it is also reported that "any attempt by the senior co-wife to subordinate the other co-wives after they have established their own households is perceived as an attack upon their positions which should be countered by the claim that they too are women and not slaves to do her bidding."[3]

There is variation not only in the amount of jealousy displayed between co-wives but also in the direction this jealousy takes. While conflicts between co-wives may reflect competition for the favors of the husband, they may also reflect a violation of the implicit solidarity which binds the women together against the husband. Similarly, if polygyny in some instances accentuates the authority of a male individual over various members of his family, it weakens his position in other in-

2. R. Linton, *The Study of Man* (New York: Appleton, Century, 1936), as quoted by Stephen, *Family in Cross Cultural Perspective*, p. 65.

3. E. Colson, "Plateau Tonga" (Social Science Research Council, Summer Seminar on Kinship, Harvard University, 1954), quoted by Stephen, *Family in Cross Cultural Perspective*, p. 64.

stances because his wives are able to unite against him.[4] In short, there seems to be a great deal of variation in relationships within a polygynous household. This suggests that there is a complex network of reciprocal influences between the technical, rational aspects of polygyny and the personal feelings which limit its rationality.

This network can be explored by an analysis of the contrasting aspects of the concepts of authority and power. Authority, as we have noted, refers to the legitimized processes by which decisions concerning the group are carried out.[5] It should be distinguished from the concept of power, which describes a capacity to elicit from another person a behavior not necessarily of his own choice.[6] Power depends on the ability of one individual to direct and exploit the behavior of another and, alternatively, on the uncertainty of the latter regarding the relevant behavior of the former.[7]

Seven factors influence the nature of the power and authority structure of familial groups found in polygynous cultures:

1. Type of descent
2. Functionality of the domestic role allocated to women

4. This situation is particularly likely to occur when the recruitment of newer wives is ensured by the senior co-wives. "You can't trust a man to inquire into a woman's character and industry. Let a man pick his own mistresses . . . but [men] are bunglers when it comes to choosing wives." This responsibility is associated with the development of strong solidarity ties between "great wives" and "little wives," the former looking after the welfare and morals of the latter. See E. Smith Bowen, *Return to Laughter* (New York: Doubleday, 1964), pp. 72ff, esp. pp. 129–30. This account about the Tiv should be contrasted with the account of Robert LeVine about the Gusii, "Culture and Personality Development in a Gusii Community," in *Six Cultures: Studies in Child Rearing*, ed. B. Whiting (New York: Wiley, 1963), pp. 38–44.

5. We will take here the simple definition of authority by L. Broom and P. Selznick, *Sociology* (New York: Harper & Row, 1963), p. 704.

6. See R. Dahl, "The Concept of Power," *Behavioral Science*, II (1957), 201–15.

7. See M. Crozier, *The Bureaucratic Phenomenon* (Chicago: University of Chicago Press, 1964), pp. 157–59. See also R. Emerson, "Power, Dependency Relation," *American Sociological Review*, XXVII, no. 1 (1962), 31–41.

3. Degree of economic independence permitted women
4. Relationships between polygyny and social hierarchy
5. Number of wives
6. Antecedents of the wives
7. Changes of residence and, more specifically, urbanization

We believe that these factors, reflecting the social organization of the cultures in which polygynous families are found, affect the strategies used by the actors of the familial scene vis-à-vis one another and, more specifically, the strategy that a senior co-wife can use in her relationship with her husband, with the other co-wives, and with her own children. We will attempt here to form some hypotheses concerning the effects of these seven dimensions on such relationships.

Type of Descent

The type of descent prevailing in the societies under consideration constitutes the first major source of variation in the relationship established between the various actors of polygynous families.[8] Institutionalization of descent groups leads not only to the systematic affiliation of members according to a specific rule, but also differentially distributes among the members the authority necessary to the functioning of the group. There is not only a line of descent but also a definite line of authority. In patrilineal societies these two lines are coordinate, since both authority and group placement are male functions. In matrilineal organizations, conversely, these two lines are separate: males exert authority in both the domestic sphere and the descent group, but the lines of descent run through women.

This lack of symmetry evident in the organization of matrilineal descent groups has at least one important consequence. Whereas a patrilineal society can forego control over its own

8. All the discussions in this section are derived from D. Schneider and K. Gough, eds., *Matrilineal Kinship* (Berkeley: University of California Press, 1961), pp. 1–27.

female members because this loss is compensated for by the acquisition of great authority over women marrying into the group, a matrilineal society must retain control over its own female members since descent is reckoned through them.

As a consequence, the degree of social absorption of a wife into her affinal group in a matrilineal society remains limited.[9] First, since a woman cannot, through marriage, ever allocate her children to any group other than her own, the only rights transferred by marriage tend to be limited to her work and to her sexual services: in short, to her uxorial functions.[10] Second, the maintenance of strict control over female members by the matrilineal descent group is not compatible with the development of lasting and intense relationships between husbands and wives. The development of such solidarity, which depends upon the number of significant experiences shared by both partners, is prevented by strict separation of their respective economic and social activites. In short, communication between spouses and the resulting authority of the husband over his wife remains highly specific. Consequently, the matrimonial compensation remains limited.

From these contrasts in the organization of matrilineal and patrilineal societies, certain inferences may be drawn concerning the functioning of their respective polygynous families. First, it may be postulated that the domestic power of a polygynous husband over his wives in a matrilineal culture will be more limited than in a patrilineal society, where all female behavior tends to be unequivocally directed toward the satisfaction of the needs of the husband and his family. This implies that the resources of a husband in a patrilineal society

9. For a definition of this concept, see L. A. Fallers, "Some Determinants of Marriage Stability in Busoga: A Reformulation of Gluckman's Hypothesis," *Africa*, XXVII (1957), 106–21.

10. For a definition of this concept, see A. Southall, "The Position of Women and the Stability of Marriage," in *Social Change in Modern Africa*, ed. A. Southall (London: Oxford University Press, 1961); see also J. C. Mitchell, "Social Change and the Stability of African Marriage in Northern Rhodesia," *ibid.*, pp. 316–29.

—and hence his power over his wives—increase directly with the number of wives. In addition, deviances from the accepted model for conjugal relationships remain limited in number. Alternatively, the lack of symmetry which is evident in the organization of descent and authority within matrilineal systems can be associated with tensions between husbands on the one hand and the male elements of the matrilineal descent group on the other. The more women married to one man, the more numerous are the potential sources of opposition to his power. Consequently, not only must the model relationship between husband and wife be more clearly defined than in patrilineal societies, but there must also be greater variation in the degree to which this model is concretely enforced, because of the plurality of decision centers and of idiosyncratic differences in the personalities of the actors involved.[11]

Similar observations can be made regarding the relationships among co-wives. In a patrilineal society, women are absorbed into their affinal group, and co-wives are likely to compete with one another to gain legitimate access to the rewards provided within this group. Conversely, the maintenance of strong loyalty ties between a married woman and her family of origin, which characterizes matrilineal societies, implies that each co-wife will compete with other female members of her own matrilineal descent group to gain legitimate access to the rewards provided in that group. Correspondingly, tensions between co-wives within a given family will remain limited both in number and in scope.

The competing nature of interests of co-wives in a patrilineal society is accompanied by a strict institutionalization of their relationships. Usually an elaborate model defines their reciprocal rights and duties. There may, however, be marked variations in the extent to which this model is enforced, de-

11. Namely the plurality of decision centers accentuates the uncertainty of the outcome of the relationships between the actors involved.

pending on the pressures that each co-wife is able to exert on the other wives as well as on the husband. Since there is less competition in the relationships developed between the co-wives of a matrilineal family, the model for their reciprocal obligations will be less explicit and deviations from that model correspondingly less numerous.

Finally, type of descent is also likely to affect demands made on children. In patrilineal societies, authority of the father over his offspring is complemented by a strong emotional attachment of the mother to her children. This bond cannot, however, subvert the authority of the father, since the position of the mother is one of subordination both in her affinal group and in her family of origin. There is a certain consistency, therefore, in the demands imposed by parents on their children. The situation is much more tenuous in matrilineal families, where the emotional quality of the bond between a father and his offspring may easily threaten the proper exercise of authority residing in the male elements of the matrilineal descent group.

We have stated that co-wives in a patrilineal society tend to compete with one another to gain legitimate access to the rewards provided within their affinal group, and that such competition could well lead them to display aggressive feelings toward one another. Since access to these rewards depends, at least in part, upon the behavior of their own children, it is possible to assume that the aggressiveness of co-wives will extend to their child-rearing practices, which will be influenced by the competitive climate which prevails in the family. Alternatively, the fact that co-wives do not compete with one another in a matrilineal family tends to keep aggressive feelings among them at a minimal level. Consequently, their child-rearing practices will be characterized by a higher level of indulgence than is found in patrilineal societies.

Following is a summary and comparison of patrilineal and matrilineal-societies:

41

1. Authority of a polygynous husband over his co-wives is usually more marked and more widespread in a patrilineal society.
2. Variance in the distribution of domestic power of a polygynous family is greater in matrilineal societies.
3. Competition is less prevalent between the co-wives of a matrilineal society.
4. Competitive relationships among co-wives in a patrilineal society tend to show greater variation.
5. The socialization demands of fathers and mothers are more inconsistent in polygynous families of matrilineal societies.
6. Aggressiveness toward children is less likely to occur among co-wives of matrilineal societies.

Functionality of the Domestic Role of Women

It has been suggested that families may be distinguished from one another in terms of their functionality, that is, in terms of the extent to which they carry out the functions necessary to the perpetuation of any social system: reproduction, production of goods and services, socialization and education, maintenance of order, and maintenance of a sense of purpose.[12] Families of great functionality are those which perform the totality of these basic societal functions. It is possible to extend this concept and to apply it to the various actors in the family scene—most specifically to the role of women. However, the rules determining the division of authority and activity along sex lines limit the significance of the concept and, as a consequence, the functionality of the domestic roles of married women can only be examined with reference to the first three functions: reproduction, production of goods and services, and socialization.

12. See R. Winch, *The Modern Family* (New York: Holt, Rinehart and Winston, 1964), pp. 33ff.

In Africa, the first two functions are closely interrelated since the economic output of a given group depends almost entirely on the size of its membership and therefore on the fertility of its women.[13] Given the strong value attached to fertility by all African societies, the functionality of the woman's role in reproduction is not dependent upon societal norms but rather upon the personal physiological and psychological characteristics of the partners.[14] The significance of her contribution to the production of goods and services, however, and hence her economic functionality will vary with the institutional arrangements that prevail in her society.

Insofar as activities of socialization involve the teaching of economic roles to the oncoming generation, the economic functionality of a married woman is conducive to her educational functionality. However, her socialization functions are also affected by (1) the sex of her offspring—she is more demanding of her daughters than of her sons—and (2) the rules for division of labor and the degree to which the tasks assigned to women and children are identical.

Although the acquisition of a new wife is a privilege reserved to individuals with a relatively high socioeconomic position, such an addition then represents either a new liability or a new asset.[15] The functionality of the domestic role of women will be low in the first instance and high in the second.

In short, a woman's functionality is determined by (1) the number of children that she has borne, (2) the extent of her participation in her husband's economic enterprises, and (3)

13. The less developed a society, the closer the relationship between the economic production of a group and the fertility of its women. On this theme, see E. Shevky and W. Bell, *Social Area Analysis* (Stanford: Stanford University Press, 1955), pp. 10–11.

14. Hence the importance attached to witchcraft as being one primary cause of sterility. This is particularly true of one of the ethnic groups to be compared here. See D. Paulme, *Une société de Côte d'Ivoire d'hier et d'aujourd'hui: les Bété* (Paris: Mouton, 1962), chaps. 8 and 10.

15. See Linton, *Study of Man*, as quoted in Stephens, *Family in Cross Cultural Perspective*, p. 50.

the extent of her participation in the socialization and the disciplining of the children placed under the legitimate control of the head of the household into which she has married. Further, this functionality is maximal when there is no alternative solution to satisfy the corresponding needs of her husband and his extended kin group.[16] Thus, it will increase as the male labor force available to a given kin group decreases and as the pool of still unmarried but marriageable women diminishes.

The first type of situation may occur wherever corporate kin groups are not permitted to exchange potential surpluses of male labor. Bottlenecks in the production of goods necessary to the survival of the society may also develop when the male segments of this society are grouped into rigid age classes, each performing specific tasks which cannot be done by another class. In all such instances, an increase in the number of women married to each male of a given kin group will maintain or reinforce the labor pool of this group, especially when the women are under the obligation to assist their husbands.[17]

The second type of situation obtains among peoples with high incidence and intensity of polygyny.

It has been suggested that the control of a familial group over its members is positively correlated with the number of basic societal functions that it performs, that is, with its func-

16. This reasoning is directly derived from the article by Emerson, "Power-Dependence Relation." For a concrete illustration in an African context, see R. Cohen, "Marriage Instability among the Kanuri of Northern Nigeria," *American Anthropologist*, LXIII (1961), 1231–49.

17. Such bottlenecks may occur in societies such as the Bété, where a young man is neither allowed to cultivate subsistence crops nor entitled to own fields of either coffee or cocoa. It might also occur among the Adioukrou of the Ivory Coast, where operations pertaining to the growth and the crop of coconuts are strictly divided along age lines and where women will assist their husbands in the performance of their tasks. See M. Dupire and J. L. Boutillier, *L'Homme Adioukrou et sa palmeraie* (Paris: Collection l'homme d'outre mer, 1958).

tionality.[18] In other words, it is argued that this control is influenced by the amount of resources that the family can make available to its individual members. As a parallel, we posit here that the domestic power of a woman over her husband increases as the functionality of her role becomes more marked, that is, as the number and significance of her contributions become greater. This increase will be more visible among monogamous than among polygynous cultures, because married males have no access to alternative sources of rewards. However, this increase will still be visible among polygynous families wherever and whenever political and economic factors prevent males from marrying an additional co-wife.

We must still analyze how variations in the functionality of the domestic roles ascribed to married women influences the relations that co-wives entertain with one another. Inasmuch as they are expected to perform a large number of significant duties, an increase in the number of females in a family requires both a more complex system for division of labor among them and a more elaborate system of delegation of authority. Consequently, the individual roles of these women will become increasingly complementary to one another, leading to more cooperation among them.[19]

Last, we must speculate about the effects of variations in the functionality of the domestic role of women on their child-rearing practices. These effects are problematic. Some authors have suggested that, in the African context, women with a high functional role are emotionally cold and unyielding and react with extreme severity to any defiance of their authority by their children. Likewise, these women are inclined to expect from their children a high degree of participation in the var-

18. See Winch, *Modern Family*, p. 29. See also R. Cavan, "Subcultural Variations and Mobility," in *Handbook of Marriage and the Family*, ed. Harold Christensen (Chicago: Rand McNally, 1964), pp. 534–81.

19. See Bowen, *Return to Laughter*, p. 72: "Little and great wives farm together, cook together and mind each other's business."

45

ious chores that they themselves must perform.[20] In short, the functional nature of the position held by a woman is supposed to be conducive to an accentuation of the instrumental aspects of the maternal role. Alternatively, however, it has been suggested that the relations displayed by women toward their offspring depend on the conflicts and contradictions that they experience in the fulfillment of their domestic duties. Women will be unstable in the demands that they impose upon their children when these conflicts and contradictions are high.

In summary, as the functionality of the domestic role of a woman increases:

1. Her power over her husband will be more manifest, particularly in the context of monogamous and polygynous families within cultures characterized by a high incidence of plural marriage.
2. She will be more likely to cooperate with the other co-wives of her spouse.
3. She will be more severe in her child-rearing practices and more unstable toward her children, particularly when her maternal functions lead to obligations which are at variance with the demands imposed upon her in the sphere of economic activities.

Degree of Economic Independence Permitted Women

In the previous section, we have suggested that the position of a woman in her affinal group gets higher as her contributions are indispensable to the welfare of this group. In this section, we are going to hold a symmetric view and propose that this position gets higher as the contributions of her affinal group to her own welfare are limited in number and significance. This

20. See L. Minturn and W. Lambert, *Six Cultures: Antecedents of Child Rearing* (New York: Wiley, 1964), pp. 240–80.

situation occurs where the degree of social absorption of married women in their affinal group is minimal. If such a situation is a dominant feature of matrilineal societies, it also characterizes certain patrilineal societies.[21]

One of the major consequences of minimal absorption of a wife into her affinal group is that frequently she is entitled to have properties of her own and to indulge in independent economic activities, the returns from which belong entirely to her. The concrete exercise of this legal right to escape from the financial domination of her husband depends on the economic conditions which prevail in her society and more specifically upon the strains and tensions which exist in the labor market. The more numerous these strains and tensions, the greater is the number of opportunities for a woman to participate autonomously in the economy. These opportunities are likewise a function of inequalities in the size of the age categories that make up the male labor force, because of migrations, for instance.[22] In turn, both the legal prerogative of a married woman to achieve a measure of financial independence from her husband and the number of economic opportunities available to her influence the extent to which she can affect the power of her husband. The more these married women gain access to the labor market and to its rewards, the less dependent they are upon their husbands. Due to the sharp segregation of roles along sex lines, economically independent co-wives are able to interact less frequently with their husbands and to be less intensely subjected to their domestic power and authority.

Among polygynous families where there is a low degree of social absorption, an additional co-wife leads to a lessening of the domestic burden imposed upon the women already present

21. On this point, see L. A. Fallers, "Some Determinants of Marriage Stability." The Yoruba patrilineal society, with a high degree of economic independence enjoyed by women, is a case in point.

22. Indeed, the migrations of the adult male population toward industrial or urban centers increases the scarcity of the labor force necessary to the survival of that part of the group remaining in its natural environment.

in the household. As these women are correspondingly more frequently able to enter into the labor market, they should be induced to adopt positive attitudes toward newcomers. Further, cooperation among co-wives in this instance should be facilitated by the corresponding decline in the domestic power and authority held by the head of the household.

Finally, we are confronted with two competing hypotheses regarding the child-rearing practices of gainfully employed co-wives. On the one hand, we could argue that the exercise of an occupation prevents these women from maintaining warm and positive relations with their children. On the other hand, however, we could propose that economic success, facilitated by the limited number of domestic obligations imposed upon the female actors of polygynous families, leads these women to have positive attitudes toward their offspring.[23] Yet, it has been observed in Africa that economically independent women tend to be emotionally unstable and irritable toward their offspring, as tends to be true of women whose domestic role is highly functional.[24] In fact, involvement in autonomous economic activities appears to accentuate this latter trait. In short, as the economic independence of married women increases:

1. The domestic power of their husbands diminishes and the social and emotional distance between conjugal partners becomes greater.
2. Cooperation between co-wives increases.
3. Sternness and irritability toward children becomes more marked.

In conclusion, it must be noted that the scales of economic independence and functionality of the domestic role of mar-

23. For a full discussion, see P. Roy, "Employment Status of Mothers and Adjustment of Adolescent Children: Rural-Urban Differences," *Marriage and Family Living*, XXI (1959), 240–44.

24. The Nupe are a case in point. See S. F. Nadel, "Witchcraft in Four African Societies: An Essay in Comparison," *American Anthropologist*, LIV (1952), 18–22.

ried women are not entirely independent. The fact that some women play a highly functional role forbids them access to economic autonomy. Alternatively, however, a woman whose domestic role has little functionality may not necessarily benefit substantially from economic independence.

Relationships between Polygyny and Social Hierarchy

The definition of matrimonial obligations is conditioned by the dominant traits of the social systems within which marriages are observed.[25] In Africa, marriage ensures the transfer of uxorial and, eventually, *in genetricem* rights in exchange for a brideprice. The form and amount of this brideprice depend on the economic activities of a particular society, but also on the degree of social differentiation which prevails, and thus on the relative scarcity of marriageable women.

Such scarcity varies with the functions of marriage. Sometimes marriage constitutes the best way for a given lineage to strengthen its alliances and hence its power over the area.[26] Where this obtains, the eldest male will marry several women from a number of less powerful families, thereby increasing the scarcity of marriageable women and making polygyny a privilege reserved exclusively to the upper segments of the social structure. This upper "class" may be defined in terms of age and seniority, as is often the case in nonstratified societies; or in terms of political and economic positions; or both. Whether polygyny primarily represents a status-symbol without political significance, or whether it also constitutes a means

25. See Claude Leví-Strauss, *Anthropologie structurale* (Paris: Plon, 1958), p. 236.
26. On this point, see G. Joseph, "La Condition de la femme en Côte d'Ivoire," *Bulletin de la Societe d'Anthropologie de Paris*, 1913, pp. 595 ff. The author argues that the political influence of an individual varies in direct proportion to the number of his marriages.

49

to greater political status, societies can still be differentiated from one another in terms of the degree to which an additional wife is merely a new liability. At one end of the continuum, the harem represents an institution in which possession of several wives consecrates the economic and political position achieved by an individual. At the other end, it is possible to conceive cultures in which polygyny exists in all or almost all of the subsegments of the society, thus decreasing in part or even wholly its symbolic properties. In this case, the incidence of polygyny will be the same among various social categories but its intensity will be low. What are the implications of these variations for the functioning of polygynous families?

As the symbolic significance attached to plural marriage increases, the organization of polygynous families becomes correspondingly skewed in a patriarchal direction.[27] In the upper segments, wives are played off against one another. In the lower categories the relative scarcity of desirable women obliges males to seek brides with a background lower than their own. Thus, younger men or commoners in a first marriage can only afford a woman whose brideprice is low, that is, an older woman, a widow, or a woman whose social and economic background is not entirely irreproachable.[28] Because of the status functions attached to polygyny, the supply of eligible brides increases as the individual rises in status within the social structure. This situation may lead to divorce as soon as such men are in a position to exercise greater choice. In societies with a low rate of divorce, increase in the size of the field of eligible brides are associated with parallel variations in the domestic power of the husband, but also with variations in the number and significance of tensions introduced in the relation-

27. See Talcott Parsons, *The Social System* (Glencoe, Ill.: Free Press, 1951), pp. 418–19.
28. See Vernon Dorjahn, "The Factor of Polygamy in African Demography," in *Continuity and Change in African Culture*, ed. M. Herskovits and W. Bascom (Chicago: University of Chicago Press, 1959), pp. 89–112.

ships between co-wives. Because of her seniority, the first co-wife is entitled to exert a certain amount of power over the newest brides of her husband, but this privilege will be limited if her social and personal antecedents are inferior. Such tensions, in addition, are likely to produce a climate of uncertainty in relationships among the various co-wives and their children.

In summary, as the symbolic value attached to polygyny increases:

1. The domestic power of the husband over his wives increases.
2. The relationships between co-wives become more competitive.
3. The child-rearing practices of co-wives are characterized by a higher level of aggressiveness and instability.

Number of Wives

Many attempts have been made by social psychologists to determine the influence of size on the productivity and cohesiveness of the small group.[29] Some authors have argued that the total resources of a group in terms of both instrumental and social skills increase in direct proportion to its size. Other scholars have suggested that a group with limited membership is characterized both by limited resources and negligible differences in the position held by individual actors. The equidistant accessibility to rewards makes all within the group competitors. As a corollary, the greater the competition among members of the group, the greater is the similarity of their activities, and the smaller are the chances for them to reward

29. See B. Collins and H. Guetzkow, *A Social Psychology of Group Processes for Decision Making* (New York: Wiley, 1964), pp. 13–55. See also R. Bales and E. Borgatta, "Size of Group as a Factor in the Interaction Profile," in *Small Groups: Studies in Social Interaction*, ed. P. Hare, E. Borgatta, and R. Bales (New York: Knopf, 1965), pp. 495–512.

one another.[30] Enlargement of the membership of a group, alternatively, demands an increased differentiation of individual roles which, in turn, tends to knit social ties more firmly.[31]

Further, the more co-wives there are in polygynous families the greater are their differences in age, usually. Their respective expectations with regard to the outcome of their interaction cannot be alike, since female functions both within and outside the domestic group vary directly with age. It may be argued that the effects of age differences among co-wives will reinforce the effects of an increase in their number. The resources available to the group as a whole being increased, their use will facilitate cooperation among the individual actors of the familial scene. Indeed, a larger group is likely to be more cohesive because chances of finding individuals with similar sets of values are improved, and because roles required for task completion and adequate maintenance can be fulfilled without additional tensions. It is, in fact, a common observation that there is a negative correlation between the amount of tension developed in a group and its size.

Evidence along these lines is not unequivocal, however. The formation of coalitions, which is always threatening to the maintenance of a maximal level of conformity, becomes more frequent as the size of the group increases.[32] In addition, it has also been observed that the rate of participation in the processes of decision-making becomes more individualized, creating inequalities in the status of the participants. Such inequalities create potential tensions which may lead to total or partial disruption of the group. Finally, marked differences in age of the various co-wives, a function of their number, may

30. See G. Homans, *Social Behavior, Its Elementary Forms* (New York: Harcourt, 1961), chap. 7.

31. See Emile Durkheim, *The Division of Labor in Society* (New York: Macmillan, 1933), pp. 313ff.

32. See, for instance, E. Thomas and C. Fink, "Effects of Group Size," in *Small Groups*, ed. Hare, Borgatta, and Bales, pp. 525–36.

lead to incompatibilities in the distribution of familial roles.[33] The youngest co-wife is quite likely to be as young as the children of the senior co-wife, a situation that is likely to foster tensions between the husband and his wives, among the women themselves, and among the children of the senior co-wife and the youngest brides.

In summary, such conflicting evidence makes difficult any consistent prediction concerning the effect of the number of wives on the functioning of polygynous families. It is possible, however, to tentatively suggest the following:

1. Theoretically, if a large number of wives is permitted within a given culture, chances are very good that there will exist a precise and formal model to define the role and status of each individual actor. Wherever there is a unique center of decision in families with many co-wives, such formalism may be associated with increased domestic power for the husband and increased cooperation among co-wives.

2. Variations in domestic power structure and in patterns of cooperation will be less marked in families with many co-wives than in those with only two co-wives.

3. As the number of wives increases, there will be an equivalent increase in the number of physical areas where familial interactions take place. This, in turn, will lead to a decline in the frequency of interaction of a woman's children both with other co-wives and with the husband. Correspondingly, the family will tend to be increasingly matrifocal in character and the role of the mother will

33. This is an extension of the functionalist argument about the factors accounting for the avoidance of sexual relationships. The more incompatible are the individual roles, the more unstable are the relationships between individual actors. As far as polygyny is concerned, the negative effects of age differences among co-wives have been indicated by S. Falade, "Women of Dakar and Surrounding Areas," in *Women of Tropical Africa,* ed. D. Paulme (Berkeley: University of California Press, 1963), p. 225.

become both instrumental—that is, turned toward the completion of the group requirements—and social-emotional—that is, turned toward the maintenance of a closer relationship among her children.[34]

Antecedents of the Wives

Some societies favor a sororal form of polygyny with its consequent greater cohesiveness among co-wives since they will tend to have common values and norms. It is difficult to assess the effect of this increased cohesiveness on the power exerted by the husband for, while it is possible to assume that power is more marked when conflicts do occur among co-wives, it is also likely that power is easier to exert when there is a great deal of conformity within the group. An observable effect of sororal polygyny, however, is a greater degree of indulgence toward the children.[35]

Another dimension to be considered here is the previous matrimonial experience of both conjugal partners, particularly that of the wives. Divorce creates difficulties insofar as the brideprice paid by the bridegroom or his family must be reimbursed by the parents of the bride. Such reimbursement may create considerable turmoil within a family, where a divorcée's younger brothers might have to forego marriage because resources which were to be used for their own brideprice have been returned to the sister's divorced husband. The father of

34. For a distinction between these concepts see M. Zelditch, "Role Differentiation in the Nuclear Family: A Comparative Study," in *Family Socialization and Interaction Processes*, ed. Talcott Parsons and Robert Bales (Glencoe, Ill.: Free Press, 1955), pp. 307–51. For an example of a situation where a woman exerts both roles simultaneously, see R. T. Smith, *The Negro Family in British Guiana* (London: Routledge and Kegan Paul, 1956), notably pp. 221–28 and 253–54.

35. See P. Murdock and J. Whiting, "Cultural Determination of Parental Attitudes, The Relationship Between the Social Structure, Particularly Family Structure, and Parental Behavior," in *Problems of Infancy and Childhood*, ed. M. Senn (New York: J. Macy Foundation, 1951), pp. 20–21.

such a family might also be placed in an awkward position if he has used available funds in some activity such as a business venture, or as a brideprice for his sons or other male dependents.[36] To avoid such embarrassment or inconvenience for her family, a divorcée will frequently remarry almost at once. Immediate remarriage diminishes her power position by reducing the kind and number of strategies she may employ in her relationship with her new husband, and also toward any bride he may afterward take. Indeed, polygyny enhances the visibility of each female actor and maximizes the consequences attached to the relative position that she occupies in the field of eligibles.

The effects of divorce vary, however, with the importance of the brideprice. In matrilineal societies, the degree of social absorption of a woman into her affinal group is limited. The brideprice is correspondingly reduced, and thus its reimbursement does not raise insurmountable difficulties. Further, in this situation the loyalties of the wife remain oriented toward her own family group, which maintains its obligation towards her regardless of her matrimonial situation. The situation of a divorcée in a patrilineal society is much more unpleasant.

Varying with the amount of brideprice paid to the wife's family, and hence with type of descent, the effects of divorce also depend upon the incidence of this phenomenon and upon the domestic role of the married woman. Divorce will only moderately affect a woman's power position in her new family if her domestic role is highly functional, if she is entitled to much economic autonomy, or if she belongs to a society where polygyny has little symbolic significance. In all these instances, her dependence on the male segment of her affinal group is

36. This situation is likely to occur among the Bété; see Paulme, *Les Bétés*, p. 71. For a general discussion on the relationships between type of descent, brideprice, and divorce see M. Gluckman, "Bridewealth and the Stability of Marriage," *Man*, 1953, p. 223. For a summary of all these problems see M. Zelditch, "Family, Marriage and Kinship," in *Handbook of Modern Sociology*, ed. R. E. L. Faris (Chicago: Rand McNally, 1964), pp. 680–773.

minimal, and changes in her matrimonial status will therefore have little influence on her new domestic position.

Given the strong attachment of an African mother to her offspring, however, it follows that divorce will tend to emphasize such an emotional bond and ultimately to reinforce the dependence of the woman on her children.[37]

As the dependence of a woman and her family on her affinal group increases:

1. The amount of power that a remarried woman may wield over her husband declines, and the extent of this decline will be more marked among polygynous families.
2. Competition with any woman later added to her new family will be more acute.
3. Dependence on her offspring, apparent in all cases, will here be maximal.

Urbanization

It has often been argued that social change makes patterns of family life uniform and induces a nuclearization of the family. Such nuclearization not only implies a severing of ties between the nuclear group and the extended kin group but also a redistribution of the roles of husband, wife, and child, and, most specifically, their increased interaction.[38] This view presupposes that simultaneous participation in modern and traditional organizations is incompatible and that as traditional values and norms lose their grip on the individual, he is more ready to adopt new sets of values and practices.[39]

37. On the significance of the relationship between an African child and his mother, see, for instance, M. T. Knappen, *L'enfant mukungo orientations de base du système éducatif et développement de la personnalité* (Paris: Nauwelaerts, 1962).

38. See W. Goode, *The Family* (Englewood Cliffs, N.J.: Prentice-Hall, 1964), chap. 10.

39. For a discussion of the views held regarding this, see P. Gutkind, "African Urban Family Life," *Cahiers d'études africaines*, II (1962), 149–207.

Yet, familial organizations do follow a pattern of change that is somewhat independent of that characterizing other institutional segments of the society. In fact, increased exposure to new norms and techniques may lead to a partial restoration of antecedent patterns of behavior; as such additional exposure facilitates access to rewards provided by the new social system, these rewards can be specifically used to reinstate and/or maintain a previously acknowledged system of social differentiation. This restoration is nevertheless selective: the patterns of behavior which are restored vary with the nature of the antecedent social structure considered.[40]

It is, therefore, necessary to place equal stress on both the convergences and divergences of the processes of social change.[41] It should be noted that since colonization was imposed and enforced by men, there was correspondingly less exposure of the female members of traditional African societies to European models, and that female participation in modern social structures has therefore been consistently lower than that of the males.[42] In the occupational structure of new African urban centers, there are on the whole few opportunities available to women; and such opportunities as do exist show marked variations in distribution. Both the volume of emigration and the general level of acculturation of the female population diminish as the locus of emigration is further from urban centers.[43] As a consequence, women from the ethnic

40. For this argument, see W. Moore, *Social Change* (Englewood Cliffs, N.J.: Prentice-Hall, 1963), pp. 106ff.

41. See A. Feldman and W. Moore, "Industrialization and Industrialism: Convergence and Differentiation," *Transactions of the Fifth World Congress of Sociology* (Washington, D.C., 1962), II, 151–69.

42. See Linton, *Study of Man*, pp. 324–46. Indeed, female enrollments in educational institutions are systematically lower than those of males. See Remi Clignet and Philip Foster, "Potential Elites in Ghana and the Ivory Coast: A Preliminary Comparison," *American Journal of Sociology*, LXX, no. 3 (1964), 349–62.

43. On this point, see D. McElrath, "Social Differentiation and Societal Scale: Accra, Ghana," in *The New Urbanization*, ed. S. Greer *et al.* (New York: Saint Martin's Press, 1968), pp. 39–51.

groups whose natural settlements are remote from the centers of urbanization do not participate in the labor force as much as those who come from shorter distances.

Regardless of these diverging effects, urbanization also has converging influences on the functioning of familial structures. First, it is associated with a decline in the amount of space which may be used by any familial group. Further, if positions of prestige and control tend to remain entirely vested in adult males, the criteria which determine the socioeconomic station of these males are increasingly heterogeneous, based on both ascription and achievement. There is a decline in the significance of the family as a force in status determination, and thus the familial group itself cannot increase the rewards to which men aspire.[44] At the same time the concentration of many males at the bottom of the occupational ladder prevents them from being able to provide their spouses and children with sufficient resources. In addition, the differential participation of the two sexes in modern educational and occupational structures reinforces the traditional cleavage between the aspirations and expectations of conjugal partners.

As a result, the position of urbanized women is highly marginal. Since African urbanized males are frequently unable or unwilling to participate regularly in family activities, there is a vacuum in the organization of the nuclear family which may be filled by women. These women face an increased amount of domestic responsibilities, without necessarily enjoying a higher status in the society at large.

Functioning of polygynous families is influenced by these converging and diverging features of urbanization. First, the social functions of plural marriage are more limited. In the urban context, additional co-wives are more likely to be additional liabilities than additional assets. Second, polygyny is necessarily less uniformly normative than in a rural environment. Thirdly, decline in the amount of domestic space is

44. See Smith, *Negro Family in British Guiana*, pp. 221–28.

going to be particularly apparent in this type of family and the chances for conflict between the co-wives are increased accordingly. Lastly, the widening of both social and emotional distance between conjugal partners should be most visible in this particular type of household. In short, of all urbanized females, co-wives of polygynous households should have the most marginal position.

The intensity of the effects of urbanization in this regard would seem to depend, however, upon two sets of factors. First, as the distance between urban centers and the locus of emigration of a married woman diminishes:

1. Polygyny should increase her chance of participating in the labor force, thereby enhancing her domestic power over her husband.
2. Polygyny should enable her to maintain frequent contacts with her own family of origin and to get from it the social and emotional support that she needs in an uncertain and ever changing environment.
3. If the shortage of space induces her to compete with the other co-wives of her husband, she is also more induced to cooperate with them, insofar as both her participation in the labor force and her absence from her husband's residence depend upon their good will.
4. Polygyny will emphasize the inconsistencies of the demands exerted on her children. Her reaffirmed contacts with her own family of origin will expose her children to the conflicting demands of their maternal and paternal relatives. In addition, her involvement in the labor market will lead her to be more severe and more unstable in her child-rearing practices. Finally, this involvement in the labor market will also be accompanied by an increase in the number of socialization agents.

Secondly, we can hold the distance between urban centers and locus of emigration as a constant and examine the effects of an increased social differentiation on the degree of social absorption of the various co-wives examined. In effect, as urbanization both increases the economic marginality of married males and reduces accordingly the effective degree of dependence of a woman on her husband and his family, we see the following:

1. Her power over her husband will be reinforced.
2. Her cooperation with the other spouses of her husband will be heightened. Indeed, their competition becomes dysfunctional since the rewards to which they aspire are no longer provided by their husbands but rather by independent sources, notably their respective families of origin.
3. Her relationships with her children will tend to be both emotional and instrumental. Indeed, the decline in the significance of the domestic role held by her husband obliges her to be more demanding of her children and to anticipate that her dependence upon them will ultimately be greater. At the same time, her children constitute the primary source of emotional rewards that she can obtain in this new environment.

Thus far, in each situation examined we have permitted only one variable at a time, maintaining all other factors as constants. In actuality, these dimensions may have conflicting effects, since they are not necessarily proceeding in parallel directions. Polygynous societies may present organizational features whose implications are not necessarily consistent. Our next task is therefore to integrate the exploration of all these dimensions into a common and dynamic framework, so that our seven major sets of hypotheses may be tested in a concrete environment. For this purpose, we will compare the functioning of monogamous and polygynous families of two ethnic groups of the Ivory Coast: the Abouré and the Bété. Since these two peoples present a certain number of systematic similarities and differences, we should be able to eliminate the factors which are irrelevant to a distinction between differing types of marriage and to scale the relative significance of the forces which affect this distinction.

CHAPTER 4

The Abouré and the Bété

The Ivory Coast constitutes a particularly favorable area for undertaking systematic comparisons, since it has the approximate shape of a square 400 miles on a side, and it can therefore be easily divided into a variety of equal-sized regions.

Geographically, it is nicely differentiated with a variety of climates. Whereas rainfall averages 80 inches per year in coastal areas, the rate of precipitation drops consistently as one moves north from the coast, to fall below 40 inches per year in the northern sections of the country. Accordingly, there are marked contrasts in the types of vegetation which cover the various regions. The rain-forest zones which are found in the southern areas of the Ivory Coast decline in size as one leaves the coast and are progressively replaced by savanna in the north. (See Figure 1.)

The Bandama River divides the Ivory Coast into two regions with distinctive types of social organization. On the eastern bank, the majority of tribes have come from nearby Ghana and their organization is matrilineal. On the western bank, the majority of peoples have emigrated from nearby Liberia and follow patrilineal rules of descent. (See Figure 2.) Patterns of economic organization further differentiate these two sections. Whereas the eastern section includes mainly fish-

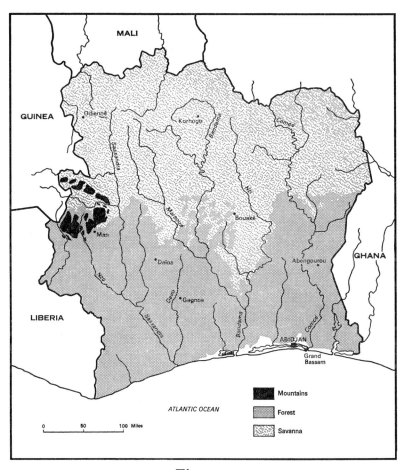

Figure 1
Ivory Coast

ermen and semi-settled farmers, many peoples of the western zone were originally warriors and hunters. This contrast implies, in turn, differences in types of settlements. In the eastern areas, villages are relatively densely populated, whereas there are large variations in the population distribution of the western zone, with a general tendency toward small settlements (Table 5).

63

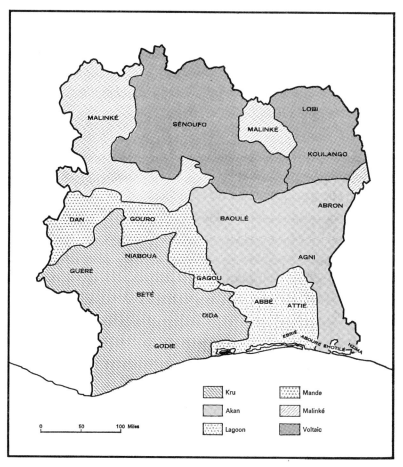

Figure 2
Ethnic Composition of the Ivory Coast

The traditional political profiles of the various components of the Ivory Coast are similarly contrasted. The political complexity of the eastern ethnic groups seems to decline as one moves northward from the coastal region; the opposite is true insofar as western tribes are concerned. The cluster of Kru peoples is politically segmented and does not present a variety of social categories with differentiated functions. In contrast,

Table 5

Distribution of Villages by population in Western and Southern Sections of Ivory Coast (Percentages)

Village Population	South (including the Abouré)	West (including the Bété)
0–99	11.3	13.2
100–299	38.2	46.3
300–599	27.6	31.4
600–1199	12.6	7.8
1200–9999	10.3	1.3
Total	100.0	100.0
N	914	936

Derived from *Côte d'Ivoire: Population 1965* (Paris, 1967), p. 37.

the Malinke of the Odienné district in the northwest are integrated within a large-scale political organization with distinctive castes which are engaged in a variety of economic and social activities.

The fact that the French colonial influences have not been exerted everywhere at the same time and/or with an equal intensity constitutes another facet of the contrast between the eastern and western regions. Contacts were established with the eastern coastal regions during the first three decades of the nineteenth century; the western zone was not really colonized before the end of the first decade of the twentieth century. In fact, resistance to French penetration persisted in the central and western parts much longer than in any other part of the country. Furthermore, the techniques of colonization have varied. In the east, French colonial authorities were eager to increase the production of cash crops by local farmers. They were accordingly willing to favor the importation by these farmers of unskilled manpower from the northern areas of the Ivory Coast or even from Upper Volta. They decided also to encourage this type of farming by stimulating competition between local ethnic groups and peoples alien to the area for a more productive use of the land available. In contrast, in the central and western zones colonial authorities encouraged the implantation of large-scale European-owned plantations. Local farmers consequently became unable to find the additional labor which they needed to increase the size of their agricultural enterprises. The unfavorable terms of this competition against large-scale plantations often obliged them either to migrate or to hire themselves out to these European concerns.

In summary, the different regions of the Ivory Coast can be distinguished from one another in terms of (1) climate and vegetation, (2) type of descent, (3) traditional political organization, and (4) exposure to modernization and patterns of economic exploitation. The present comparison is concerned with an examination of two peoples: the matrilineal Abouré of the southeastern part of the country and the patrilineal Bété of the southwest. Analysis of the distinctive traits of each of these two tribes will enable us to determine which factors can be used as constants, that is, which factors are irrelevant to the distinction between monogamy and polygyny. Alternatively, we should be able to analyze which differences in the organization of these peoples are associated with variations in the dominant traits of their monogamous and polygynous households. Initially, we will examine the traditional environment of each one of these peoples; we will thereafter investigate the circumstances of their participation in urbanization.

The Abouré

The Abouré are presently located in the immediate hinterland of the former capital of the Ivory Coast, Grand Bassam. This is a flat land crossed by two relatively important rivers: the Comoe and the Mee, and it is divided by various lagoons in a maze of islands of various size.

Like their neighbors, the Agni, the Abouré come from Ghana and were originally attached to the cluster of Akan-speaking peoples. According to local myths and legends, the Abouré once constituted a part of an important Ashanti kingdom, but decided to emigrate when the taxes levied upon them by the king became unbearable. Migration toward their present setting involved three successive steps. The first one brought them from Ghana to a place called Ebobo, where another fugitive people, the Ehotilé, who settled there during the early part of the eighteenth century, had preceded them. The Abouré sought the protection of this people against the numerous acts of warfare carried out by the nearby Nzima. Later, Abouré leaders deemed outrageous the price demanded for this protection and decided to move westward into the area of Adiaké. There, continuous conflicts with both Ehotilé and Agni forced them to move once more in a southwestwardly direction. The third step of their migrations brought them to their ultimate settlement, around Bonoua, to a place where they could practice both agricultural and fishing activities [1] (Figure 3). Although the main features of their social organization do not differ from those of Ehotilé and Agni peoples, historical factors seem to explain the hostile sentiments which oppose these various tribes to one another. To a large extent, Abouré feel that they have been deprived of their natural assets by their more powerful neighbors.

Political Organization

This people, numbering between 12,000 and 18,000, is divided into three subgroups.[2] The largest of these subgroups, the *Ehiwe,* occupies seven villages and hamlets scattered around Bonoua, whose population today exceeds 5,000 inhabitants. Originally engaged in the cultivation of palm trees, this sub-

1. See G. Rougerie, "Les Pays Agnis du sud est de la Côte d'Ivoire forestiere," *Etudes éburnéennes,* VI (1957), 55–57.

2. The arguments developed from here on are summarized from G. Niangoran Bouah, "Le Village Aburé," *Cahiers d'études africaines,* I (1960), 113–27.

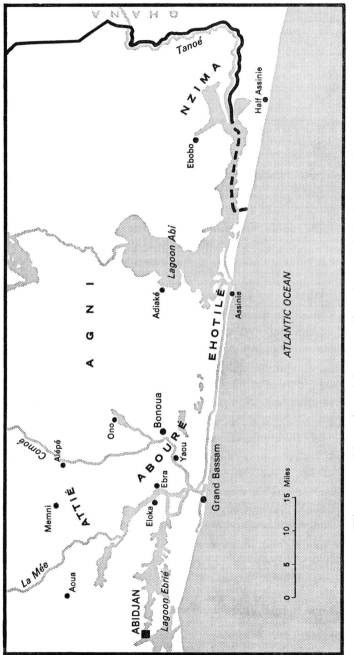

Figure 3 Abouré and Surrounding Areas of the Ivory Coast

group has progressively abandoned this activity to become involved in the cultivation of industrial products: coffee, cocoa and pineapple. The *Ehe,* whose most important village is Yaou, are settled between Bonoua and Mossou. This group, which initially specialized in military functions, includes 3,000 individuals. The last subgroup, the *Ossuom,* comprises fewer than 2,000 individuals grouped in one single village, Ebra, where the bulk of the population has always been engaged in fishing activities. In short, Abouré peoples are characterized by both the densely populated character of their villages and the relative diversity of their occupational organization.

These three subgroups were independent of one another. Each had its own political organization directed by a king who was subject to a complex system of checks and balances exerted by a council comprised of the headmen of the seven founding families (*mendres*). Each one of these subgroups was divided into four social categories: (1) The *Edye* included all individuals able to trace their affiliations back to the seven forefathers of the village. All these individuals had equal rights and participated extensively in all decisions pertaining to the welfare of the community. (2) The *Ohopwe* were all individuals alien to the original community. They could settle in a village only after having been granted permission by an older member of one of the original families. The offspring of an Edye female and of an Ohopwe male remained Edye; conversely, a child born of an Ohopwe woman remained Ohopwe himself but was entitled to demand his affiliation to a given family which would insure his protection. (3) The *Kaha* included all the slaves. Although they participated in the various age and familial groups, individuals of this category could not occupy any position of authority. The high female-male ratio of this component of the Abouré population was probably the result of the high value attached to the child-bearing properties and economic activities of female individuals. (4) The *Appoliens* included the offspring of all Kaha individuals. Unlike Kahas, individuals placed in this category could assume important responsibilities in the familial group. Like the Kaha, however, they were not entitled to hold leadership in a given age group. The most important feature of this categorization is the fact that, among the Abouré, slaves had to be recruited from the outside.

The division of Abouré into age groups took place within a collective cycle which was completed when the members of a whole generation fell below a certain number. At the onset of each cycle, adult males were placed into one of the four age groups in which roles were clearly defined. First, these age groups performed military functions: in war time the eldest (above age 60) was in charge of administering the village. A second group (45 to 60 years of age) had defensive functions and was supposed to ensure the protection of the village. Younger groups (25 to 45 years of age) assumed offensive responsibilities, while the junior members of the cycle (under 25) were asked to provide the army with food and equipment and to take care of the wounded. The various age groups also had economic functions, and members of the same category were expected to help one another, for instance, in the clearing of new patches of land for cultivation. Age groups also played social roles; members of the same group contributed to the expenses for the burial of one of their peers. Similarly, they owed one another financial support in case of sickness, when the services of a medicine man were needed. Finally, they were involved in the negotiations pertaining to the divorce or re-marriage of any of their peers. The socioeconomic solidarity which used to bind together the members of a given age group remains partly evident today. Among the Abouré, as among many other African peoples, members of the same age class often pool their individual resources, which each person can then utilize in turn.

Each generation elected its own headman who was con-firmed in his function by the ultimate approval of his own kin group. This procedure was essential, because this headman was asked to act as a mediator among *mendres* when they deadlocked over an important issue needing resolution.

Each change of generation was accompanied by the reconstruction of the village. The necessity of periodically renewing the territorial organization of a community did not raise any difficulties so long as houses were built of light material. The increased use of concrete and the differentiation in construction styles which have accompanied the introduction of a cash economy have multiplied the tensions and strains between generations. Since disparity in the level of economic success quite markedly follows age lines, complementarity between generations has declined, while solidarity between age peers seems to have enabled many individuals to resist the disruptive forces associated with social and economic change.

Each village stretches in an east-west direction. Each contains two distinct neighborhoods called *Kumassi* and *Begnini,* appellations which are probably a part of the Ghanaian legacy of this people. On the whole, Abouré villages are a necklace of compounds with restricted access to the common grounds of the village. Although evidence is scanty on this particular point, it appears that Abouré generally tend to follow patrilocal rules of residence. In the past, each individual had two residences: (1) The *opukoble,* the house of the headman of the patriclan, was the place for ceremonies devoted to the cult of ancestors and the place where the whole clan gathered when its members were confronted with issues of collective interest. (2) The *opuko,* the residence of the head of each lineage, comprised a minimum of two houses: one with kitchen facilities for the women, and one for the men. The nuclear family had no individualized residence.

The Economic Organization of the Abouré

In their economic organization, the Abouré represent a combination of the two polar types found among the cluster of Akan-speaking peoples. Like the Ashanti, they are known as good farmers and valiant warriors. Like the Nzimas, they are

71

considered daring sailors and efficient fishermen.[3] With social change, the importance of a cash-crop economy has increased, and today agriculture constitutes the predominant livelihood for the inhabitants of Abouré villages. The Abouré face the same difficulties in their farming enterprises as their neighbors, the Agni. Although entrepreneurial in their orientation, they are limited in their progress by the scarcity of land. As a result, in the most recent decades they have tended to locate their culture hamlets farther and farther away from their place of origin; thus, the number of Abouré farmers in the Adiaké area keeps growing.

Agricultural production in the Abouré region is highly diversified. Farmers are assisted by unskilled laborers coming from Upper Volta. Many of these farmers use their profits to enlarge the size of their holdings, to modernize their equipment, to increase the size of their labor force, or to invest in commercial, industrial, or housing concerns. Like the Agnis, the Abouré are indeed shrewd financial operators.[4] They have increasingly abandoned the cultivation of subsistence products to their wives, who often receive assistance from unskilled laborers hired for preparing or harvesting cash crops.

The high level of Abouré participation in a cash-crop economy is paralleled by the high level of their participation in formal schooling.[5] There are at least two reasons for this: The first public school opened by French colonial authorities was located in Assinie, only twenty miles from Bonoua. This

3. See Rougerie, "Les Pays Agnis," pp. 83 and 121–22.

4. *Ibid.* See also A. Kobben, "Le Planteur noir," *Études éburnéennes*, V (1956), chaps. 5 and 8. The organization of Agni farms is treated in a comparative perspective by Marguerite Dupire, "Planteurs autochtones et étrangers en basse Côte d'Ivoire orientale," *ibid.*, VIII (1960), pt. 3.

5. See *Supplement trimestriel au bulletin mensuel de statistiques* Vol. I (Abidjan: Ministere des Affaires Economiques, des Finances et du Plan, 1961), for an analysis of primary school enrollments by area. These results are not given by ethnic groups, but it is still quite obvious that the area of Grand Bassam which is predominantly populated by Abouré has one of the highest enrollment rates in the entire country.

school was opened in 1886 and at least four generations have therefore already had a primary education. This span of time is large enough to make the Abouré aware of the processes of individual upward mobility engendered by primary schooling. They have accordingly increased their participation in educational structures, and today the background of the average Abouré student's parents is quite similar to the mean socioeconomic profile of the entire Abouré population. In addition, the size of school enrollments has certainly been influenced by the proximity of Abidjan and its important labor market. Increases in school enrollment have in turn contributed to a marked diversification in the occupational profile of the peoples of the southeastern section of the country.

Family Organization

Like the Ashanti, the Abouré believe that two elements necessarily enter into the development of the human embryo; spirit is provided by the father and blood by the mother. Thus, certain taboos and certain technical crafts are transmitted along paternal lines. Placement of the individual along maternal lines is, however, the most significant determinant of his role and obligations. The transmission of assets and of status follows the lines of blood, that is, the structure of the matrilineal descent group.[6]

Domestic relationships reflect the pre-eminence of this latter descent group. Matrimonial negotiations involve the participation of the bride's maternal uncle, who is the recipient of a large part of the brideprice. The loyalties of the bride after her marriage remain directed toward her own family. Her ties with her brothers, particularly with the eldest, remain very strong, since her offspring will be his heirs and will be bound by various obligations toward him as soon as they reach adulthood. Uxorial rights transmitted by marriage remain limited,

6. G. Niangoran Bouah, Études sur les Aburés, personal communication to the author.

73

because Abouré wives are entitled to engage in economic activities on their own and are therefore characterized by a low level of dependence on their husbands. Their income, derived mostly from the sale of subsistence products and, more recently, cash crops, is increased by their participation in additional trading activities.

The low level of absorption of the wife into her affinal group is associated with the payment of a limited brideprice by the bridegroom or his family. In 1958 this brideprice did not exceed 2000 francs ($8) in the Mossou area and was often limited to 25 francs (10¢) in the region of Bonoua (perhaps because at the beginning of the colonial period this sum was a silver coin). The symbolic components of this brideprice (gin and palm wine) tend to be more important than the speculative exchanges of cash which accompany marriage among many West African peoples.

Low degree of social absorption and low value of the brideprice are often associated with a high level of divorce.[7] Indeed, Abouré follow this particular pattern. Of all marriages concluded in Mossou between 1945 and 1955, only 5 per cent were still undissolved in 1958. Almost one-half of the brides married during this period were involved in a third marriage in 1958; 29 per cent were married for the second time; and 8 per cent, although divorced, had not yet remarried.

The observance of patrilocal rules of residence is accompanied by the subordination of the bride to the various members of her affinal group. For example, she must assist her mother-in-law with domestic chores and must participate in the mourning ceremonies following the death of an affine. This subordination, however, is limited in both scope and intensity. The solidarity between the bride and her family is in fact much

7. For a full discussion of this point, see L. Fallers, "Some Determinants of Marriage Stability in Busoga: A Reformulation of Gluckman's Hypothesis," *Africa*, XXVII (1957), 106–21. See also D. Schneider, "A Note on Bridewealth and the Stability of Marriage," *Man*, 1953, pp. 54–58.

greater than that between the bride and her mate. For example, at the time of marriage most Abouré families provide their daughters with a dowry of pots and pans, which not only reflects the sharpness of division of labor along sex lines but also the obligation of the bride's family to participate in those duties incumbent upon the bride herself. In contrast, the bridegroom rarely offers a wedding present to his betrothed.

The circumstances surrounding the delivery of a child constitute another example of the social distance between conjugal partners. Whenever a woman endures a painful childbirth, her husband is called to assist her. Should he fail to facilitate the delivery, this is a sign that the child is illegitimate. The wife must confess the name of her lover, who will then have to take care of her and her child. Even in less dramatic circumstances, the orientations of the conjugal partners toward children are at variance. Women prefer to have female children who will increase the size of their matriclan, while their husbands would rather they have male children. Furthermore, as in other matrilineal societies, latent inconsistencies in the orientations of both partners lead to difficulties in bringing up these children. Although a child is affiliated with his maternal descent group through his maternal uncle, he is raised by his father, and his early socialization is often taken care of by his paternal grandparents, uncles, and aunts.

Currently, marriage cannot take place without the consent of the bride. After her first menstruation a young girl is washed and groomed by her age mates. After her third menstruation she is confined for a week and then becomes marriageable. Any child born before official puberty rites will be illegitimate and will be given away to a childless family. The determination of a male's marriageability is more informal. There is no ceremony marking his coming of age, and his adulthood is socially recognized when he is able to fully participate in agricultural tasks and build a house.

Marriage does not involve the bride's moving immediately

to her husband's residence. She must first take leave of her own family; this is an opportunity for her maternal grandmother to express symbolically the similarity of their respective fates and their ensuing solidarity. The maternal grandmother gives the bride a hen; the number of chickens hatched by this hen will indicate the number of children that the newly married woman will have. Indeed, fertility is crucial in determining the outcome of marital relationships. Members of a woman's matrilineal descent group are entitled to ask for a divorce if the marriage is childless after eighteen months.

Polygyny is not a rare institution among the Abouré. In 1958 almost one-third of married women in Mossou were married to polygynist individuals. However, the intensity of plural marriage was limited, and more than 80 per cent of women married to polygynist husbands had only one co-wife. The motivations underlying polygyny in this society are varied. Abouré males are anxious to have as many male children as possible, often believing that this goal can be achieved through an increase in the number of women they marry. Second, these males are not entitled to resume sexual relations with a wife before the end of a three-year period following her last childbirth. Although nowadays this obligation is less frequently fulfilled, it is still invoked as a motive for plural marriage. Finally, polygyny is a mark of prestige about which many males are sensitive. Because of the low degree of social absorption accompanying marriage, an additional wife is not an extra source of labor among this people, but she remains, however, a sign of wealth enhancing the status position that an individual occupies within his community. The relatively high level of economic development of this people leads the Abouré male individuals to contract plural marriage more frequently than their counterparts from the nearby and similar Agni area. No less than 45 per cent of the women interviewed in rural areas in the course of this survey were married to polygynist individuals; in a sample of Agni farmers from the

Bongouanou area, the corresponding figure was only 25 per cent.[8]

There are few restrictions on the recruitment of additional co-wives. As in most polygynous cultures, the senior co-wife must be consulted. In fact, she is entitled to occupy a position of authority over the additional spouses acquired later by her husband. On the whole, however, relationships between co-wives are friendly and cooperative. The cultural model underlying their interaction is that of the bond between sisters of varying age.

The Bété

The Bété belong to the Kru cluster which occupies the western part of the Ivory Coast and the eastern part of Liberia. Numbering 184,000 inhabitants, the Bété are scattered among the districts of Gagnoa, Daloa, and a part of the district of Sassandra. (See Figure 4.) The overall population density of this section of the Ivory Coast is very low. Averaging 8 inhabitants per square kilometer, it is less than one-third of that observable in the Grand Bassam area where the Abouré are concentrated. This pattern of settlement reflects the original inhospitability of the rainforests which even today cover a large part of the three districts.

Political Organization

Originally the political organization of the Bété was highly segmented. The most important part of social relationships has always been dominated by kinship organization, a feature which results from the scattered territorial organization of

8. See *Enquête nutrition niveau de vie: subdivision de Boungouanou* (Abidjan: Service de la Statistique, 1958), p. 32. Variations in the figures given here raise the whole question of the variability of the patterns of marriage for a given ethnic group. Of course, this variability can hardly be assessed by the traditional methods of ethnography.

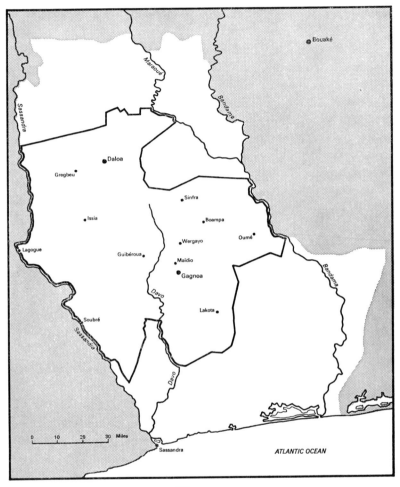

Figure 4
Bété Area of the Ivory Coast

this people. Thus, the largest unit among the Bété is the clan (*digpi*), whose functions have consistently declined since the early days of the colonial period. On the whole a clan comprises between one and two thousand individuals, scattered among five or six villages. A clan generally includes a limited number of families able to trace their origins back to a common ancestor, but there are exceptions to this general principle, since, in the hostile environment of the tropical forest, proximity often involves the sharing of similarly threatening experiences, neighboring familial units are often tempted to consider themselves as constituting one single kin group. For this people, the similarities of a present experience are more important than those associated with the past.[9]

The absence of traditional political integration beyond a limited number of villages probably accounts for the lack of "national" identity which characterizes the Bété even today. The segments of the Bété population which live in the Daloa area regard themselves as entirely distinctive from those segments living in the regions of Gagnoa or Soubre. Although a neighboring tribe, the Niaboua, present organizational traits virtually identical to those of the Bété, the latter consider them aliens. In short, both the low density of this area and the coterminous character of territorial and familial organizations are conducive to the emergence of strong centrifugal forces. Bété villages are more differentiated and individualized among themselves than comparable geographical units among the Abouré.

Today social integration does not exceed the boundaries of a single village, which is therefore the maximal unit that requires study. Villages tend to be divided into distinctive neighborhoods, which are occupied by distinct sublineages or sometimes even by complete lineages. Within these large units, called *grebo,* there are several *kc:su,* or extended families which include several nuclear families grouped around the eldest living male member. A *kc:su* comprises (1) this senior individual, (2) his wives, (3) his male children, married or unmarried, (4) their wives and their offspring, (5) his unmarried female offspring, and (6) his female siblings and ascend-

---

9. For a full description of the Bété, see D. Paulme, *Une societé de Côte d'Ivoire d'hier et d'aujourd'hui: les Bétés* (Paris: Mouton, 1962).

ants, single or widowed. This demonstrates the patrilocal character of the Bété people.

The political organization of the Bété villages is geronto-cratic in nature. Although their power has declined, the heads of the *kc:su* still make all important decisions. Solidarity between members of the same age group is minimal, since they do not exert any significant functions for the sake of the community as a whole. Initially, when Bété villages were frequently engaged in warfare operations, youngest adult males were grouped into a common class whose functions were exclusively military. Later, with the disappearance of military activities, the amount of interaction between age-group members declined markedly. Young adult males have never been allowed to own land; neither have they ever been allowed to cultivate subsistence crops, an activity which is reserved for married women. This rule has reduced possible cooperation among age peers and accentuated the subordination of each of them toward the head of his own *kc:su*. Indeed the most significant social networks among the Bété are to be found within extended families and are shaped according to sex, age, and seniority. Contacts among *kc:sus* involved only their respective heads; these contacts have always been concerned with problems of inheritance or exploitation of the land attached to the village. Economic changes, however, have introduced a variety of strains in this type of familial structure.[10]

Economic Organization

As long as Bété villages were engaged in warfare, hunting, and gathering activities, conflicts about land use arose more frequently between villages than within a village, for Bété villages were corporate units and no individual family was ever

---

10. These strains are fully described in Kobben, "Le Planteur noir"; in Paulme, *Les Bétés;* and in H. Raulin, *Mission d'étude des groupements immigres en Côte d'Ivoire: problems fonciers dans les regions de Gagnoa et Daloa* (Paris: ORSTOM, 1957).

in a position to exert an individual claim on a given piece of land. The introduction of subsistence cultivation hardly modified this situation, because this type of activity has not traditionally concerned the most influential members of Bété communities, its elder males. The introduction of a cash economy, however, changed the types of relations prevailing both among *kc:sus* and within them.

Among the Bété, as among other peoples, rights of private property can be divided into three parts: *jus utendi* (the right to the use of an asset), *jus fruendi* (the right to the returns of this asset), and *jus abutendi* (the right to dispose of this asset). In many traditional African cultures, the last component—*jus abutendi*—was subject to important restrictions, because land was attached to the group as a whole and presented sacred properties which made its sale illegitimate and illegal. This particular *jus* was a function of inheritance rules, and its exercise has often been conducive to the formation of new political subunits. The only right to be clearly individualized was the *jus utendi*. A familial unit which had been allowed to clear a patch of land was entitled to cultivate it for an indeterminate period of time, and to keep for its own use the ensuing crop. *Jus fruendi* had hardly any significance, since there was no cash economy.

The systematic introduction of coffee and cocoa into this area has drastically modified these three parts of the right to property. With the commercialization of farming, the exercise of *jus utendi* and *jus fruendi* has implied a considerable increase in the amount of cash which an individual or a familial group can dispose of. This, in turn, has been associated with a growing individualization of the claims exerted on a given piece of land and on its products. Consequently, this individualization has induced strains between generational groups which did not exist at earlier periods, or which were, at least, less acute, since there was a clear *quid pro quo* underlying the relations between individual members of such groups. In addition, the increase in the amount of cash circulating in the Bété area has modified the content of many familial obligations, such as the payment of the brideprice.

Jus abutendi has been equally affected by the introduction of cash crops. Unable or unwilling to increase the initially low level of participation of Bété peoples in a modern economy, French authorities ensured the economic development of this region by favoring the settlement of European-owned large-scale plantations and, later on, of individual African farmers alien to the area. These immigrant farmers have never met any difficulties in obtaining initial approval to settle on a given piece of land. Problems tend to arise, however, as to the exact nature of this approval. Immigrant farmers frequently consider the agreement as a bill of sale and never expect to be bound by any further obligations toward the individual or the familial group with whom they have dealt. As long as these farmers are engaged in subsistence activities, their Bété interlocutors are not likely to raise any question about the nature of the agreement concluded; this usually ceases to be true when the immigrant becomes involved in the production of cash crops. At this point, many Bété individuals are tempted to ask for a permanent sharing of these cash crops; their demands are based on the fact that, in the absence of an individualized *jus abutendi* in the Bété traditional law, the agreement concluded is necessarily a lease and not a sale. The permanent character of the share so demanded indicates that the transaction established with the immigrant farmer is definitely based upon relations between renters and tenants rather than between sellers and buyers.

Whatever the real nature of the right acquired by the immigrant farmer, it still presents a precarious character. Indeed, if the land that he acquires has ever been cultivated by or assigned to a given segment of a *kc:su,* individuals of that segment claim that the lease belongs to them as a result of the *jus utendi* that they have previously acquired. This claim, however, is often challenged by the eldest member of the *kc:su* present in the village, who argues that *jus utendi* does not lead to the right to lease the land used. This elder consequently regards as illegal the occupation of the piece of land under consideration, as long as he is not given a treatment similar to that obtained by the holders of *jus utendi,* who were the initial negotiators. To sum up, the introduction of a cash economy in the Bété area has been accompanied by a variety of strains between local and immigrant peoples. The frequency and intensity of such strains are accentuated by the deep involvement of immigrant farmers in a cash economy. This involvement leads them to cultivate more sizable estates, to acquire a larger labor force, and to enjoy higher returns from their enterprises than do local populations. Clearly, these strains are also a function of the relative scarcity of land still available for cultivation in a particular village.[11]

The introduction of a cash economy has fostered tensions not only between immigrant and locally born peoples but also within the latter category itself. While the tensions which develop within Bété familial groups often concern the use of benefits derived from the land transactions concluded with immigrant farmers, they are also likely to result from inheritance problems. On the one hand, the head of a *kc:su* often claims that he should receive the largest part of the estate of the deceased person, because of the number of obligations incumbent upon him. Not only must he pay for the ceremonies which accompany the death, but he also must take care of the individuals dependent upon the deceased. In addition, he is also obliged to administer a fund large enough to pay the brideprices for all the male members of the group who are subject to his authority. On the other hand, the individualization of the work performed on a given estate and the profits acquired through this work make the present tenants of the

11. For this point, see more particularly Kobben, "Le Planteur noir," chap. 9.

estate wish to perpetuate the personal advantages that they have acquired. Having gained an unexpected access to cash, these occupants are unwilling to resume their subordinate position vis-à-vis the eldest member of the familial group. In short, the power held by the senior members of a Bété village becomes increasingly jeopardized. They no longer have an absolute control over the main resources of the village, the partial use of which they were previously able to exchange with the junior members of the community against the latter's work in their own fields. In this originally gerontocratic society, economic change has increased the intensity of socially and economically centrifugal forces between generational groups.

The low involvement of the Bété people in a modern economy presents many facets. First, the ratio of cash to subsistence crops is lower than in the Grand Bassam area. In effect, the participation of Bété farmers in agricultural activities turned exclusively toward subsistence products is much higher than of their Abouré counterparts. About 20 per cent of them do not grow coffee and cocoa. In part, this lack of involvement in the modern sector of agriculture reflects the insufficient access of Bété farmers to the agricultural labor market. The only labor force that they can use includes their wife or co-wives and members of their immediate family. Second, cash economy is much less diversified than in the Abouré region, where the cultivation of cocoa occupies larger areas and where the outputs of pineapple, banana, and kola are more sizable. Third, the lack of involvement of Bété farmers in a modern economy is demonstrated by their use of the cash derived from their activities for social rather than economic purposes (payment and refund of brideprices, litigations of all sorts). In effect, the number of legal feuds (divorce, land tenure, and so on) varies throughout the year and reaches a peak in the period immediately following the sale of crops.[12] This social use of cash prevents many farmers from reinvesting their

12. *Ibid.*

profits in their enterprises and from reaching, accordingly, a level of productivity comparable to that obtained by Abouré farmers.

This low level of participation of the Bété people in a modern economy is in turn associated with primary school enrollments lower than those in the Grand Bassam area.[13] Although colonial authorities in the late 1950's and the new government have made serious efforts to increase the number of schools and teachers in the entire West, the gap between the figures for Daloa and Gagnoa districts on the one hand, and Bassam on the other, has only moderately declined. In addition, there is some evidence to suggest that the recruitment of Bété students in the school system is socially selective, for the social profile of Bété secondary students differs markedly from that of the total Bété population.[14] The marginal character of the educated Bété leads them to become more geographically mobile than the corresponding segment of the eastern peoples.

Familial Organization

The Bété are both patrilocal and patrilineal in their organization. This insures a particularly apparent preeminence of the patrilineal descent group. The patrilineal nature of the Bété does not, however, enhance relations between fathers and sons since familial assets and liabilities are transmitted to the eldest member of the senior segment of the familial group. For this reason, ties between agnatic brothers are often more crucial than those between a father and his male offspring. The restrained and tense character of the ties established between the various generations of a paternal descent group is, however, compensated for by the smoother nature of the bonds interwoven between an individual and his matrilineal descent

13. See *Supplement trimestriel au bulletin mensuel de statistiques.*
14. This interaction between social differentiation and ethnicity is discussed in Remi Clignet, "Ethnicity, Social Differentiation, and Secondary School in West Africa," *Cahiers d'études africaines*, XXVII (1967), 361–76.

group. An individual is in a position to expect as much from his maternal uncles and cousins as he is from his agnates.

The assets of the head of a *kc:su* consist of the labor performed in his fields by the male members of his familial group. They also involve the brideprice that he collects from the affinal groups of the female members of the village. His liabilities include the payment of brideprices which will enable the male members of his group to marry. He must also allocate distinctive pieces of land to the various nuclear groups which are parts of the *kc:su* and intervene in conflicts between individuals or nuclear families over land tenure or domestic difficulties. He has never exerted any religious authority.

In precolonial times, exchanges of brideprice did not raise any difficulties insofar as its value was stable and hardly negotiable. These two features obviously facilitated the preeminence of the role of the head of the *kc:su* over that held by any other member of the familial group. There are evidences that the value of the brideprice has increased since the early days of colonization; furthermore, it is increasingly delivered in cash. For several reasons, this tends to undermine the superordinate position of the head of the *kc:su*. First, he might be tempted to divert the funds collected toward the satisfaction of his own needs. When he does so, he is not in a position either to arrange the marriage of the male members of his group or to facilitate the divorce of its female members by refunding the brideprice paid at the time of their marriage. Thus, he often alienates from himself the junior members of the group.[15] In addition, his own situation is jeopardized by the fact that in an increasing number of cases the brideprice paid for a female of the *kc:su* tends to be cashed by her own father, who nevertheless refuses to use the corresponding funds for marrying his own sons, arguing that such a payment is definitely the main duty of the head of the *kc:su*. In this particular instance also,

15. For a discussion of the role performed by the head of the *kc:su* in this regard, see Paulme, *Les Bétés*, chaps. 3 and 4.

the introduction of a cash economy seems to be accompanied by the development of multiple strains between generations. Each generation tends to retain tradition when this entails benefits and to dismiss it when it implies a persistence of unfortunate obligations.

Since in theory the brideprice paid for the marriage of a girl is used to pay that for the marriage of her brother, particularly strong ties emerge between siblings of opposite sex. The eldest sister or the first-married sister imposes exacting demands on her young male siblings; her demands must be satisfied before those of their own wives. Whereas relations between Abouré brothers and sisters are accompanied by a permanent flow of reciprocal obligations and rights, corresponding ties among the Bété are characterized by the successive nature of the obligations engendered. A young Bété woman is under pressure from her brothers to marry as early as possible. Married, she is in a position to retaliate against her brothers.

Her retaliations are also likely to result from the frustrations that she experiences in her affinal village. There she must comply with the wishes and demands of her sisters-in-law, whose position is superordinate to her own. Such frustrations are aggravated by the distance which separates her new residence from that of her own group. Indeed, a woman marries most often outside of her own *digpi*. The rules of exogamy applicable to Bété individuals not only forbid marriages between individuals of a familial group but also between partners with grandparents of a similar origin. Accordingly, the extent of these exogamy rules leads Bété to find their spouses quite far from their own village, although there are variations among subareas in this regard.

Retaining her loyalties toward her own family of origin after her marriage, a Bété wife is still characterized by the high degree of her absorption into her affinal group. First, she is the backbone of the labor force of which her husband disposes. "We do not hire unskilled laborers on our farms," say many Bété respondents, "since our wives can perform the tasks which need to be done." [16] Second, there is no equivocation as to the nature of the rights transmitted by marriage. The child born of a Bété wife belongs to the family of her husband. In case of divorce she is no longer entitled to this child.

The high degree of social absorption of the Bété wife is in turn associated with the payment of a high brideprice. While this brideprice value has increased over time, it is still not clear whether this reflects an increased participation of Bété women in the agricultural activities of their affinal group or simply results from a modification in the nature of matrimonial relations, the brideprice becoming an object of financial speculation rather than a compensation for the loss experienced by the bride's family. The high degree of social absorption of their wives leads many Bété males to offer wedding presents to their spouses, a practice which is not usually observed among the Abouré. Furthermore, among the somewhat rare Bété families who provide their daughters with a dowry, its nature differs markedly from that offered by their Abouré counterparts. The persistence of close-knit ties between an Abouré woman and her family of origin leads her family to provide her with pots and pans, in short, with the tools necessary for the performance of her domestic chores. By contrast, among the Bété, such presents (when they exist) are much more personalized and tend to enhance the esthetic and social value of the bride. Accordingly, they include mainly prestige items (clothes, jewelry, cosmetics, and so on).

If there is a close association between degree of social absorption and brideprice among the Bété, the relationship is far from being so clear between either one of these two variables and divorce. Indeed, many observers of this particular people have noted the high incidence of divorce,[17] which can be partly accounted for by the conflicts which arise concerning the

16. Kobben, "Le Planteur noir," p. 129.
17. Among others, Kobben, *ibid.*, and Paulme, *Les Bétés*.

final destination of the brideprice. Frequently, several individuals who are "influential" in the *kc:su* are simultaneously negotiating the marriage of a given female member of their familial group. The conflict of interests evident here is often solved by the elopement of the bride-to-be, which takes place with her own consent and that of one of the more powerful members of her familial group. Changes in the power structure of the *kc:su* may lead to a challenge of a marriage concluded through such devious means. The bride may divorce to remarry the partner suggested by the previously weakest male member of her group. In short, the growing tensions among the various generations of a single Bété familial group are probably one of the most decisive factors accounting for the high incidence of divorce among this people. Two caveats must be entered at this point: The high incidence of elopement and of divorce should not be considered as symbolic of the low status occupied by Bété women in their own familial group as well as among their affines. Often enough, women take advantage of matrimonial mobility to enhance their own position. In addition, the term "high incidence" requires qualification. From an examination of the present data, divorces among this people still appear to be less frequent than among the Abouré.

For a limited sample (N = 67) Kobben indicates that 68 per cent of married males are polygnist. The rates indicated by Paulme for four villages around Daloa are much lower and range between a maximum of 51 per cent and a minimum of 33 per cent. Such variations probably reflect the size of the agricultural enterprises of the villages examined and also depend upon the age structure of the male population of these settlements (Table 6). The older a male, the greater the number of wives that he has. The significance of age in this regard is due to the operation of two factors: First, social status increases with age, and the number of wives in African societies is indeed a precise indicator of the social rank of a particular person. Second, it should also be remembered that among the Bété recruitment of co-wives takes place through the institution of

Table 6

Incidence of Plural Marriage in the Bété Village of Zepreguhe, by Age of Husband (Percentages)

| | Number of Wives | | | |
Age of Husband	One	Two	Three	Four or more
Under 35 years	35.5	30.7	11.1	0.0
Between 36 and 50	35.5	46.0	55.5	22.3
Over 50	29.0	23.3	33.4	77.7
Total	100.0	100.0	100.0	100.0
N	31	13	9	9

Computed from D. Paulme, *Une société de Côte d'Ivoire d'hier et d'aujourd'hui: Les Bété* (Paris: Mouton, 1962), pp. 47–61.

levirate, by which the wives of a deceased person are transmitted to his heir along with the other components of his estate. Insofar as elderly persons are more likely to be heirs than are their younger counterparts, their number of wives is also likely to be proportionately larger.

Polygyny among this people is also associated with parity of age between husbands and their senior co-wives. Thus, in the sample drawn by Paulme, only 22 per cent of the monogamous males have a wife who is of their own age or even older. For the polygnists, the corresponding proportion is exactly one-half. It may be that this differential reflects changes over time in the norms underlying optimal age differences between spouses. In this case, then, the contrast is not likely to reflect cleavages between differing types of families but rather opposition between generations. On the other hand, it can also be argued that in the context of a gerontocratic society, the first woman married by a polygynist individual is not necessarily the most attractive (a woman who belongs to the same age group as her husband or who is even older than he is does not indeed occupy a first-choice position in the field of eligibles).

The traditional rights and obligations of the husband and

of each of his co-wives are rather explicitly defined by Bété customs.[18] First, the Bété husband can forbid each of his wives to utilize subsistence crops for purposes other than feeding the household. In other words, the sale of such crops depends on the good will of the husband and is therefore subject to his legitimate approval. Co-wives are placed into two categories. When the household is limited in size, the senior co-wife (the *zoa da*) experts an absolute control over the activities of all other women present in the house. When the household is large, she is assisted by the second co-wife (*zoa keikei*), who thus enjoys a higher status. Both women exert a right on the agricultural production of the junior co-wives and are entitled to assign them to the various pieces of land which are to be cultivated. Senior co-wives are supposed to distribute the domestic chores among junior co-wives and, more specifically, to decide who should cook for the whole family. They are entitled to be the first of the women to be served at mealtime and are allowed to eat apart. They may also require junior co-wives to wash them and are supposedly in a position to control the offering of presents by the husband to his junior spouses. In addition, they decide with what wife and for how long the husband will sleep. This latter prerogative is particularly important in view of the fact that the husband visits his wives and not the contrary. Indeed, it can be postulated that the obligation of a wife to receive her husband in her own private room accentuates his power as well as that exerted by the senior co-wife. Finally, the senior co-wife is entitled to contract debts.

Thus the organization of Bété polygynous families recognizes the preeminent position occupied by the senior co-wife, as it results from her seniority in the home. This preeminence, however, is lessened by differences between her background and that of junior co-wives, who in the field of eligible pros-

18. For a full discussion of these rights and duties, see E. Dunglas, *Moeurs et coutumes des Bétés* (Paris: Larose, 1939).

91

pects, tended to be more socially valuable. This contradiction fosters tensions which are clearly elaborated upon by the women interviewed by Paulme. Regardless of the character of the households in which they are married, every Bété woman considers her present matrimonial status as temporary and feels that she would likely divorce her present husband if he starts neglecting her in favor of a newcomer.[19] Indeed, the model underlying the relations between Abouré co-wives is that of sisters; the model applicable to the Bété domestic scene is that of rivals.

Summary of the Contrasts between the Abouré and the Bété

In summary, there are three major differences between the Abouré and the Bété. They differ (1) in their traditional political organization, (2) in the extent of their respective participation in the modern sector of the economy, and (3) in the rules of descent that they follow.

First, Abouré individuals must fulfill obligations which are not exclusively familial, and they are integrated in social units which are larger than kin groups. The effects of this social integration are likely to be accentuated by the dense character of settlements in this particular area, so that there will be a high degree of pressure toward conformity. As a result, one can anticipate that there will be less variation in the power structure of the Abouré rural domestic groups than in the corresponding power structures among the Bété.

Second, the Abouré, as a group, have been more deeply involved in the processes of modernization. The level of their school enrollments is higher than than that of the Bété. The size of their agricultural enterprises is usually larger and their participation in the labor force is more diversified. This differ-

19. See Paulme, *Les Bétés*, pp. 79–82.

ence leads us to establish two competing hypotheses regarding the variability of the familial organizations prevailing in each one of them. Thus, one can argue that the greater involvement of Abouré individuals in modernization enhances the number of choices that they can make with regard to familial styles of life. We would expect that, when provided with new resources, some Abouré individuals would be anxious to acquire modern patterns of behavior, whereas others would be prone to restore traditional sets of norms and attitudes. Alternatively, however, one can propose that the latter involvement of the Bété in processes of social change leads this people to be temporarily more disorganized and hence to display a larger degree of inconsistency, as far as patterns of familial interaction are concerned.

Thirdly, the Abouré follow matrilineal descent lines whereas the Bété are patrilineal in character. This contrast has the following implications: (a) The rights that Bété husbands acquire in their wives by marriage are more numerous. Bété children are placed in paternal descent groups, and Bété women constitute an important element of the labor force of which their husbands dispose. (b) We can tentatively suggest that variations in the number and significance of rights transmitted by marriage are also associated with variations in sleeping arrangements. Abouré women are obliged to visit their husbands, whereas the pattern is reversed among the Bété. One can argue that the control of Bété husbands is therefore maximal, since their spouses have no privacy. Correspondingly, one can propose that the control of Abouré married males is spatially more limited and that this limitation reflects the lower degree of social absorption of their wife or wives. In any event, contrasts in sleeping arrangements would seem to induce different types of strains in the relations between mothers and children, between co-wives, and between conjugal partners. (c) Because of the persistence of the duties of a married woman toward her own family, Abouré brothers and sisters are tied by a continuous flow of reciprocal obligations. Among the Bété, marriage is associated with a reversal in the direction of such obligations. Before marriage a woman is subordinate to her brother; after her marriage, he must comply with her demands and wishes. (d) Correspondingly, the brideprice payed by Bété males tends to be higher than that payed by Abouré. In addition, differences in the number and significance of rights transmitted by marriage and in the amount of matrimonial compensations are accompanied by corresponding disparities in the incidence of divorce, which is more frequent among the Abouré.

All these contrasts should have implications on our comparison between monogamous and polygynous families. Thus, the incidence of plural marriage should be and is lower among the Abouré. Second, the functions ascribed to plural marriage should be and are more limited among the Abouré. It is mainly an instrument of social differentiation and does not enable Abouré males to enjoy a larger amount of resources. Third, the authority and power invested in Bété polygynist males is more diffuse and more significant; similarly, the control exerted by Bété senior co-wives over junior spouses is greater than that enjoyed by their Abouré counterparts. The patrilineal nature of the Bété people accounts for the high significance of age and seniority as criteria for the placement of individuals in familial structures. As a result, there is a hierarchy in the status of the various Bété co-wives and of their offspring, a hierarchy which can be jeopardized whenever there are marked disparities in the social origins of the various co-wives. This last situation is likely to be particularly frequent in view of the normative character of plural marriage among the Bété. In contrast, the low degree of social absorption of Abouré co-wives into their affinal group and the persistence of strong loyalties between each of them and their respective families of origin minimizes their competitive orientations and introduces a certain equalitarianism in their patterns of interaction.

Thus far we have indicated how the traditional social organization of the two peoples differs, and we have accordingly disregarded variations in their respective patterns of residence. In other words, we have examined only the rural elements of these two peoples, under the assumption that similarities and contrasts there reflect parallels and differences between the archetypes of the two cultures. Yet, both peoples also live in a variety of cities. Urbanization introduces new strains in the organization of families of these two peoples, and encourages the disappearance of former tensions. We shall therefore examine the structural properties of Abidjan, the largest city of the Ivory Coast, where the urbanized segments of the Bété and the Abouré are concentrated.

The Urban Milieu

Abidjan, the capital city of the Ivory Coast, owes certain of its characteristics to the nature of the distribution of urban centers in the entire country. Thus, the urbanized segment of the population is concentrated in that one city, and the index of primacy for the Ivory Coast exceeds 70 per cent and is by far superior to that of nearby Ghana, where patterns of economic development and of ethnic differentiation are nevertheless like those of the Ivory Coast.[20]

The primate nature of the distribution of urban centers in the Ivory Coast accounts for the high concentration in Abidjan of industrial, commercial, and cultural concerns. There is only one large factory in the hinterland, and the vast majority of educational institutions are located either in the capital or in its immediate surroundings. Accordingly, wage earners are particularly numerous in Abidjan. Thus, in 1961, 57 percent of Ivory Coast salaried employees were residents of Abidjan, and this proportion rose to 59 per cent in 1962, and to 62 per

20. For a discussion of the term *primacy*, see Bryan Berry, "City Size Distribution and Economic Development," *Economic Development and Cultural Change,* IX (1961), 573–87.

cent in 1963.[21] This trend suggests that the rate of economic development is geographically uneven throughout the country, and that social contrasts between the coastal zone and the hinterlands are more likely to increase than to decrease.

Because of the concentration of economic development in Abidjan, the population of the city has grown quite fast. From 5,000 inhabitants in 1921, it became a city of 130,000 inhabitants in 1945, and reached 250,000 inhabitants in 1963. This growth is mainly due to migrations; in 1963, only 62,000 of the total population of Abidjan had been born there. Two factors must therefore be taken into account in analyzing the actual composition of the city's population. On the one hand, the economic and political development of the entire Ivory Coast takes place mainly within this coastal area; it is there, accordingly, that the corollary manifestations of social differentiation should be the most apparent. On the other hand, the present characteristics of the population of Abidjan also depend upon the city's rate of growth. In short, contemporary statistics of the capital have to be compared not only with those of the other urban centers and of the country as a whole, but also with the corresponding statistics for the past.

The Selective Character of Migrations

Since the growth of the population of Abidjan results mainly from immigration, it is necessary to analyze the manifold aspects of the selectivity which underlies migration patterns.

First, migration involves more men than women. For the entire population of Abidjan, the male-female ratio averaged 124 in 1963, a value which far exceeded that of the ratio of the entire country—101 in 1961.[22] In the four most important cities of the hinterland, Bouaké, Gagnoa, Daloa, and Man, the

21. Derived from *Statistiques mensuelles de l'Office de la Main d'Oeuvre* (Abidjan: Ministere du Travail, n.d.). I am grateful to Henri Benoit of the ILO who did the actual computation.

22. See *Étude socio economique de la zone urbaine d'Abidjan* (Paris: Societe d'Études et de Mathematiques Appliquees, 1965), report no. 3.

corresponding figures were 103, 120, 104, and 103, respectively.[23] Thus, the selectivity of migration along sex lines was most manifest in the largest urban center of the country. This selectivity has, however, declined throughout time; in 1955, the male-female ratio for Abidjan was 139.

Second, migration primarily involves the younger and more active elements of the population. In 1963 the groups between 15 and 59 years of age constituted 61 per cent of the entire male and 56 per cent of the entire female population of the city. For the Ivory Coast as a whole, the corresponding figures were 51 and 55 per cent, respectively. Selectivity along age lines was therefore more manifest for the male than for the female segments of the population. This selectivity was more evident in Abidjan than in Bouaké, the second city of the country, where the 15 to 59 segment represented 57 per cent of all males and 58 per cent of all females. However, this form of selectivity characteristic of migrations toward Abidjan has declined over time; in 1955, this group constituted 71 per cent of the male population of Abidjan and 68 per cent of the female. Thus, the economic development of the capital city enables the active population to support more dependents. In addition, it enables this active population to be increasingly sedentary. Although immigration remains important, and although almost two-thirds of the immigrants have spent less than 5 years in the capital city, the relative contribution of migration to the growth of Abidjan is presently more limited than it used to be.

Third, the various regions of the hinterland do not participate evenly in the flow of migrations toward Abidjan. Table 7 shows that the extent of the participation of various zones of the Ivory Coast in urban structures varies negatively with their distance from the capital; on the whole, Ivory Coast migrants come from the zones adjacent to Abidjan. However,

23. See "Enquête socio economique sur la ville de Bouaké," report no. 1, mimeo. (Paris: SEDES, n.d.); and "Villes de Côte d'Ivoire: Man, Daloa, Gagnoa," mimeo. (Paris: SEDES, n.d.).

Table 7

Population Distribution of Local Areas of the Ivory Coast and of Abidjan, by Sex (Percentages)

Zones	Hinterland [a]		Abidjan [b]		Selectivity Ratio [c]	
	M	F	M	F	M	F
	(i)	(ii)	(iii)	(iv)		
Ivory Coast					—	
East Forest	18.6	17.3	40.4	44.3	2.2	2.6
West Forest	35.3	35.2	15.5	15.7	0.4	0.4
Savanna	26.4	27.0	7.2	11.3	0.3	0.4
Sudanian	19.7	20.5	4.2	3.9	0.2	0.2
Mali and Upper Volta	—	—	22.2	14.1		
Other African Areas	—	—	10.5	10.7		
Total	100.0	100.0	100.0	100.0		

[a] Derived from *Supplement trimestriel du bulletin mensuel de statistiques*, vol. VIII (Abidjan: Ministere des Affaires Economiques, des Finances et du Plan, 1966), p. 9.

[b] Computed from *Étude socio economique de la zone urbaine d'Abidjan*, mimeo. (Paris: SEMA, 1964), report no. 3.

[c] The selectivity ratios are equal to (iii) divided by (i) and (iv) divided by (ii).

migrants are also derived in large numbers from other countries. In other words, the distribution of migrants by distance between place of origin and place of destination is bimodal. The majority of these individuals come both from the most adjacent and the most remote areas. It is likely that, depending on the distance between their villages of origin and Abidjan, they are not derived from similar social backgrounds; further, we will demonstrate that they do not participate evenly in the residential, educational, and occupational struc-

Table 8

Ethnic Groups in Abidjan (Percentages)

Ethnic Groups	Hinterland [a]		Abidjan [b]	
	M	F	M	F
Lagoon	8.1	8.2	13.7	14.7
Agni-Tchi	26.4	26.8	21.3	28.0
Kru	17.9	18.2	17.0	17.4
Mande	27.1	25.5	17.5	18.0
Voltaic	18.0	18.4	22.5	16.0
Other	2.5	2.9	8.0	5.9
Total	100.0	100.0	100.0	100.0

[a] Computed from *Supplement trimestriel du bulletin mensuel de statistiques*, vol. VIII, p. 27.

[b] Computed from *Étude socio economique*.

tures of the capital city. Lastly, the same table indicates that women are more likely than their male counterparts to be derived from the zones immediately surrounding the capital. The flow of male and female migrations, however, is affected not only by distance but also by cultural factors: thus, among the ethnic clusters whose natural habitat is far away from Abidjan, Voltaic females are proportionately less numerous in Abidjan than in the hinterland whereas the opposite is true with regard to other foreign women (Table 8). Alternatively, among ethnic clusters naturally located closer to the capital,

Agni-Tchi women are not only more numerous in the city than their male counterparts but their relative representation in Abidjan is larger than in the Ivory Coast as a whole. The differential participation of men and women who come from areas unevenly distant from Abidjan and culturally distinct should affect their styles of life and particularly their familial status. Indeed, the scarcity of marriageable women affects in differing degrees the various types of male migrants.

Changes in style of family life are also produced, however, by variations in the degree of individual commitment toward the modern sector of the economy.[24] Of course, this commitment is more striking in urban than ruarl populations.

Thus, the residents of Abidjan have a higher level of schooling than the general population of the Ivory Coast, and in 1963 no less than 36 per cent of the adult males of the capital city were able at least to read and write French, vis-à-vis only 5 per cent for the entire country. Yet, there has been an increase not only in the average educational level of the adult male population of the capital city but also in the proportion of individuals with a post-primary education. In 1963, 5 per cent of the adult males of Abidjan had completed part or all of their post-primary studies. In 1955, the corresponding percentage was 2.5 whereas the proportion of adult males able to read and write French did not exceed 23 per cent.

The level of commitment of the female population is, naturally, significantly lower, and the proportion of adult females able to read and write French did not exceed 10 per cent in 1963. Of course, this percentage is higher than that observable for the country as a whole and is twice as large as the corresponding figure for 1955. The gap between the educational achievements of the adult male and female populations of Abidjan has nevertheless become wider. The problem is to

24. For a full definition of the term, see W. Moore and A. Feldman, *Labor Commitment in Developing Areas* (New York: Social Science Research Council, 1950), chaps. 1 and 2.

determine whether such a gap leads to significant changes in familial style of life or, alternatively, whether it is conducive to a persistence of traditional models and hence to the persistence of plural marriage.

Degree of commitment toward industrial and modern organizations is of course assessed more accurately through an evaluation of occupational status. First, as already indicated, there is a concentration of salaried personnel and wage earners in Abidjan, where two-thirds of the active males enter in this particular occupational category as against only 36 per cent of their counterparts in the main secondary cities of the hinterland. Correspondingly, farmers and fishermen, who represent 10 per cent of the labor force of these inland centers, constitute barely 3 per cent of the working population of Abidjan. The salaried and wage-earning population of Abidjan tends, in addition, to be concentrated in large-scale businesses. Indeed, between 1960 and 1961, the number of firms employing more than 20 persons grew from 296 to 323.[25] Finally, all these changes have been accompanied by an increased differentiation of occupational statuses and, more specifically, by a widening of the range of skills present in the labor market. Among clerical workers, the number of unskilled individuals in 1963 was only 1.5 times larger than that for 1961. In contrast, the number of senior supervisors quadrupled during the same period.[26] In brief, African adult males enjoy a growing number of opportunities to reach the higher rungs of the occupational ladder.

There has also been an increased participation of women in the labor force. Whereas only 6 per cent of the adult female population of Abidjan worked in 1955, this grew to 13 per cent in 1963. Of course, this participation remains skewed in character, and 40 per cent of the adult women actually active

25. Derived from "Caisse de compensations et prestations familiales: rapport d'activite, 1960 et 1961," mimeo. (Abidjan, n.d.).
26. Derived from *Statistiques mensuelles de l'Office de la Main d'Oeuvre.*

are still engaged in trading and small-scale activities. Still, this last figure is somewhat lower than that for 1955, and women seem increasingly able to enter a variety of occupations.

Differences in the levels of participation of the two sexes in the most rewarding slots of the occupational structure seem to increase in magnitude, and one can speculate about the degree to which such inequalities lead to changes in familial organizations or, alternatively, encourage a persistence of traditional patterns of familial interaction, including polygyny.

Migration, Labor Commitment, and Familial Status

There is no doubt that in the long run social change is accompanied by the emergence of a nuclear type of family and hence by a decline in the incidence of plural marriage.[27]

First, in the Ivory Coast, as elsewhere in Africa, modernization has been accompanied by the development of a cash economy and by a corresponding increase in the mobility of economic rights. With this growing individualization of the rights held in land, extended families are increasingly unable to control the behavior of their individual members and to control the fulfillment of the obligations incumbent upon the heirs of a given testator. Accordingly, one would expect a decline in the incidence of traditional forms of polygyny, such as levirate.

Second, economic development has accelerated the rate of occupational mobility. An increasing number of adult roles are learned in the context of modern educational and economic institutions, with a corresponding decrease in the significance of the socialization functions carried through familial units.

27. On this general point, see the propositions made by W. Goode, *World Revolution and Family Patterns* (New York: Free Press, 1963), chap. 1. The points covered in the following section are derived from Remi Clignet and J. Sween, "Social Change and Type of Marriage," *American Journal of Sociology*, LXXIV (1969), 123–45.

As a consequence, traditional values should lose their initial salience and polygyny should cease to be uniformly normative.

Further, patterns of economic development have enhanced the volume and the range of migrations toward African urban centers. Since the population of such centers grows faster than their respective labor markets, individual migrants need to be highly mobile and hence to support few dependents. As a result large families, including polygynous households, may become dysfunctional. In addition, the number of economic opportunities offered to married women in urban centers remains limited. Although it is still a potential symbol of success, urban polygyny is hardly instrumental in enhancing wealth. This decline in the functions of plural marriage should be paralleled by a corresponding decrease in its incidence.

Lastly, as achievement succeeds ascription as a mechanism for placement in occupational structures, familial actors experience new anxieties and frustrations, which should induce changes in familial functions. Acting as mechanisms of tension management, families have to help release the emotions and strains accompanying participation in more trying economic and social structures.[28] Polygynous marriages hardly facilitate the new style of familial interaction, which requires that the number of familial actors remain limited, and that mate selection to be governed by principles of social homogamy. Due to the scarcity of eligible women in African urban areas, polygynous arrangements entail increased contrasts in the age, ethic, and social characteristics of conjugal partners. Thus, plural marriage is likely to satisfy only one type of complementary need pattern (the father-daughter or Pygmalion model) which does not necessarily correspond with the diversified and equalitarian demands of urban life.

---

28. For a more complete treatment of this question, see J. Pitts's introduction to "Personality and the Social System," in *Theories of Society*, ed. Talcott Parsons *et al.* (New York: Free Press, 1961), pp. 712–13.

Differential Rates of Nuclearization of Familial Institutions

Even if we assume that African polygyny is doomed to disappear, it is still necessary to evaluate its rate of decline and to determine, correspondingly, the sequence in which various African subgroups will forego plural marriage. We propose that this sequence is a function of (1) the erosive power of urbanization and modernization, and (2) the antecedent social structures from which urban inhabitants originate.

Conflicting Hypotheses Regarding the Erosive Power of Urbanization

Given the fact that plural marriage is traditionally a privilege attached to age and seniority, there are two conflicting hypotheses regarding the effects exerted by urbanization upon its distribution. According to one hypothesis, polygyny should decline as one moves from the least to the most modernized segments of the population. Participation in the most economically and socially rewarding occupations, hence in the modern sector of the economy, selectively characterizes individuals with a primary or post-primary education and, therefore, individuals derived from those ethnic and socioeconomic groups already exposed to modernizing influences. Persons gaining access to new means and resources are likely to simultaneously acquire new ends and aspire to a western familial life-style. We can expect, therefore, that (1) the most intensely urbanized segments of both Abouré and Bété will be characterized by the highest proportions of monogamous marriages, and (2) differences in the proportions of monogamous families between Abouré and Bété can be explained in terms of inequalities in the relative overall participation of these two peoples in modern structures.

According to a second hypothesis, however, the relationship between modernization and type of marriage should be curvilinear. Monogamy should characterize only new immigrants into urban places, and individuals placed at the bottom of the modern occupational hierarchy (unskilled manual workers). Polygyny is too costly an institution in the new circumstances faced by such new groups. Males enjoy limited resources, while females are almost entirely barred from the labor market.

Alternatively, the incidence of polygyny should be highest among both the most traditional and the most modernized individuals. Among the most traditional subsistence farmers, petty traders, and tribal leaders, rewards are still distributed along age lines and there are few alternative choices for familial life-style. Elders continue to favor traditional amenities, including plural marriage; indeed polygyny is often instrumental in the attainment of their resources. Having more resources, the most modernized segments of the population have also more choices with regard to life style. They are nevertheless likely to maintain polygynous arrangements, insofar as access to the top positions of a modern hierarchy reflects the influence of age and seniority, and hence, the continuity of traditional orientations.

In summary, the second hypothesis implies a clear distinction between modernization of means and modernization of ends. Whereas the first hypothesis assumes that matrimonial status is mainly influenced by the origin of the resources allocated to the individual and hence by exposure to modern values, the second hypothesis views matrimonial status as merely determined by the amount of these resources. By the first hypothesis, the erosive power of modernization is deemed to have permanent and regularly increasing effects. According to the second hypothesis, this erosive power is perceived as temporary and selective.

From this second hypothesis, we can infer the following propositions: (a) It is among the least urbanized segments of both the Abouré and Bété that we will observe the highest proportions of monogamous families. (b) The lower level of the Bété's participation in modern structures will be accompanied by a corresponding lower incidence of polygynous families within the migrant segments of the Bété.

105

Conflicting Hypotheses
Regarding the Vulnerability
of Antecedent Social Structures

Changes in the incidence of plural marriage depend upon both the intensity of modernizing forces and the vulnerability of traditional polygynous arrangements. In turn, variations in the vulnerability of these arrangements reflect variations in the following:

1. The initial degree of social integration. African peoples enjoy differing degrees of political, social and religious cohesiveness and therefore exert uneven pressures toward conformity upon their individual members.

2. The initial salience of plural marriage. Initially the incidence of polygyny varies with ethnic groups and this incidence is highest among those societies which follow patrilocal rules of residence, allocate significant economic functions to women, and/or have a system of privileges transmitted along hereditary lines.

3. The initial functions performed by plural marriage. Traditional polygyny may be perceived as a source of wealth, a result of wealth, or both.

The problem remains to assess the effect of such variations upon present choices of polygynous or monogamous marriage. One can argue that rates of innovation in matrimonial behavior will be maximal among peoples where demands initially imposed upon familial actors are consistent with the requirements resulting from urbanization.[29] Yet, one can also expect these rates of innovation to be maximal whenever and wherever traditional and modern demands are perceived as mutually exclusive by migrants.

In effect, these two hypotheses reflect conflicting views about the recruitment patterns of urban immigrants. In the first case, the majority of urban dwellers are expected to come from the

29. See Goode, *World Revolution and Family Patterns*, chap. 1.

mainstream of peoples whose traditional life style favors rapid and easy adaptation to new conditions. In the second case, one expects this majority to originate from marginal segments of ethnic groups whose traditional organization is least compatible with participation in modernizing structures. These marginal segments have, indeed, the most to gain from an urban experience.

These hypotheses also reflect conflicting views on the processes of familial innovation. In the first case, one assumes that the urbanized individuals who adopt monogamy first are likely to belong to peoples for whom polygyny has never been a prime norm, has always involved limited segments of the population, and has served few functions. In the second case, one conversely assumes that the first urban dwellers to remain monogamous are those whose adaptation to an urban life style has necessitated a thoroughgoing transformation of norms and values. Such individuals tend to be derived from peoples where polygyny was initially highly normative, frequent, and served a variety of purposes.

In short, the first hypothesis explains familial innovations exclusively in terms of the dominant traits of antecedent social structures, while the second hypothesis attaches equal importance to the position occupied by individuals within such structures.

Thus, in the context of the first hypothesis, urbanization and industrialization should reinforce the significance of the factors which have traditionally limited the incidence of plural marriage among the Abouré. In contrast, there should be fewer differences in the distribution of rural and urban Bété family types.

Alternatively, however, the second hypothesis assumes that the erosion of traditional familial arrangements is maximal among the Bété. Insofar as the type of control maintained by Bété elders and the obligations imposed upon the married women of this group are at variance with the possibilities offered by an urban environment, Bété immigrants toward

Abidjan would seem to be obliged to change their style of family life to a greater extent than their Abouré counterparts. More specifically, the relative declines in the amount of control exerted by elders, in the extent of domestic obligations imposed upon married women, and hence in the incidence of plural marriage—all should be more marked among the Bété.[30]

Distance between the places of origin and destination should, however, be expected to affect the extent of the influence exerted by the congruence or the incompatibilities between traditional and modern demands. Does the large distance separating the southwest of the Ivory Coast from Abidjan lead to an accomodation of Bété migrants to the requirements of a modernizing and ever changing environment, or does it alternatively lead to their "encapsulation" in the city and to the corollary reinforcement of their traditional patterns of value and behavior?[31] Again we are confronted with two competing arguments. If it can be assumed that geographic distance weakens familial ties and hence the power of traditional norms, it can also be suggested that it may reinforce the cohesiveness prevailing among migrants.

In addition, the persistence of traditional norms and values is also dependent upon the degree of ethnic segregation prevailing in the urban milieu itself. To be sure, some segregation seems to exist, but the overrepresentation of Bété and Abouré in certain areas of the city are comparable (Table 9). Thus Abouré are three times more numerous in the modern town-developments of Adjame, on the northwest fringe of Abidjan and eleven times more numerous in those of Treichville in the

30. This proposition suggests then that Bété migrants are more likely to occupy marginal positions in their social structure of origin, but this raises a type of problem which we will not analyze here. One can say that the average proportion of polygynist males will be particularly low among the Bété. One can also say, however, that the variance of the distribution of plural marriage among this group will be particularly high.

31. For a full treatment, see P. Mayer, *Tribesmen or Townsmen* (Capetown: Oxford University Press, 1961).

Table 9

Geographic Distribution of Adult Abouré and Bété in Abidjan (Percentages)

	Districts	Abouré Male	Abouré Female	Bété Male	Bété Female	Total Population Male	Total Population Female
West	Abgan-Attiekoube	1.4	1.1	9.2	8.7	4.8	5.8
	Town developments (Adjame)	9.8	9.8	11.4	12.5	5.7	6.5
	Adjame	6.6	5.8	14.6	16.5	28.1	26.9
North	Cocody	2.3	2.1	3.5	2.8	8.7	8.8
East	Town developments (Treichville)	34.9	37.7	28.1	29.0	10.6	12.2
	Koumassi	6.6	7.7	6.8	5.9	6.8	5.8
	Treichville	33.1	31.0	19.8	17.3	26.7	24.9
	Vridi Port–Bouet	5.3	4.8	6.6	7.3	8.6	9.1
	Total	100.0	100.0	100.0	100.0	100.0	100.0
	Proportion of City Population	2.7	3.3	6.6	7.1		
	N	438	377	1,065	816	16,171	11,504

Note: All the information presented in Tables 9 to 19 is derived from the analysis of the magnetic tape onto which the census of 1963 has been transcribed. We have included in the following tables African respondents between 14 and 99 years of age living in those census tracts with identification numbers between 20 and 85. The population of other areas has been eliminated, because of differences in sampling ratios; the sampling ratio of the census tracts examined here is one-fifth; that of the excluded subareas is one-tenth. This tape was obtained through the kind generosity of the Ministre des Affaires Economiques et du Plan of the Ivory Coast.

Table 10

Distribution by Matrimonial Status of the Abouré and Bété Female and Male Populations of Abidjan and of the Hinterland

Male

Matrimonial Status	Abouré		Bété		Total Population	
	Abidjan	Hinterland[a]	Abidjan	Hinterland[a]	Abidjan	Hinterland[a]
Monogamous	90.9	77.8	80.7	62.4	85.3	71.0
Bigamous	8.5	18.0	16.0	25.6	12.6	21.6
3 wives and more	0.6	4.2	3.3	12.0	2.1	7.4
Total	100.0	100.0	100.0	100.0	100.0	100.0
N	193	43,900	532	93,000	17,074	508,900

Female

Matrimonial Status	Abidjan	Hinterland[a]	Abidjan	Hinterland[a]	Abidjan	Hinterland[a]
Monogamous	79.2	—	62.8	—	72.0	
Senior co-wife	11.1	—	18.5	—	14.1	
Junior co-wives	9.7	—	18.7	—	13.9	
Total	100.0		100.0		100.0	
N	217		572		8,142	

[a] Derived from *Supplement Trimestriel du Bulletin Mensuel de Statistiques*, p. 41. The figures indicated here as given for ethnic clusters and differ from those obtained in the sample used for the present study.

northeast sections of the city, than they are in Abidjan as a whole. The Bété, correspondingly, are a little under two times more numerous in the former sites and a little over four times in the latter ones than they are in the population at large. Insofar as a modern habitat is indicative of a high socioeconomic status, both Abouré and Bété are equally well off in comparison with the remainder of the population. Yet, the economic position of the Abouré is superior to that of the Bété. Table 9 also suggests that migrants tend to remain attached to neighborhoods from which they have easy access to their places of origin: Bété are more numerous than Abouré in the west sections of Abidjan, whereas Abouré are more frequently found in the eastern sections of the city. Yet, nowhere is the segregation of these two peoples sufficient to enable them to rigidly maintain their traditional styles of life.[32]

In fact, the persistence of traditional matrimonial behavior does not seem affected by distance of migration nor by the segregation prevailing in Abdjan and our data show that neither of the two hypotheses presented earlier are substantiated. Indeed, urbanization is associated with a comparable decline in plural marriage for both of the peoples investigated (Table 10).

Urban Influences on Plural Marriage

Urbanization implies both changes in the demographic structures of each migrant group and an increased differentiation in their respective residential, educational, and occupational experiences. We will examine in turn the relative influence of these factors on the distribution of monogamy and polygyny among the Abouré and Bété residents of Abidjan.

32. The index of isolation, as defined by E. Shevky and W. Bell, *Social Area Analysis* (Stanford: Stanford University Press, 1955), pp. 44ff, does not exceed .114 for the Bété and .081 for the Abouré; these two values are inferior to those observed for other ethnic groups.

Composition of the Abouré and Bété Populations in Abidjan

We have argued that plural marriage tends to be a privilege acquired by senior males. Early stages of urban growth should tend to prevent the spread of polygynous families, for male urban residents are much younger than average and occupy marginal positions in both traditional and modern environments. Although there are no differences in the age distribution of adult Abouré and Bété residents of Abidjan, Table 11 indicates nevertheless that the relationship between age and matrimonial status is far clearer among the Bété than among the Abouré. This suggests that seniority, which is so important in rural areas, still dominates the organization of Bété urban families.

The incidence of plural marriage also depends, however, upon the number of women available and hence upon the size of the field of eligibles. Given the fact that there are substantial age differences between African conjugal partners, particularly in the context of polygynous families, we should assess the importance of disparities in the number of women of a certain age and in the number of elder males. Table 12 shows quite clearly that the number of potential female partners is larger among the Abouré than among the Bété. This explains at least in part why matrimonial competition is more acute among the Bété, leading to a marked correlation between the age and the matrimonial status of the men of this people. Further, this competition is reinforced by the fact that only 12 per cent of Bété adult women in Abidjan are single as against no less than 25 per cent for the Abouré.

As a result, the field of eligibles among the Abouré can be narrower. Abouré males are not necessarily obliged to marry women from other ethnic backgrounds. Nor are they obliged to recruit their wives from the hinterland. In brief, early stages of urbanization present obstacles to the persistence of plural marriage, but these obstacles disappear later on. In-

Table 11

Relationship between Age and Matrimonial Status in Abouré and Bété Male Residents of Abidjan (Percentages)

Age	Abouré		Bété		Total Population	
	Propor-tion of Total	Incidence of Polygyny	Propor-tion of Total	Incidence of Polygyny	Propor-tion of Total	Incidence of Polygyny
20–29	48.2	6.7	52.8	11.9	46.2	6.8
30–39	34.4	8.8	28.6	20.8	34.2	14.6
40–44	6.0	21.4	6.1	25.0	7.5	23.2
45–49	4.2	25.0	5.9	32.6	5.2	25.4
Above 49	7.2	5.8	6.6	37.5	6.9	22.3
Total	100.0	—	100.0	—	100.0	—
N	282		761		12,989	

Table 12

Relationship between Age and Matrimonial Status in Abouré and Bété Female Residents of Abidjan (Percentages)

| | | | Matrimonial Status | | |
Age	Sex Ratio [a]	Propor- tion of Total	Single Spouse	Senior Co- wife	Junior Co- wife [b]
			Abouré		
Below 25	114	50.0	49.3	37.5	38.1
25–34	79	33.7	39.5	41.6	47.6
35–44	81	10.1	8.7	20.9	14.3
45 and over	161	6.2	2.5	—	—
Total		100.0	100.0	100.0	100.0
N		376	172	24	21
			Bété		
Below 25	119	62.7	61.6	37.7	59.8
25–34	182	30.5	33.2	52.8	33.6
35–44	260	4.3	4.2	6.6	6.6
45 and over	433	2.5	1.0	2.9	0.0
Total		100.0	100.0	100.0	100.0
N		812	355	106	107
			Total Population		
Below 25	198	51.4	51.2	28.7	54.4
25–34	139	34.1	36.6	47.9	34.8
35–44	209	10.4	9.3	18.2	7.3
45 and over	402	4.1	2.9	5.2	3.5
Total		100.0	100.0	100.0	100.0
N		11,442	5,812	1,152	1,136

[a] Given age differentials between conjugal partners, we have computed the sex ratio as 100 times the number of males with age x divided by the number of women with age $(x - 1)$.
[b] Theoretically, there should be at least as many junior co-wives as senior co-wives. Logical errors in the construction of the code used in the census have obliged us to derive the rank-order of wives through an inspection of entire households. Because of this, some data for junior co-wives has been lost.

114

deed, the higher the participation of an ethnic group in urban structures, the more even will be its male-female ratio and the larger will be the proportion of singles in the overall female population. The percentage of single women rose from 13 to 18 per cent between 1955 and 1963, and it is probable that this increase is most apparent among peoples such as the Abouré, who have been exposed to the forces of modernization and urbanization most intensely and for the longest time.

Table 12 also summarizes the age distribution of monogamous senior and junior wives in the entire population, as well as among the urbanized segments of the Abouré and Bété. On the whole, single spouses tend to be derived from younger age groups, but the significance of age in this respect remains equivocal.[33] On the one hand it may be argued that age remains an important determinant of the position occupied by individuals both in familial and in larger structures and that senior co-wives are necessarily found in older age categories. On the other hand it might be proposed that age mainly reflects the influence of historical factors. Senior co-wives are older just because they are the remnants of an obsolescent system of familial relationships. The fact that there are few differences in the age characteristics of single spouses and of junior wives tends to suggest that the first assumption is more correct than the second one. Thus far, monogamous families remain potentially polygynous.

There are, however, marked contrasts in the age distribution of Abouré and Bété women with differing matrimonial status. Bété senior co-wives are significantly older than their junior counterparts, and this should enable them to occupy more easily the preeminent position to which they are tradi-

33. For a discussion of the factors which limit the significance of age as a meaningful demographic indicator, see J. C. Caldwell, "Population's General Characteristics" and "Population Change," in *A Study of Contemporary Ghana*, ed. W. Birmingham, I. Neustadt, and E. Omaboe, Vol. II, *Some Aspects of Social Structure* (Evanston, Ill.: Northwestern University Press, 1967).

tionally entitled. By contrast, age is a better predictor of the type of marriage entered by Abouré women than of their matrimonial rank; Abouré single spouses are younger than co-wives, regardless of their rank.

As a result, one can predict that cleavages in the organization of monogamous and polygynous families will be more marked among the Abouré than among the Bété. In addition, one can speculate about the extent to which the absence of age differences between Abouré junior and senior co-wives will facilitate the emergence of cooperative patterns of interaction among them. Age similarities may aggravate competition for access to the rewards offered by familial and larger environments. They may also lead to the emergence of a class consciousness and reinforce the equalitarian tendencies already latent among traditional polygynous Abouré households. We will discuss these competing hypotheses more thoroughly in Chapter 8.

Length of Residence in Abidjan

The amount of urban experience acquired by an individual constitutes a more accurate indicator of his exposure to Western norms and values. A substantial proportion of adult males have spent less than 5 years in the capital city, and this proportion is essentially the same for the two peoples compared here (Table 13). It is quite clear that, by itself, exposure to an urban milieu is not sufficient to cause changes in the familial organization of African migrants. The incidence of plural marriage is highest among individuals whose exposure to such norms has been the longest. In other words, a higher participation in urban structures increases the number of alternative choices that individuals can adopt with regard to familial life style, including the restoration of the *status quo ante*.

It is quite obvious, however, that there are some differences in this respect between Abouré and Bété. In the case of the second group, access to the top position of the urban hierarchy (as indicated by the length of time spent in Abidjan) is used to

Table 13

Relationship between Length of Urban Residence and Incidence of Polygyny in Abouré and Bété Male Residents of Abidjan (Percentages)

Length of Urban Residence	Abouré		Bété		Total Population	
	Propor-tion of Total	Incidence of Polygyny	Propor-tion of Total	Incidence of Polygyny	Propor-tion of Total	Incidence of Polygyny
Less than 1 year	18.0	0.0	18.3	9.0	19.1	8.0
1 to 5 years	38.3	9.1	34.9	17.5	31.4	12.9
6 to 10 years	13.8	6.8	18.0	14.3	19.9	11.5
More than 10 years	21.9	14.3	24.4	25.7	22.7	20.6
Born in Abidjan	8.0	0.0	4.4	18.7	6.9	11.1
Total	100.0	—	100.0	—	100.0	—
N	438		1,065		16,101	

acquire traditional symbols of power and prestige, including additional wives. Association between urban experience and matrimonial status is far less clear among the Abouré, and this shows that the higher involvement of Abouré in modernization leads them to adopt new systems of values. We have argued that the main result of an increased exposure to European norms and practices is an increase in the number of choices that an individual can make with regard to style of life. Our data support this contention. Differences in the incidence of plural marriage between Bété and Abouré are greater in the case of individuals who have spent the longest periods of time in Abidjan than in the case of newcomers to the capital city. This results from the fact that Bété choices remain predominantly oriented toward the principles of a traditional hierarchy system, while Abouré choices are apparently more diversified.

Table 14 shows that Abouré women have, on the whole, lived in the urban environment of Abidjan longer than their Bété counterparts, but a comparison with Table 15 shows that the amount of Abouré urban experience hardly varies along sex lines. Interestingly enough, a long exposure to the urban environment does not prevent Abouré women from entering polygynous marriages, and in fact, women married to monogamous males are more likely to be newcomers to Abidjan than are either senior or junior co-wives (between whom there are no significant differences in this respect). The situation is quite different among the Bété, since only 44 per cent of the senior co-wives of this people have spent less than five years in the capital city, as against no less than 63 per cent of their junior counterparts.

In summary, differences in the scarcity of valuable women within an urban environment lead to variations in the matrimonial status to which they can aspire. Bété women with a high urban experience are rare enough to make the position of senior co-wives more prestigious and their high exposure to the practices of the new environment probably reinforces the

118

Table 14

Relationship between Length of Urban Residence and Matrimonial Status in Abouré and Bété Female Residents of Abidjan (Percentages)

Length of Urban Residence	Propor-tion of Total	Matrimonial Status		
		Single Spouse	Senior Co-wife	Junior Co-wife
Abouré				
Less than 1 year	17.0	14.0	0.0	5.2
1 to 5 years	37.7	39.6	59.1	47.3
6 to 10 years	19.4	25.0	4.6	26.3
More than 10 years	25.9	21.4	36.3	21.2
Total	100.0	100.0	100.0	100.0
N_1	346	164	22	19
Born in Abidjan	8.2	4.7	8.3	9.5
N_2	377	172	24	21
Bété				
Less than 1 year	22.7	18.7	11.6	19.2
1 to 5 years	39.8	40.3	32.0	43.5
6 to 10 years	19.1	21.6	28.2	20.2
More than 10 years	18.4	19.4	28.2	17.1
Total	100.0	100.0	100.0	100.0
N_1	778	342	103	104
Born in Abidjan	44.5	4.5	2.8	2.8
N_2	816	358	106	107
Total Population				
Less than 1 year	23.3	21.6	12.0	21.9
1 to 5 years	36.2	37.9	29.7	39.0
6 to 10 years	19.6	21.4	24.1	21.6
More than 10 years	20.9	19.1	34.2	17.5
Total	100.0	100.0	100.0	100.0
N_1	10,612	5,788	1,149	1,061
Born in Abidjan	9.2	7.7	5.2	6.2
N_2	11,684	5,833	1,169	1,131

privileged position guaranteed to them by traditional norms. Their "achievement" maximizes the significance of the ascriptive nature of their preeminent role in familial structures. Correspondingly, men are obliged to import new or additional wives from the hinterland. As a result, there should be a certain continuity in the organization of Bété rural and urban polygynous families.

In contrast, the relative abundance of Abouré marriageable women in the urban context reduces their matrimonial choices and contributes to limit the emergence of any differentiation in the status of junior and senior co-wives. This leads us to predict that among the Abouré: (1) there will be sharp contrasts in the organization of rural and urban polygynous families, since the hinterland contributes moderately to the recruitment of additional urban co-wives; (2) the domestic power structure of urban polygynous families will be highly fluid since the equal amount of urban experience acquired by senior and junior co-wives may accentuate competition or, alternatively, cooperation between them; and (3) urban monogamous and polygynous families will differ markedly in their functioning since monogamously married women have proportionately less urban experience.

Education

As suggested earlier, there are marked differences in the educational level of urban and rural male populations. There are also sharp inequalities in the relative amounts of schooling acquired by different migrant groups: whereas one-half of the Abouré adult males have completed at least their primary education, this is true for only 27 per cent of the corresponding Bété population. This, of course, results from disparities in the degree to which Bété and Abouré hinterlands have been exposed to European influences. Nevertheless, both groups have an average level of educational attainment superior to that of the urban population at large.

Table 15 shows that the distributions of educational

Table 15

Relationship between Educational Status and Matrimonial Status of Abouré and Bété Male Residents of Abidjan (Percentages)

Educational Status	Abouré		Bété		Total Population	
	Propor-tion of Total	Incidence of Polygyny [a]	Propor-tion of Total	Incidence of Polygyny [a]	Propor-tion of Total	Incidence of Polygyny [a]
Illiterate	25.7	2.1	42.1	19.9	63.8	24.8
Completed some primary studies	23.8	13.7	30.9	25.2	18.0	17.5
Completed all primary studies	39.4	9.4	18.9	19.6	12.6	15.2
Went beyond primary studies	11.1	13.4	8.1	25.0	5.6	13.3
Total	100.0	—	100.0	—	100.0	—
N	432		1,055		16,039	

[a] Among illiterates, the relative incidence of plural marriage among persons unable to speak French is 0.0 per cent for the Abouré, 4.3 per cent for the Bété, and 10.3 per cent for the population at large.

achievement and of plural marriage appear to be negatively correlated. The evidence is less conclusive, however, when one takes into consideration the relative numbers of persons with differing schooling levels.[34] More important is the observation that, among both peoples compared here, variations in educational attainment exert little influence on the incidence of plural marriage. A higher education does not necessarily affect the system of familial values adopted by Abouré and Bété males, and, at least up to a certain point, both seem to perceive academic experiences in instrumental terms, that is, as means enabling them to achieve high positions in a hierarchy of a traditional type. Thus, the socialization functions of schools should not be exaggerated. It is probably only after the completion of the first cycle of post-primary studies that students begin to perceive new systems of values and norms.[35]

As suggested earlier, the educational level of the adult females in Abidjan is significantly lower than that of males and does not vary markedly along ethnic lines (Table 16). Yet, the influence of academic experiences on the matrimonial status of adult women is not the same for the Abouré and for the Bété.

Among the first people, monogamous wives are more frequently able to speak French than are the women in polygynous households, while there are no differences in this respect between junior and senior co-wives. This difference in exposure to French language confirms our prediction that there will be contrasts in the organization of Abouré monogamous and polygynous families, whereas the identical experiences of senior and junior co-wives along these lines will prevent the institu-

34. Thus the correlation between the distribution of educated males and of polygyny throughout the various census tracts of Abidjan does not exceed —.095.
35. Even at this point there are still some differences along ethnic lines in the attitudes adopted by students. See Clignet, "Ethnicity, Social Differentiation, and Secondary School in West Africa."

Table 16

Relationship between Educational Status and Matrimonial Status in Abouré and Bété Female Residents of Abidjan (Percentages)

Educational Status	Proportion of Total	Matrimonial Status		
		Single Spouse	Senior Co-wife	Junior Co-wife
Abouré				
Do not speak French	39.8	41.5	58.3	52.3
Speak French but illiterate	40.6	47.3	33.3	38.1
Completed some primary studies	6.4	1.8	4.2	0.0
Completed all primary studies	10.2	7.0	4.2	4.8
Went beyond primary studies	3.0	2.4	0.0	4.8
Total	100.0	100.0	100.0	100.0
N	374	171	24	21
Bété				
Do not speak French	47.6	49.4	45.7	54.6
Speak French but illiterate	41.2	43.0	50.5	42.4
Completed some primary studies	5.8	3.9	1.9	3.0
Completed all primary studies	4.1	3.1	1.9	0.0
Went beyond primary studies	1.3	0.6	0.0	0.0
Total	100.0	100.0	100.0	100.0
N	807	356	105	106
Total Population				
Do not speak French	68.6	73.3	73.4	76.0
Speak French but illiterate	23.2	21.3	24.1	21.6
Completed some primary studies	4.1	2.6	1.4	1.5
Completed all primary studies	2.9	2.1	0.9	0.6
Went beyond primary studies	1.2	0.7	0.2	0.3
Total	100.0	100.0	100.0	100.0
N	11,584	5,833	1,169	1,131

tionalization of any form of hierarchical rank-ordering between them.

The distribution of Bété married women by level of formal schooling presents a slightly different profile. There are no differences between monogamous and polygynous women in this regard, but senior co-wives tend to be more frequently exposed to French as a means of communication than the co-wives with a lower matrimonial rank.

At another level, we can see that differences in the relative scarcity of educated women condition the extent of their matrimonial choices. Among the Bété, the proportion of individuals with at least a primary education declines as one moves from single spouses to junior co-wives. Among the Abouré, conversely, over 9 per cent of both single spouses and junior co-wives have reached this particular level of studies. This tends indirectly to support the view that increased disparities in the level of formal schooling achieved by adult males and females may contribute to maintain the incidence of plural marriage at a relatively high level.

In summary, our two indicators of exposure to modernizing forces show that this exposure *per se* does not lead to a decline in the incidence of plural marriage. A long urban experience enables men to maintain this institution, the popularity of which is apparently not affected by their participation in educational structures. Similarly, it is not so much the relative exposure of women to modernizing forces which shapes their matrimonial status, but rather their numbers, especially in comparison to males with similar characteristics.

This suggests that the second hypothesis formulated earlier tends to be upheld and that the subgroups which are both least and most exposed to modernizing forces retain currently a high incidence of plural marriage.

The testing of this hypothesis also requires an examination both of the changes in value systems fostered by modernization and of the degree to which such changes alter traditional familial styles of life. Indeed, changes in value systems are

124

likely to be accompanied by changes in the types of rewards desired and obtained by individuals. We will analyze in this respect the influence of religious and occupational affiliations, keeping in mind, of course, that they are as much representative of distinctive systems of values and rewards as of differing levels of exposure to social change.

Religious Affiliations

The distribution of religious affiliations in the population of Abidjan is parallel to the distribution of flows of migrations. We have seen that migrants are predominantly derived from the southern sections of the Ivory Coast and from the countries located north of the Ivory Coast. As a result, the majority of residents are Christian (missions have been particularly active in coastal areas) or Muslim (the influence of Islam is particularly visible in the northwest sections of the Ivory Coast, in Mali, and in Upper Volta).

There are, accordingly, few religious differences between Abouré and Bété. The latter people is, however, slightly more oriented toward animist practices or toward a diversity of faith-healing churches.[36] The influence of Catholicism on the style of familial life of the two peoples compared here is nevertheless distinctive. Among the Bété, no less than 85 per cent of monogamous males are Catholic. The corresponding figure is 79 per cent among those who have two wives and 78 per cent among those who have more than two wives. Conversely, 89 per cent of the monogamous Abouré males are Catholic, and this proportion increases to 95 per cent among their polygynist counterparts.

The religious affiliations of the female population are a relatively significant determinant of their matrimonial status. Thus, junior co-wives are more frequently derived from non-Christian backgrounds than are senior co-wives or women married to monogamous males. This is equally true of the two

36. On this point, see Paulme, *Les Bété*, chaps. 9 and 10.

Table 17

Relationship between Religious Affiliation and Matrimonial Status in Abouré and Bété Female Residents of Abidjan (Percentages)

Religious Affiliation	Proportion of Total	Matrimonial Status		
		Single Spouse	Senior Co-wife	Junior Co-wife
Abouré				
Animist	1.0	0.6	0.0	4.7
Muslim	3.1	4.1	0.0	4.7
Harrist [a]	0.9	1.7	0.0	0.0
Christian	89.1	86.0	83.3	85.9
Other	5.9	7.6	16.7	4.7
Total	100.0	100.0	100.0	100.0
N	377	172	24	21
Bété				
Animist	6.0	4.2	8.5	12.3
Muslim	0.9	1.9	0.0	0.0
Harrist	0.2	0.0	0.0	0.0
Christian	83.3	86.1	83.0	71.9
Other	9.6	7.8	8.5	15.8
Total	100.0	100.0	100.0	100.0
N	816	359	106	106
Total Population				
Animist	6.3	5.8	7.4	8.9
Muslim	35.2	42.3	45.1	47.3
Harrist	1.2	1.0	1.0	0.7
Christian	49.9	43.8	39.4	35.2
Other	7.4	7.1	7.1	7.9
Total	100.0	100.0	100.0	100.0
N	11,411	5,798	1,142	1,133

[a] A syncretic cult practiced on the west coast of Africa. See B. Holas, "Bref aperçu sur les principaux cultes syncrétiques de Côte d'Ivoire," *Africa*, XXIV (1954), 55–61.

peoples compared here (Table 17). More important, however, for our study, Bété junior co-wives are significantly less often Christian than their Abouré counterparts. Such differences in turn should affect the strains imposed upon the rank-ordering of Abouré and Bété co-wives.

Occupation

In spite of recent changes in the structure of the labor market, Table 18 shows quite clearly that the active male population of Abidjan is more frequently engaged in manual than in clerical activities and tends to be concentrated in the lower rungs of these two occupational hierarchies.

Differences in the over-all degree of modernization of the two peoples compared here are accompanied by disparities in their forms of participation in the labor market. First, the proportion of unemployed males is larger among the Abouré, which suggests that overurbanization tends to be more characteristic of the groups of migrants who have had the longest and most rewarding contacts with the modern sector of the economy.[37] Second, Bété are proportionately more numerous in manual occupations, as a result of their lower level of formal schooling. Third, the Bété are for the same reason more concentrated in the lower echelons of both manual and clerical hierarchies. Finally, their participation in military and uniformed services (customs, police, etc.) is higher, and this reflects the particular patterns of recruitment followed by administrative authorities during the colonial period.

37. Correspondingly, one can note that individuals with a high social rank are quite likely to support a large number of dependents. In fact, correlation between social rank and size of household is .485. Similarly, one must note that the amount of time necessary for an individual migrant to shelter new migrants has declined over time. Thus, domestic groups whose heads arrived Abidjan between 1930 and 1944 required twenty years to have a membership of three adult units. For groups whose heads arrived between 1945 and 1954, the corresponding amount of time was seven years; For groups whose heads arrived after 1955, this time-span was only four years. See *Structures et transformations des groupements domestiques d'Abidjan* (Paris: SEMA, 1965), p. 87.

Table 18

Relationship between Occupational Status and Incidence of Polygyny in Abouré and Bété Male Residents of Abidjan (Percentages)

Occupational Status	Abouré		Bété		Total Population	
	Proportion of Total	Incidence of Polygyny	Proportion of Total	Incidence of Polygyny	Proportion of Total	Incidence of Polygyny
Unemployed	(31.5)	0.0	(22.9)	11.1	(15.0)	10.4
Farmers, fishermen	1.4	0.0	0.8		2.9	12.1
Artisans, traders	5.5	0.0	3.4	0.0	16.0	20.3
Manual workers						
skilled	4.1	0.0	19.5	28.6	32.2	9.6
semi-skilled	24.7	7.1	24.4	22.2	19.2	13.4
unskilled	6.8	0.0	11.8	9.5	7.4	12.4
White collar workers						
semi-skilled and unskilled	27.5	5.9	13.9	22.7	8.0	12.8
skilled	12.3	14.3	6.3	30.0	4.2	17.5
Managers, professionals	15.0	10.0	11.0	19.2	6.7	17.3
Military and uniformed workers	2.7	50.0	8.9	38.1	3.4	28.5
Total	100.0		100.0		100.0	
N_1[a]	438		1,065		16,000	
N_2[b]	73		237		3,914	

[a] Total census used to compute proportions of unemployed.

[b] Limited sample of all Abidjan residents (as established by the Societe d'Études et de Mathematique Appliquees) used to compute other percentages.

An examination of the association between the occupational and matrimonial status of adult males confirms the validity of the thesis that the incidence of plural marriage depends more upon the resources owned by an individual than upon the prerequisites underlying access to these resources. In fact, incidence of polygyny is higher among clerical than among manual workers. It is higher among skilled than among unskilled persons. Lastly, it characterizes both successful self-employed individuals, such as traders and artisans, and adults who enjoy both stable and relatively high incomes, such as those engaged in uniformed services.

As expected, the influence of occupational status on the distribution of polygyny is not alike for the Abouré and the Bété. In fact, differences in the proportions of polygynists among these two peoples get wider as one moves from manual to clerical occupations or from lower to higher skill levels. As indicated earlier, the widening of these differences reflects increases in the number of choices that they can make with regard to familial styles of life. Among the Bété, occupational mobility is used as a means for maintaining or restoring traditional symbols of power and prestige including plural marriage. Among the Abouré, occupational mobility is more likely to be viewed as a reward in itself, and, as a result, the modernization of *means,* achieved through access to occupations which yield both high prestige and high and stable incomes, is more coterminous with a modernization of *ends,* that is, with the acquisition of "modern" aspirations and values.[38]

Both the differentiation of occupations and the differential incidence of plural marriage among various occupational categories should affect the power structure of polygynous families. The demands exerted on a white-collar worker are different from those experienced by a farmer; in turn, these differences should be accompanied by parallel contrasts in the

38. On the distinction between means and ends, see Moore and Feldman, *Labor Commitment,* chap. 1; and R. Aron, *The Industrial Society* (New York: Praeger, 1967).

organization of the familial groups of these individuals. Further, the degree to which a particular form of polygyny is modified by urbanization also depends upon the extent to which the corresponding segments of the migrant population participate evenly in the variety of occupations offered by an urban environment. Since the incidence of plural marriage is more limited among urbanized Abouré than among urbanized Bété, and since the participation of Abouré males in modern occupations is both higher and more diversified than that of the Bété, one would expect contrasts in the organization of rural and urban polygynous households to be more significant among the Abouré than among the Bété.

As indicated earlier, the participation of urbanized women in the labor market is more moderate than that of adult males (Table 19). In all cases, this participation is determined by the matrimonial status of the individuals investigated, and, as we could have anticipated, single women are in a better position to find gainful employment. Among married women, those married to monogamous males are more frequently able to participate in the highly skilled occupations of the modern sector of the economy than the various co-wives of polygynous households. Conversely, trading activities are proportionately more frequently undertaken by the spouses of polygynists, and especially by junior co-wives.

Yet, the association between matrimonial and occupational status is not identical for Abouré and Bété married women. Among the Abouré, monogamous wives are more likely to be gainfully employed than women in polygynous households, and this should be associated with a marked contrast in the organization of the relevant types of families. On the whole, urbanized Abouré women have a lower participation in the labor force than their rural counterparts and should be, therefore, increasingly dependent upon their husbands. In addition, this dependence should be particularly evident among senior cowives, since of all married women they are the least likely to have independent sources of income. In fact, there should be

Table 19

Relationship between Occupational Status and Matrimonial Status in Abouré and Bété Female Residents of Abidjan (Percentages)

Occupational Status	Un-married	Single Spouse	Senior Co-wife	Junior Co-wife
		Abouré		
Unemployed	(78.1)	(83.1)	(95.8)	(85.7)
Manual	17.1	38.0	0.0	0.0
Clerical and sales	62.8	48.3	100.0	100.0
Service	6.2	0.0	0.0	0.0
Professional, technical, and civil service	6.2	13.7	0.0	0.0
Other	7.7	0.0	0.0	0.0
Total	100.0	100.0	100.0	100.0
N_1 (total)	160	172	20	21
N_2 (total employed)	35	29	1	3
		Bété		
Unemployed	(84.4)	(91.4)	(93.4)	(95.2)
Manual	21.6	41.9	28.6	66.7
Clerical and sales	35.1	48.3	28.6	33.3
Service	29.7	0.0	0.0	0.0
Professional, technical, and civil service	13.6	9.8	42.8	0.0
Other	0.0	0.0	0.0	0.0
Total	100.0	100.0	100.0	100.0
N_1 (total)	244	359	106	107
N_2 (total employed)	37	31	7	6
		Total Population		
Unemployed	(76.4)	(90.8)	(90.1)	(92.9)
Manual	20.3	19.4	22.8	15.0
Clerical and sales	46.4	49.2	67.5	81.3
Service	7.0	1.0	0.1	0.0
Professional, technical, and civil service	7.9	10.6	8.2	3.7
Other	18.4	19.8	1.4	0.0
Total	100.0	100.0	100.0	100.0
N_1 (total)	3,362	5,238	1,135	1,138
N_2 (total employed)	792	536	114	80

increased tensions between senior and junior co-wives, due to their uneven level of participation in the labor market.

In contrast, there is no difference in the occupational status of Bété women in the different types of marriage. Although limited, the participation of all Bété urban women is higher than that of their rural counterparts. Their dependence upon their husband should decline accordingly. Further, since this decline is equally experienced by all women, regardless of their rank-order in the familial structure, there should be fewer conflicts among them than in rural areas.

Plural Marriage and Urbanization: A Final Review

As a first step, we have analyzed the selective character of migrations toward Abidjan and examined the possible implications of this selectivity on both the incidence and the significance of plural marriage.

We have demonstrated that the male-female ratio of the Abouré is more even than that of the Bété; we have indicated that the age distributions of male and female populations of the first ethnic group are more alike than is the case among the Bété. Lastly, we have demonstrated that the educational and occupational levels of the Abouré are higher than those of the Bété. In a second step, we have analyzed how the differing levels of modernization of these two peoples affect their respective types of marriage. We have, for example, observed that urbanization uniformly reduces the incidence of polygyny and that the distribution of this institution retains distinctive profiles among the urbanized segments of the two peoples. We have also noted that the influence of social differentiation on this distribution varies markedly along ethnic lines.

To be sure, early stages of urbanization, both at the individual and collective levels, are accompanied by a decline in plural marriage because of the numerous strains which accompany an accentuated division of labor and rapid changes in style of life.

The corresponding emergence of an autonomous nuclear family may nonetheless be a temporary phenomenon. A successful adjustment to the demands and opportunities of the urban milieu enables certain peoples, including the Bété, to restore their traditional patterns of familial organization—specifically, plural marriage. Conversely, the definitive emergence of a Western-like nuclear family cannot take place before the natural increase of the urban population exceeds increases due to migrations. In other words, it cannot take place before the second and third generations of urban dwellers are numerous enough to unequivocally absorb the psychological implications of a modern, urban way of life, and obviously the Abouré are closer to this threshold than are the Bété.

Under such conditions it is meaningful to examine the degree to which the urban and rural forms of plural marriage found among these two peoples differ from one another.

In this respect, we have seen that in Abidjan the matrimonial status of Bété male individuals is determined by ascriptive factors such as age, but also by exposure to an urban environment, and by levels of education and occupation. The incidence of polygyny is highest among older males, among individuals who have been longest exposed to an urban way of life and who have achieved a high educational and occupational position. In this particular case, then, plural marriage is a privilege acquired by individuals able to reach the top positions of the social hierarchy as defined in both modern and traditional terms. This should introduce a certain amount of continuity in the organization of rural and urban polygynous families. In both cases, polygyny should reinforce the patriarchal orientations of this particular people. In urban as in rural areas, the degree of domestic authority and power claimed by a Bété individual should vary as a direct function of the number of his wives.

In contrast, Abouré urbanized individuals are proportionately more numerous, and the relative size of the most modernized segments of the Abouré population living in Abidjan should be associated with the emergence of a style of life drastically different from that prevailing in the rural locations of this particular people. Further, the incidence of polygyny among this people has fallen below a critical threshold to the point that it has become a marginal phenomenon. Lastly, plural marriage is more randomly distributed among the various socioeconomic segments of the Abouré urbanized population than among the distinctive subgroups of Bété migrants. For these three reasons we can expect more significant differences in the organization of rural and urban Abouré polygynous families.

The extent of these differences, however, not only depends upon the characteristics of the male population but also on the disparities between these characteristics and the corresponding features of the female population and on the relative scarcity of valuable women.

Abouré women who are born in Abidjan, or who have lived there for a long period of time and have attained the highest rungs of the educational ladder open to them, are proportionately more numerous than their Bété counterparts. Their relative number should be associated with the spread of negative attitudes toward polygyny. As a result, there are certain differences in the recruitment patterns of single spouses and of co-wives, and such differences in turn should be associated with marked contrasts in the organization of monogamous and polygynous families. At the same time, however, possible differences in the characteristics of various types of Abouré co-wives have declined in size. Senior and junior co-wives tend to have the same age, the same amount of urban experience, and the same level of exposure to French language. The decline in the number of economic opportunities available in the urban setting as compared with the rural, is however more manifest for senior than for junior co-wives. As a result, the greater degree of dependence on their husbands which urbanization forces on Abouré married women should be more intensely experienced by senior co-wives. This accentuated dependence, in

134

turn, should cause a large number of tensions and strains between these women, their husbands, and their junior co-wives.

In contrast, the number of "modernized" Bété females remains more limited, and their scarcity is particularly important in view of the persistence of positive attitudes toward plural marriage among this people. Modernized Bété women do not consider the status of single spouse to be necessarily more rewarding than that of senior co-wife, but there are marked differences in the recruitment patters of senior and junior co-wives. Senior co-wives tend to be slightly more educated and to have a higher level of exposure to urban norms and practices. Their preeminence along these lines should reinforce the superiority of the domestic position that their seniority entitles them to occupy. Urban Bété women are more likely to have independent sources of income than their rural counterparts and to be accordingly less dependent upon their husbands, and the decline of this dependence is as characteristic of junior as of senior co-wives.

At the beginning of our discussion concerning the effects of urbanization on the distribution of plural marriage, we argued that the decline of this institution would depend both on the susceptibility of antecedent social structures to the eroding power of the forces of social change and on variations in the intensity of this eroding power.

We have been unable to test differences in the vulnerability of the polygynous arrangements prevailing among the Abouré and the Bété. Urbanization fosters parallel declines in the importance of plural marriage among these two peoples. At the same time, however, social differentiation is accompanied by greater variations in the distribution of this institution both among the various subgroups of a particular ethnic group and between the two groups themselves. The most significant contrasts observable along these lines concern the recruitment of monogamous and polygynous spouses in the case of the Abouré, but concern the recruitment of senior and junior co-wives among the Bété.

We have suggested that differences in recruitment will lead in turn to contrasts in the patterns of interaction prevailing among the various types of family investigated here. To sum up our hypotheses, we predict the following:

1. Differences in the average age and in the urban, educational, and occupational status of Abouré and Bété monogamous, senior, and junior co-wives will be associated with the emergence of cleavages in their respective styles of familial interaction.
2. Contrasts in the organization of monogamous and polygynous families will be most evident among the urbanized segments of the Abouré population.
3. Contrasts in the organization of urban and rural polygynous families will be most visible among the Abouré.
4. The domestic authority and power structure of Bété polygynous families will be less fluid and less frequently challenged than that of the Abouré.

We will examine each one of these hypotheses in Chapter 8.

CHAPTER 5

Power and Authority: a Preliminary Comparison

We have formulated a variety of hypotheses to account for variations in the distribution of power and authority among polygynous families, and we have sketched the cultural contexts in which we will test these hypotheses. We must now define the instruments that we will use, that is, we must operationalize our dependent variables—power and authority.

First of all, the definitions of both the power and the authority held by an individual depend on the range within which his culture defines subordinate and superordinate positions. In effect, the potential discrepancy between power and authority probably varies with the distance separating these two positions. The larger this distance, the more power and authority will coincide. Many ethnographic accounts indicate that African women occupy a subordinate position in their social structure, and that they are more objects than subjects of rights. But what is meant by subordinate? Are we comparing the rights and duties attached to their positions with the characteristics of the roles held by their husbands? Or are we contrasting their rights and obligations with those of the male members of their own familial group? Superordinate and subordinate positions are always relative. The first step in the analysis of domestic power structure must therefore deal with a definition of the various ways which are used to determine subordinate and superordinate positions.

An initial evaluation of the status of African women rests upon an examination of their position vis-à-vis their husbands. Although in general it is low, this position is subject to variation. Cultures differ in the amount and intensity of duties which are expected of married women. On a second axis, we can compare the relative positions occupied by women and by the male members of their own kin group. The Abouré and the Bété do not place these two sets of roles at constant intervals on the scales of power and authority. The third axis is that of seniority, which underlies most forms of social participation in Africa. Among all African peoples, senior co-wives occupy a position which is superior to that of their junior counterparts; the extent of this preeminence, however, is variable. Lastly, although their relations with many adult males is one of subordination, women are still entitled to receive respect and deference from their own offspring. Yet the quality of the bond between a mother and her children varies from culture to culture.

It is likely that the placements of individual females on each one of the dimensions sketched above are interdependent. Thus, variations in the degree of social absorption of a married woman into her affinal group are associated with variations in the forms and the degree of subservience that she must observe both toward the various members of her affinal group and those of her own kin group. In short there is a negative relationship between the relative power held by a husband and his bride's brother. Further the more the bond established between a woman and her brother is characterized by ease and informality, the more the tie between the same woman and her husband will be marked by a high degree of formality and restraint. However, are this proposition and its reciprocal universal? Cold and instrumental relations between brothers and sisters are not necessarily balanced by the emergence of friendly and informal relations between husbands and wives.

Rather, the tensions associated with the former bonds may be compensated for by the emergence of cooperative and equalitarian feelings among co-wives. In short, assessment of the regularities underlying the distribution of power within domestic groups requires an examination of the variety of networks of communication existing among the actors present in such groups.

Regardless of the specific mechanisms of equilibrium used within familial organizations, power and authority are always internally differentiated. One form of authority and of power refers to the attainment of both individual and collective goals and is called *instrumental.* The other form, which concerns the maintenance of a maximal amount of cohesiveness within the group of actors under consideration, is called *expressive,* or *social-emotional.* There are regularities in the development of instrumental and expressive forms of authority and power, since variations in the extent of instrumental leadership are paralleled by similar variations in the manifestations of expressive leadership. Indeed, it has been suggested that the function of expressive leadership is to reduce the tensions created by the exercise of instrumental power and authority.[1]

This point being established, is it possible to define a composite measure of the instrumental and expressive leadership exerted by a given individual in the context of his familial relations? It may very well be that an individual or a group holds an instrumental power or authority with regard to the performance of a specific familial function and is invested in a role of expressive leadership as far as the exercise of another function is concerned. The role of the husband can be instrumental with regard to the economic functions of the household but expressive with regard to child-rearing practices. The next step of the analysis concerns, therefore, an examination of certain familial functions, considering one single dyad at a

1. For a full discussion of this point, see M. Freilich, "The Natural Triad in Kinship and Complex Systems," *American Sociological Review,* XXIX, no. 4 (1964), 529–40.

time. This examination should enable us to assess the dominant characteristics of the familial relations prevailing among the two cultures compared here. It will also enable us to determine the degree to which theoretical contrasts between polygynous and monogamous families are substantiated by empirical evidences.

Instrumental Relations between Husbands and Wives

Obviously, the extent of the instrumental leadership exerted by a husband over his wife should be influenced by economic circumstances. The economic dominance of husbands should be inversely related to the participation of their wives in the labor force: the more a married woman is in a position to earn an independent income, the less marked should be the instrumental leadership of her husband. Only one-third of the women in the sample are engaged in occupations outside their household; thus the majority of respondents are therefore likely to be dependent upon their husbands' resources. There are no significant differences along these lines between the wives of monogamous and polygynous males: 35 per cent of single spouses and 32 per cent of the senior wives of polygynists participate in the labor market.

Other avenues are available to married women anxious to acquire a certain economic independence. An increased functionality in their domestic role should enable them to achieve the same goal. This functionality is, however, not necessarily easy to measure. A first indicator can be provided by an examination of the fertility of our respondents. Insofar as the chances of survival of a familial group depends on the size of its membership, it can be argued that the functionality of the domestic role of a woman increases with the number of children that she bears. There are, however, no differences along these lines between the women in monogamous families and the senior co-wives of polygynous households. One-fourth of the women included in these two types of families have had three or more children.[2] A second indicator of the functionality of the domestic role of a married woman is provided by an analysis of the residence of familial groups whose wives do not participate in the labor force and are therefore housewives. The functionality of rural housewives is greater than that of their urban counterparts, because the former must perform a greater variety of tasks and are expected, in addition, to participate in the economic enterprises of their husbands.[3] High functionality is more characteristic of co-wives than of women entering monogamous marriages. More than two-thirds of housewives in polygynous families have a rural residence and, accordingly, a high functionality, as against only 56 per cent of monogamous wives.

What are the implications of these similarities and differences upon the various aspects of the domestic power structures of families? Table 20 summarizes the patterns which characterize the handling of familial resources. This table shows that the perceived authority of husbands over familial resources is not commensurate with the extent of their contributions. Only 38 per cent of the women interviewed report that their husbands exert an absolute control over the budget

2. These results are at variance with those indicated by E. Van de Valle, "Marriage in African Censuses and Inquiries," in *The Demography of Tropical Africa*, ed. W. Brass *et al.* (Princeton: Princeton University Press, 1968), pp. 231–32; and with those reported by H. V. Muhsam, "Fertility of Polygamous Marriages," *Population Studies*, X (1956), 3–16. These two observations are confirmed by the results of the demographic survey of the Ivory Coast population at large. For the entire country, the fertility rate of monogamous wives averages 261. This drops to 235 for women in bigamous families, and to 182 for the wives of polygynists who have at least three co-wives. See *Supplement trimestriel au bulletin mensuel de statistiques*, vol. VIII (Abidjan: Ministere des Affaires Economiques, des Finances et du Plan, 1966), p. 74. However, such statistics do not necessarily take into account the differences in age of the various co-wives.

3. On this point, see the responses given to A. Kobben by his Bété informants in "Le Planteur noir," *Études éburnéennes*, V (1956), 129.

141

Table 20

Distribution of Control over Familial Budget (Percentages)

	Monogamous Families	Polygynous Families
Separate budgets	35.5	33.5
Dominance of husband	37.7	41.4
Dominance of wife	21.1	20.8
Equality between spouses	4.2	2.9
Other, no answer	1.5	1.4
Total	100.0	100.0
N	1,012	759

and are therefore the only ones to hold the family purse-strings. One-fifth of the women interviewed consider themselves able to control the spending of family funds, either because of the relative power that they have acquired over their husbands, owing to their functionality or to their economic independence, or because of the delegation of financial responsibilities by the husband. However, the proportion of households where the budgets of conjugal partners are separate averages one-third, which is analogous to that of wives engaged in independent economic activities. At first glance, these two dimensions seem to be interrelated. We will show that, in fact, the women who participate in the labor force handle their budgets separately from that of their husbands.[4] More important, however, the same table indicates that monogamous and polygynous families do not differ from one another in this respect; polygyny hardly accentuates the financial authority of the husband over his senior co-wife.

To be responsible for the handling of familial resources is, however, only one facet of financial authority and power. It is

4. Regardless of ethnicity, half of the women participating in the labor force have autonomous budgets, as against only one-fourth of those who are unemployed.

equally important to determine which spouse exerts the right to initiate expenses. This right can be exerted by the individual partner who holds the family purse-strings, or it can be claimed by his or her mate. Further, its exercise is likely to vary with the item to be bought. Here, we will consider only the processes by which the decision to buy clothes for the respondent herself is taken. Since she is the beneficiary of this particular expense, one can anticipate that she will be prone to affirm her autonomy in this respect. Her confession that relevant initiatives are taken by her husband should therefore be considered a strong indicator of his actual authority.[5] Interestingly enough, the proportion of women recognizing the financial authority of their husbands in these matters is a little less than one-half. Thus, the extent of this particular manifestation of the dominance of African husbands is rather limited. Further, there does not seem to be a close association between the women's perception of the domestic power structure and their participation in the labor force. Neither is there any apparent parallel between the distributions of which partner controls

Table 21

Distribution of Initiative to Purchase Clothes for the Wife (Percentages)

Initiative Exerted by	Monogamous Families	Polygynous Families
Husband	46.6	50.3
Wife	27.0	26.1
Either one	23.2	20.6
No answer	3.2	3.0
Total	100.0	100.0
N	1012	759

5. The wording of the item did not enable us to establish necessary distinctions between decision-making processes and influences. Although the actual purchase may have been made by the husband, he may still have been influenced by his wife.

familial resources and of which one initiates certain types of expenses. Table 21 indicates that the particular form of authority represented by the right to purchase clothes is similarly distributed among polygynous and monogamous families.

Social and Emotional Relations between Spouses

Thus far, we have seen that there is an over-all economic dominance of the husband over his wife or wives but that the intensity of this dominance is not consistent. Indeed, the fact that a married woman is a housewife does not necessarily mean that her husband controls familial resources; neither does it imply that she is subjected to the control of her spouse when she wants to acquire new clothes. Moreover, the degree of dominance exerted by these African husbands seems to be independent of plural marriage.

Are there mechanisms to compensate for the effects of this dominance? Does this dominance affect the social and emotional climate of the family? A possible answer to these questions might be provided by an examination of the types of quarrels occurring in the various types of households investigated. Table 22 shows that the economic dominance of African husbands is seldom accompanied by domestic quarrels of a financial nature. Rather, the males' superordinate position is challenged on other grounds. Frequently, each partner suspects his or her spouse to be unfaithful. Similarly, a husband often accuses his wife of responding more gracefully to the demands of her own relatives than to the requests of his family, and the wife herself often holds corresponding grievances. In short, the nature of most frequent domestic quarrels reveals the particular nature of the social and emotional involvement of African conjugal partners in their matrimonial life; each one perceives the loyalties of his or her mate to be unduly

144

Table 22

Subjects of Domestic Quarrels (Percentages)		
	Monogamous Families	Polygynous Families
Sexual and emotional interaction	35.0	35.6
Child rearing	11.6	10.3
Money	19.4	19.0
Division of labor	7.3	9.5
Relations with affines	23.2	21.3
Others	3.5	4.2
No answer	—	0.1
Total	100.0	100.0
N	1012	759

turned toward their original family or toward potential rivals. Indeed, the differentiation of rights and obligations attached to kin groups on the one hand and to the sexes on the other minimizes the cohesiveness of the nuclear family. Plural marriage, however, does not modify the types of tensions which oppose spouses to one another.

Given the economic dominance of her husband and the nature of the strains evident between spouses, male authority may remain unquestioned or may be subjected to a variety of challenges. In effect, power and authority are not necessarily coterminous: a wife may feel that the outcome of most domestic quarrels modifies in her favor her bargaining position with her husband, or alternatively that such quarrels reinforce the latter's dominance. Table 23 shows that the proportion of wives yielding to their husbands is greater than the reverse. Interestingly enough, patterns of budgetary control and perceived outcome of domestic strains are distributed in a similar manner; an examination of these two forms of domestic relations shows that African familial orientations and values are

145

Table 23

Outcome of Family Quarrels, as Perceived by the Wife (Percentages)

Person Perceived as Yielding Most Frequently	Monogamous Families	Polygynous Families
Husband	36.7	34.7
Wife	42.8	48.1
Both	9.7	8.0
None	2.6	2.1
No answer	8.2	7.1
Total	100.0	100.0
N	1012	759

not equalitarian. Control over familial resources is likely to be exclusively exerted by either the husband or the wife. Similarly, domestic tensions constitute opportunities for the preeminent partner to reaffirm the superordinate character of his or her position. In both contexts, familial relations are exemplified by a zero-sum model. Competition, rather than cooperation, is the main determinant of the system of interaction between spouses. This lack of equalitarian orientations characterizes all types of households under analysis. The outcome of domestic quarrels is alike for both polygynous and monogamous families; plural marriage barely accentuates the power exerted by African husbands.

The lack of equalitarian orientations is associated with the emergence of double-standard rules. For example, less than one-half of the respondents consider that adultery presents implications independent of the sex of the offender. One-fourth, on the contrary, believe male adultery to be a worse domestic offense, whereas the remaining one-fourth regard female adultery as the most serious breach in conjugal morality. The even division of opinion on this topic certainly accounts for the high incidence of domestic quarrels pertaining to illegitimate sexual relations. Social norms appear to be particularly unclear on this point, but the high proportion of women who accept double-standard rules of domestic behavior nevertheless confirms our previous observation that familial relations are barely influenced by equalitarian orientations. Marriage is regarded as a necessary evil, an institution leading to power struggles both between familial groups and individuals. Whether married to monogamous or polygynous individuals, the women included in our sample are characterized by the low degree of their social and emotional absorption into their affinal family.

The large emotional and social distance between spouses also leads married women to display a high level of indifference toward the occupational status of their husbands. Few respondents are eager to see their spouse acquire a more rewarding occupation or to earn more money in his present job. There is, a slight difference in this regard between monogamous and polygynous wives: 17 per cent of monogamous respondents report that they are concerned with the upward mobility of their husbands, as against 13 per cent of their polygynous counterparts. However minimal, this contrast tends to indicate that plural marriage requires men to be socially and economically successful, which reduces the amount of economic anxieties eventually experienced by their wives.

Among the peoples under consideration, as among most African cultures, there is an institutionalization of male preeminence. Mealtime etiquette, for example, symbolizes the superordinate position of men, who eat alone and are served first. Plural marriage sharpens the social distance between sexes in this context and only 8 per cent of the senior co-wives included in the sample eat with their husbands and children, as against 16 per cent of their monogamous counterparts. In short, plural marriage leads married women to display more apparent deference toward their husbands.

Relations between Wives and Their Families of Origin

At the beginning of this chapter, we assumed that there is an inverse relationship between the relative power exerted on a married woman by her affines on the one hand and by her own family on the other. The testing of this hypothesis requires an examination of not only the power held by husbands but also the control retained by the family of origin of the respondents in the sample. It is to this point, therefore, that we must now turn our attention. Since all the children born of a woman must be legitimately placed in a descent group, the location where this woman gives birth may provide an indication of the extent to which she maintains obligations toward her own family. Of course, the fulfillment of such an obligation depends on a series of factors, such as age and number of previous matrimonial experiences. It also depends on the rules of descent followed by the group to which she belongs and on the distance between her place of origin and the village of her husband. Table 24 shows that a little less than one-fourth of all respondents return to their mother's residence to deliver their first child, yet it does not enable us to analyze the nature of the associa-

Table 24

Place of Delivery of the First-Born Child (Percentages)		
	Monogamous Families	Polygynous Families
Hospital or maternity ward	29.4	26.4
Husband's residence	25.1	29.5
Mother's residence	23.2	19.0
Elsewhere	8.4	10.3
Unapplicable, no answer	13.9	14.8
Total	100.0	100.0
N	1012	759

148

tion between the power held by a husband and that maintained by his affines.[6] The table does show, however, that plural marriage has no effect on the loyalties maintained by a married woman with her own family of origin.

The ability for a married woman to take a post-partum leave from her husband can be treated as a second indicator of the power that her family exerts over her. Table 25 shows that

Table 25

Length of Post-Partum Leave Taken after Delivery of First-Born Child (Percentages)

Length of Leave	Monogamous Families	Polygynous Families
None	21.7	25.0
Less than a month	13.6	15.8
A month and more	40.2	36.3
Not applicable, no answer	24.5	22.9
Total	100.0	100.0
N	1012	759

more than one-half of the respondents return to their place of origin for a varying period of time. This proportion is higher than that of women giving birth at their mother's place and is illustrative therefore of the centrifugal forces exerted on African nuclear families. Since fertility is a crucial determinant of the domestic status of married women and increases their chances of being rewarded, it is likely that a large number of them will return to their own family, which dispenses the most valuable rewards. In this group, indeed, women enjoy a greater number of privileges and, in addition, a far clearer position than is assigned to them by their affines. Table 25 does not enable us to determine whether the ability of a married woman to take such a leave is inversely associated with

6. For this point, see Chapter 6.

the authority and power of her husband. It confirms nevertheless that polygyny does not significantly modify the degree to
which a married woman affirms her solidarity with her family
of origin.

An examination of the institutionalized forms of communication between a married woman and her own family is, however, not sufficient for our purposes. We must also consider
more spontaneous forms of interaction between these actors.
In effect we have not only made the assumption that the
relative degrees of power exerted on a married woman by her
husband and by her kin will be inversely related but have also
contended that these two forms of power will be qualitatively
different. How can we, however, measure the strength of noninstitutionalized forms of familial solidarity?

African folktales contain vivid descriptions of the difficulties that an individual encounters when he must choose
between following his own inclinations and fulfilling his obligations. For example, there is the Bura story of a man who has
found seven eyes, out of which he has kept two for himself and
two for his wife. Since there are only three eyes left, his
problem is to decide whether he should give two to his own
mother, in which case he will feel ashamed toward his wife and
her mother, or whether he should give two to his mother-in-
law, in which case he does not express his true feelings.[7] There
is a similar Bété story, where a man is crossing a river on a
boat with his wife, his mother, his mother-in-law, and his
sisters. If he is the only one who knows how to swim, and if
the boat overturns, whom does he save?[8] In the present survey, this particular story was presented as a question and was
adapted to the sex of the respondents who were asked whether
they would save their mothers or their husbands.

7. See S. Feldmann, ed., *African Myths and Tales* (New York: Dell,
1963), p. 201.
8. See D. Paulme "Litterature orale et comportements sociaux," *L'Homme*,
I (1961), 37–49.

Given the amount of tension between conjugal partners and the low degree of emotional absorption of the respondents in their affinal group, one could have anticipated that a large proportion of the women would prefer to save their own mothers. This expectation was ill-founded, and in fact three-fourths of the women included in the sample indicated that they would save their husbands. Their motives for doing so were very explicit. To give priority to one's own mother in this situation would constitute a serious breach in the obligations expected of a married woman. Such a breach would accordingly expose not only the women but their entire familial group to the legitimate retaliations of the husband's family. Thus, this particular item gives some indication about the feelings of obligation to the norms of wifely behavior and suggests the conditions within which noninstitutionalized forms of solidarity may conflict with the obligations imposed upon a woman because of her marriage. It also indicates that the presence of one or several other co-wives does not influence the expression of the feelings displayed by married women toward their mothers and their husbands: the proportion of women saving their husbands is alike for both monogamous and polygynous families.

Relations among Co-wives

The extent of the domestic dominance exerted by husbands is alike for polygynous and monogamous families. The degree to which women from these two types of households maintain their loyalty toward their family of origin is similar. Yet, the responses of polygynous families to the strains resulting from the distance separating spouses from one another may still present some original features. Such strains can induce the development of informal and easy ties among the co-wives themselves. Alternatively, these strains can be conducive to the emergence of competitive feelings among co-wives. Table 26

Table 26

Frequency and Origin of Quarrels among Co-wives
(Percentages)

Frequency [a]		Origin [a]	
High	26.9	Dealings with husbands	41.3
Medium	27.4	Misbehavior of children	18.2
Low	45.7	Lack of solidarity between co-wives	23.3
		Others	17.2
Total	100.0	Total	100.0
N_1	373	N_1	373
No Answer	386	No Answer	386

---

[a] All the analyses of these questions have been conducted after elimination of the "no answers" category.

shows that almost half the senior co-wives perceive quarrels among other co-wives as infrequent. This response rebuts the stereotype according to which relations among co-wives are uniformly tense and strained. The variance of this distribution is, however, quite large and its size should enable us to determine whether frequency of quarrels among co-wives is associated with the extent of the domestic dominance exerted by the husband.

An examination of this association also requires an investigation of the perceived sources of conflicts among co-wives. Whatever its intensity, competition among them can be induced by their husband's attitudes and patterns of behavior or can be the product of dysfunctions in the group that they form by themselves. Table 26 shows that the most frequent quarrel among co-wives concerns their attitudes and behavior toward their husband. The treatment that each of them can obtain from the head of the household seems to be the most important determinant of the form of their interaction. A little less than one-fourth of the respondents indicate, however, that such conflicts also arise when co-wives do not respect their mutual obligations. More specifically, they refer in this context to the instances where women refuse to perform their own share of domestic chores. But this remains a minor factor affecting the form of relations among the women of a polygynous household.

Table 27

Child-Rearing Patterns among Co-wives (Percentages)

Authority Exerted by

Each mother separately	25.2
All mothers jointly, or by turns	33.8
Senior co-wife	32.7
Others	1.2
No answer	7.1
Total	100.0
N	759

Table 27 indirectly suggests certain interactions are unavoidable between co-wives; in one-third of the cases, the first co-wife is entitled, because of her seniority, to control the socialization of *all* children present in the household. Frequent interactions between co-wives also result from more spontaneous cooperation in the same field of child-rearing practices: thus, another third of the senior co-wives included in the sample report that all co-wives raise their children jointly, which enables each of them to engage in trading or farming activities and to be less vulnerable to the pressures which can be developed by the head of the household. In short, this table shows that the stereotyped view that polygyny necessarily reinforces the particular bond between the mother and her offspring is ill-founded. In fact, even as polygyny minimizes the impact of adult males on children, it accentuates the significance of the relations between all the women present in the household and the offspring of each one; such relations are collective, and not

153

individualized. The instances where co-wives are able to raise their own children separately are limited in number, not exceeding one-fourth of the cases.

To sum up, the three items of the questionnaire pertaining to the organization of familial relations in the context of polygynous families demonstrate that such relations are highly variable. The frequency and the object of quarrels among co-wives and the patterns of interaction between them with regard to child-rearing practices are distributed in a way which suggest that there is not one but several types of arrangements prevailing in this particular form of family. Our task remains to analyze the determinants of these types.

Polygyny and Child-Rearing Practices

We have seen that relations among family members are not systematically distributed according to family type, but that the organization of polygynous and monogamous families is essentially alike. Can we infer that the child-rearing practices prevailing in these two types of families are not different either?

We have indeed argued that the bonds established by married women with a variety of familial actors are interdependent. One might, however, speculate about the extent to which the dominance of the husband generalizes to his relations with his offspring. Instrumental when they pertain to his interaction with his wife or wives, are his power and authority over his children also instrumental in nature? If so, does this mean that the authority and the power claimed by an African mother over her children are essentially expressive? One might also speculate about the consequences of the presence in the household of at least two adult females on the nature of the bond that each one develops with her children. It has been argued that polygyny leads to matrifocality: does this equation imply that wives of polygynist men are invested with both instrumental and expressive roles in their relations with their children?

The importance of the emotional ties developed between a mother and her offspring can be indirectly measured by the length of the nursing period. The longer this period, the more expressive the maternal role. In fact, a substantial proportion of the mothers included in the sample nursed their children for a period exceeding one year. (See Table 28.) But there are

Table 28

Length of Nursing Period of the Last-Born Child (Percentages)

Length	Monogamous Families	Polygynous Families
Less than one year	10.3	7.2
Between 1 and 2 years	36.0	33.6
More than 2 years	25.0	31.4
Interrupted by new pregnancy	10.9	11.2
Unapplicable, no answer	17.8	16.6
Total	100.0	100.0
N	1012	759

hardly any significant differences between monogamous and polygynous families along these lines. The expressive character of the maternal role does not seem to be affected by plural marriage. This is not a surprise since we have already seen that it does not enhance the instrumental character of men's domestic leadership, either.

The stress put upon the expressive nature of the maternal role can also be measured by the length of the initial indulgence period, that is, the period during which no control of any sort is exerted upon the young child. In the present sample, weaning and the end of this period are not simultaneous. Further, whereas the distribution of the nursing period has a large variance, that of the initial indulgence period is highly concentrated. Almost two-thirds of the respondents start disciplining their children when the latter start talking. Only one-fifth of the mothers end the initial indulgence period when the child begins walking, and only one-tenth of them indicate that they do not exert any control over their children before they begin attending school. This second indicator of the expressive nature of the maternal role does not reveal any difference between monogamous and polygynous families. Plural marriage does not seem to affect the nature of the bond interwoven between mothers and children.

The expressive nature of the maternal role should prevent African women from participating in the instrumental decisions pertaining to their children. Decision to send children to school is a case in point. Because of their minimal exposure to European norms and practices, most African women lack the necessary skills to control the behavior of their offspring in this regard.[9] Table 29 confirms the validity of our assump-

Table 29

Distribution of Decision-Making Patterns concerning the Schooling of Children (Percentages)

Who Decides	Monogamous Families	Polygynous Families
Father	58.6	63.4
Mother	11.6	10.2
Both	23.7	20.3
Unapplicable, no answer	6.1	6.1
Total	100.0	100.0
N	1012	759

9. The participation of the two sexes in educational institutions differs markedly from one another. See, on this point, Remi Clignet and Philip Foster, *The Fortunate Few* (Evanston, Ill.: Northwestern University Press, 1966), chaps. 3 and 4. Depending upon their own educational level, the participation of married women in the decisions pertaining to the formal schooling of their offspring is also influenced by the rules underlying division of roles and of power in domestic groups. This point is suggested by E. and M. C. Ortigues, *Oedipe Africain* (Paris: Plon, 1966), p. 25.

tions. The dominance of African fathers in this particular area is even more evident than their control over the purchase of clothes for their wives. In other words, the dominance of African males affects not only their relations with their wives but their relations with their children as well. We have seen that there are no differences between monogamous and polygynous families regarding the extent of the financial dominance exerted by husbands over their wives. Nor is there any marked cleavage between these two types of families concerning the instrumental control of children.

However, because of the rigidity of the division of domestic roles along sex lines and because of the lack of equalitarian orientations among conjugal partners, one might speculate about the extent to which both parents have similar expectations concerning the participation of their children in modern activities. Since mothers rarely participate in the decision to send children to school, do they perceive clearly the mechanisms by which the academic behavior of their children is controlled? Table 30 shows that such a control tends to be most often perceived as a husband's attribute. It also indicates that, in many cases, the distance between both generations and sexes prevents wives from clearly perceiving who in the family is supposed to punish a child who does not meet the require-

Table 30

Punishment of Children Who Fail to Meet Academic Standards (Percentages)

Punishment Exerted by	Monogamous Families	Polygynous Families
Father	37.5	41.0
Mother	10.5	12.4
Either one	13.2	11.6
No punishment	38.8	35.0
Total	100.0	100.0
N	1012	759

157

ments of the academic system. This is one of the major difficulties with which African families must cope in their adjustment to the demands of modernization. The diverging rates of participation of the two sexes in modern occupational and educational structures prevent parents from exerting consistent demands on their children. Indeed, these disparities reinforce the rigidity which characterizes the division of domestic roles along sex lines.

One could anticipate a close association between the role of the mother toward her children and the nature of the strategies that she uses to punish them. Because of the expressive nature of her role, one can hypothesize that she will primarily use love withdrawal to cope with deviance. Among cultures oriented toward shame rather than guilt, and where the strains and dangers faced by the individual are both numerous and serious, the emotional isolation of the child is a formidable threat.

However, Table 31 shows that this withdrawal is not the sole strategy used by the respondents. In fact, the proportions of mothers who use emotional and physical punishments are highly comparable. In the first group have been placed not

Table 31

Type of Punishment Used by Mothers (Percentages)		
	Monogamous Families	**Polygynous Families**
Physical punishment	34.5	34.5
Expressive punishment	34.9	44.0
Deprivational punishment	3.9	1.4
Other	7.9	7.1
None	18.8	13.0
Total	100.0	100.0
N	1012	759
Index of dissimilarity between fathers' and mothers' punishment	4.5	6.0

only all the respondents who use love withdrawal but also all those who manipulate in one form or another the important need of the child for social affiliations. In the second category are grouped the mothers who use as punishments (a) spanking, (b) more traditional techniques such as rubbing parts of the deviant's body with irritating substances (for instance, red pepper), and (c) maintaining the child in an uncomfortable position for a long period of time: for example, with his arms outstretched. Deprivational punishments are not frequently used; perhaps poverty makes this particular technique of control inappropriate.

Polygynous mothers are slightly more prone than their monogamous counterparts to use expressive punishments and to manipulate the needs of their children for social affiliation. We have seen that mothers from both forms of families use expressive sanctions equally in their dealings with their *young* children. However slight, the difference indicated above suggests that this similarity tends to decline as children grow older. The slight emphasis on expressive punishments by polygynous mothers indirectly confirms the high significance of the bonds that they maintain with their children. The point remains that this eventual contrast between the two types of mothers is not immediate and does not take place before their respective children have grown beyond a certain age.

Interestingly enough, all respondents consider the socializing strategies adopted by their husbands to be similar to their own. The distributions of the punishments used by the respondents and of those that they attribute to their husbands have low indices of dissimilarity. Further, these indices are alike for both monogamous and polygynous families. In short, plural marriage does not modify the perceptions that women have about the relations developed by their husbands toward their children. This is not surprising: we have already observed that plural marriage does not modify the perceptions of women about the extent of the domestic dominance exerted by their husbands.

159

Table 32

Relative Importance of Demands Imposed upon Children
(Percentages)

Demand Considered Most Important	Monogamous Families	Polygynous Families
Respect for parents and elders	29.1	29.4
Participation in domestic chores	8.6	7.9
Academic achievement	48.1	49.2
Other	4.3	4.9
No answer	9.9	8.6
Total	100.0	100.0
N	1012	759

Granted that the role of African mothers is, on the whole, expressive, does this affect the demands exerted upon the children? The answer is negative (Table 32). For example, all respondents are aware of the high rewards attached to formal schooling, and academic success is what they most expect from their children—even though they are not necessarily clear about the mechanisms of social control most likely to produce this hoped-for achievement. Respect for elders and parents is the second most important demand of these mothers. This reflects the transitional conditions in which contemporary Africa is actually placed. Families are expected both to promote upward mobility and to maintain a high level of familial loyalty, in order to insure a maximal amount of stability in traditional organizations. Change is never total. An emphasis on modernization requires social organizations to be strong enough to support the strains associated with change. Table 32 also indicates that the demands of mothers do not vary with the type of family to which they are affiliated. In particular, polygyny is not at all conducive to a lessening of maternal aspirations concerning the participation of their offspring in educational enterprises. This confirms our observation made elsewhere that monogamous and polygynous families tend to be evenly represented in the secondary-school system of the Ivory Coast.[10]

One can hypothesize, however, that the socializing functions of African mothers are likely to vary with the mobility imposed upon the child. These functions should differ when the child is raised primarily in the household of his immediate parents or when he is placed under the successive authority of a variety of relatives, in which case he drifts from one compound to another. Since polygyny characterizes individuals who already occupy a high position in the social structure, one would expect their children to be less mobile and more likely to be raised at home than the offspring of monogamous families. This assumption is not borne out, for polygynous and monogamous families do not differ from one another along these lines. (See Table 33.) In only one-half the cases are the children of the respondents consistently raised in the household of their immediate parents. In other words, the socialization of children does not necessarily take place within the nuclear family; it involves a large number of agents, and this prevents children

Table 33

Relative Importance of Nuclear and Extended Families in Raising Children

Children Raised by	Monogamous Families	Polygynous Families
Parents	46.7	43.1
Maternal kin group	11.5	12.5
Paternal kin group	14.7	12.3
Others	23.5	27.8
No answer	3.6	4.3
Total	100.0	100.0
N	1012	759

10. On this point see Clignet and Foster, *The Fortunate Few*, chaps. 3, 4, and 6.

from identifying strongly with an adult role because they are ultimately exposed to a variety of conflicting models.

We have tried to explore various aspects of the problems raised by the socialization of children among cultures which are undergoing transitional experiences. The problem remains to determine how the adult actors involved in the situation perceive their interaction; more specifically, to assess the consistent character of their aspirations with regard to the requirements attached to their roles as socialization agents. In spite of the minimal amount of cooperation among conjugal partners, and in spite of the maximal emotional distance between them, wives are aware that effective socialization requires a maximal amount of interaction between spouses. A little over two-thirds of the women report the belief that both parents should participate *evenly* in the socialization of the oncoming generation. Only one-fifth think that this socialization should be exclusively carried out by one of the two parents, regardless of the sex of the child, whereas the proportion of respondents indicating that socialization should only involve actors of the same sex does not exceed 10 per cent. To sum up, socialization is the only area of familial life where the need for cooperation is considered important by the respondents. Their concern with this specific form of cooperation is independent of the form of the household to which they belong. Insofar as segregation of domestic roles along sex lines is a feature of traditional African families, it is noteworthy that senior co-wives are as eager to reject this pattern as are monogamous wives.

Conclusions

The purpose of this chapter was to identify the four dimensions which will be used to determine the relative position occupied by married women in the context of monogamous and polygynous households. We will analyze relations between these women and their husbands, relations between these women and their family of origin, relations among co-wives in polygynous households, and, finally, relations between these women and their offspring. The data presented in this chapter have not enabled us to determine the interdependent character of these four dimensions. However, examination of the relations between women and men has revealed the uniformly sizeable distance which separates husbands and wives. On the whole, African husbands are likely to exert a strong leadership on both their wives and their offspring. The same data have also shown the lack of equalitarian orientations in the functioning of African familial groups. The analysis of the interaction between married women and their family of origin has enabled us to demonstrate that (1) the control maintained by the family of origin of the respondents is far from negligible, (2) this control may interfere with the domestic power of the husband, and (3) this interference is probably due to differences in the authority and the power of the two familial groups involved rather than to differences in the power and the authority of the individual actors. Further, the variability of the relations developed between co-wives has led us to hypothesize that there is not *one* but *several* types of polygynous families. Lastly, the data concerning child-rearing practices have enabled us to assess the significance of the expressive role of African mothers toward their children.

More important, however, this chapter was also intended to examine the validity of the stereotype according to which it is possible to build universal contrasts between polygynous and monogamous households. The data included in the present chapter show that, as they may be derived from the relevant perceptions of married women, the organizations of monogamous and polygynous families are alike. To be sure, there are slight differences between these two types of households, and they run consistently in the same direction. They uniformly suggest that the husband's power and authority are more apparent among polygynous families; yet none of the differences is significant.

Two competing hypotheses may account for the absence of such significant contrasts. First, we may assume that contrasts between the requirements attached to single and to plural marriages cannot be explained at the level of familial groups but at the level of cultures. In short, we should not expect differences between monogamous and polygynous families but rather between monogamous and polygynous cultures. In the present study, the two cultures from which the respondents have been derived are both polygynous. It is therefore normal that we cannot isolate any meaningful contrast between the two forms of households that we compare. We suppose in this context that monogamous families are merely potential polygynous families, and that the influence of plural marriage as a model is so pervasive that it shapes the perceptions and attitudes of individual actors regardless of the actual composition of the familial group in which they are involved.

The second hypothesis views polygyny as an intervening rather than as an independent variable. It posits that the variance in the distribution of the various traits characteristic of domestic power structures differ so much between the two cultures compared here that the contrast between monogamy and polygyny is blurred. In other words, we assume that the intensity and direction of the differences between polygyny and monogamy vary by ethnic group and that generalization across cultures is impossible. Our next task, therefore, is to examine how both polygyny and monogamy operate in the two cultures constituting our universe. It is only then that we will be able to determine the limits within which contrasts between monogamous and polygynous families are meaningful; only then will we be able to measure the factors accounting for the variance in the distribution of the various traits recorded here.

CHAPTER 6

Type of Descent, Type of Marriage

The two ethnic groups being compared here have distinctive forms of familial organization. The Abouré follow matrilineal lines of descent, whereas Bété families are patrilineal in nature. Moreover, the positions occupied by the women of these two peoples in their respective affinal groups are not comparable. Abouré wives are less absorbed into the family of their husbands than are their Bété counterparts. Because of this low absorption, the marriage of their daughters represents, for Abouré parents, losses which are both quantitatively and qualitatively limited: (1) quantitatively limited, because the children born of an Abouré woman are parts of the labor force that her own kin group can utilize, and because the income that she derives from the exercise of an independent occupation can be diverted into the resources of her own family; (2) qualitatively limited, because an Abouré woman maintains a variety of obligations toward the male and female members of her own extended family. Accordingly, her own parents are not in a position to expect a high brideprice from the bridegroom or his relatives. Over one-half of the Abouré respondents indicate that their marriage has not apparently been accompanied by the payment of any form of matrimonial compensation. The corresponding proportion is much lower

165

among the Bété, where only a little more than one-third of the respondents give a similar answer. Contrasts between Abouré and Bété along these lines are the same for both monogamous and polygynous families.

The presence of differences in the brideprice paid for Abouré and Bété women, along with the absence of contrasts in the matrimonial compensation paid by monogamous and polygynist males, suggest that the social value of a woman varies with cultural factors but is not influenced by the type of marriage that she contracts. They also lead to the hypothesis that the losses incurred by the bride's family because of her marriage are determined by cultural norms but remain independent of the type of household into which the bride enters. This is not surprising; after all, we have argued that in the context of the two cultures compared here many monogamous families should be regarded as potential polygynous families.

Differences do appear when one takes the time dimension into consideration. Over time, polygyny affects the size of the losses that the family of origin of the respondents have experienced. Thus, Table 34 indicates clearly not only that Abouré married women are more likely than their Bété counterparts to participate in labor force, but also that the

Table 34

Participation of Married Women in Labor Force (Percentages)

	Monogamous families		Polygynous families	
	Abouré	Bété	Abouré	Bété
Engaged in independent activities	62.5	12.2	76.2	5.4
Not engaged in independent activities	37.5	87.8	23.8	94.6
Total	100.0	100.0	100.0	100.0
N	464	548	281	478

contrast between the two peoples along these lines is sharper between polygynous than between monogamous families. In fact, an Abouré senior co-wife has more chances than a single spouse to exert an independent activity; the reverse is true among the Bété. In other words, it seems that plural marriage increases the degree of social absorption of Bété senior co-wives into their affinal groups but has an opposite effect on their Abouré counterparts. This leads us to suspect that plural marriage has a differential impact on the familial organization of the two peoples and that it exaggerates the existing cleavages between their cultural orientations.

Economic and Instrumental Leadership of the Husbands

In Table 35, we have summarized the various aspects of the relations developed between husbands and wives, between these wives and their family of origin, between these co-wives themselves, and last, between them and their offspring. An inspection of columns (1) and (2) or of (3) and (4) illustrates the contrasts and similarities between the general familial organizations of the Abouré and the Bété. The examination of the differences between (1) and (2) on the one hand and (3) and (4) on the other provides some indication as to the degree to which polygyny reduces or increases such contrasts. Since polygyny limits the extent to which Bété married women are able to participate independently of their husbands in the labor market but has the opposite effect among the Abouré, it is not surprising to note that the financial authority of husbands is more manifest among polygynous than monogamous Bété families, whereas the same authority is less apparent among polygynous than monogamous Abouré families. Thus, Bété husbands are more likely to exert an absolute control over the resources of their family and this is particularly so when they have more than one wife. In contrast, the

167

Table 35

Relationship between Type of Marriage and Various Other Aspects of Family Life (Percentages)

	Monogamous families		Polygynous families	
	(1) Abouré	(2) Bété	(3) Abouré	(4) Bété
Conjugal Relations				
Incidence of women reporting:				
1. Exclusive control of family budget by husband	22.4	50.5	11.7	58.8
2. Exclusive control of clothing expenditures by husband	34.9	56.6	25.6	64.6
3. Domestic quarrels mainly caused by adultery	50.9	21.7	59.8	21.3
4. Exclusive dominance of husband in domestic quarrels	25.0	58.0	21.7	63.6
5. Single standard on conjugal morality	62.5	32.5	67.6	27.8
6. High concern with the upward mobility of their husbands	10.8	21.5	11.4	14.0
7. Patterned segregation at mealtime	83.9	84.5	89.0	91.8
Relations between Wives and their Families				
Incidence of women reporting:				
8. Preeminent status of their mothers	18.8	30.3	21.4	24.1
9. Their mother's residence as the place where they delivered their first child	42.9	6.6	45.2	3.6
10. Post-partum leaves from their husband	59.1	49.3	58.4	48.3

Table 35—(Continued)

	Monogamous Families		Polygynous Families	
	(1) Abouré	(2) Bété	(3) Abouré	(4) Bété
Incidence of women reporting:				
11. Cooperative practices in raising children	—	—	57.3	20.1
12. "Frequent" quarrels among co-wives	—	—	15.6	30.6
13. Quarrels mainly caused by jealousy toward husband	—	—	30.2	45.1
Relations between Women and Children				
Incidence of women reporting:				
14. Nursing period of last-born child less than two years	53.0	40.6	51.3	34.7
15. Initial indulgence period ceasing with talking	68.8	58.6	76.5	56.5
16. Exclusive control of father over schooling of children [a]	64.2	53.8	65.4	62.3
17. Exclusive control of father over academic behavior of children [b]	35.1	39.6	32.4	46.0
18. Exclusive use of physical punishment	25.5	41.4	26.7	39.1
19. Academic achievement as the most important parental demand	44.4	51.5	43.8	52.5
20. Socialization of children exclusively carried by the nuclear family	53.4	41.1	54.1	36.6

Table 35—(Continued)

	Monogamous Families		Polygynous Families	
	(1) Abouré	(2) Bété	(3) Abouré	(4) Bété
21. Preferences for joint parental control over children	77.8	65.1	74.4	59.4
N	464	548	281	478

ᵃ It should be noted that the difference between polygynous families results from the fact that only 2 per cent of Abouré senior co-wives make this decision alone, as against 15 per cent of their Bété counterparts.
ᵇ The significant differences result from the fact that the percentages of cases where respondents are unable to indicate who punishes a deviant child are the following: (1) 51.3, (2) 28.1, (3) 54.3, (4) 23.6.

proportion of Abouré families where each spouse has a distinctive budget increases from 69 per cent among monogamous households to 83 per cent among polygynous families, whereas the corresponding proportions among the Bété drop from 7 to 5 per cent.

The right to purchase clothes for the respondents is subject to parallel changes. Bété husbands exert their control not only on the handling of familial resources but on familial expenditures as well. This second form of financial authority is particularly manifest among polygynous Bété families. It is conversely less evident among the corresponding Abouré households. Among the latter people, 47 per cent of senior co-wives perceive that the initiative to purchase clothes is shared by spouses or exerted by either one of them indifferently, as against only 40 per cent of the Abouré women married to monogamous males. Among the Bété, the corresponding figures are only 5 and 9 per cent respectively.

Interestingly enough, the distributions of these distinctive manifestations of financial authority within each one of the two peoples investigated here have no comparable variances: Abouré and Bété respondents do not have the same propensity to single out one of the answers to the relevant items of the questionnaire. The variance of the distribution of patterns of budgetary control is narrower for the Abouré than for the Bété, and the skewed character of the distribution of Abouré responses is particularly manifest within the subsample of polygynous families. However, the reverse is true concerning the distribution of the initiatives to buy clothes for the respondents. Bété women experience stronger pressures toward conformity, especially when they have entered into a polygynous household. The effects of the high absorption of Bété women into their affinal group are consistent with the implications of the preeminence of men over women, and polygyny reinforces this consistency. The converging direction of the demands associated with these organizational principles limits the number of possible deviances from the prevailing cultural model. Conversely, the large variance observable among the Abouré reflects the inconsistent character of the demands attached to a low degree of social absorption on the one hand and those attached to male preeminence on the other. In this latter context, polygyny accentuates existing inconsistencies.

Expressive Leadership of the Husband

The intensity and the diffuseness of the authority that husbands are entitled to exert over the domestic activities of their wives influences the nature of familial quarrels. The less marked this authority, the more domestic quarrels are likely to result from reciprocal suspicions about real or imaginary breaches in conjugal loyalty. Indeed, within such families, sexual and reproductive activities remain the only significant functions of marriage. Thus, Abouré women quarrel most frequently with their husbands about sexual behavior, whereas this type of conflict occurs less frequently among the Bété. The incidence of quarrels of this nature is higher among polygynous than among monogamous Abouré families; it is conversely more limited among the Bété polygynous families than among their monogamous counterparts. A high degree of social absorption implies joint participation of spouses in a greater variety of activities and is hence conducive to a greater diversity in the origin of possible conflicts between them. Accordingly, the variance of the distribution of types of domestic quarrels is larger for the Bété than for the Abouré. It is even larger among the polygynous families of the former group since the effects of polygyny reinforce those attached to a high degree of social absorption.

As a consequence, Bété partners are, for example, more likely than the Abouré to quarrel about the division of domestic roles and obligations. Thus, 13 per cent of Bété monogamous wives indicate that this constitutes the most frequent source of domestic tensions as against a little under 1 per cent of the Abouré. Similarly, 15 per cent of Bété senior co-wives report division of labor to be the most frequent source of conflict between themselves and their husbands, whereas this answer characterizes only 0.4 per cent of the Abouré senior co-wives.

Polygyny, however, does not systematically accentuate differences in all types of domestic quarrels prevailing among the two peoples compared here; for example, financial quarrels are consistently less frequent among the polygynous than among the monogamous families of the two peoples. The incidence of such tensions is an inverse function of the amount of resources available to familial groups and actors, and in fact polygynous families are necessarily wealthier than their monogamous counterparts.

Variations in the degree of social absorption of a married woman into her affinal group are associated with variations both in the amount of domestic authority and power held by husbands. Of Abouré women in monogamous families, 48 per cent indicate that their husbands yield most of the time to their own requests; the corresponding proportion increases to 54 per cent for senior co-wives. On the other hand, only 27 per

cent of the Bété women married to monogamous men perceived themselves as exerting power over their husbands, a
view which is taken by even fewer—only 23 per cent—of the
senior co-wives from the same ethnic background.

The variance of the distribution of domestic power is narrower among the Bété. The greater concentration of answers
among the respondents of this culture reflects once more the
reinforcing effects of social absorption on the one hand and
male preeminence on the other. In other words, the norms
underlying this particular aspect of familial relations are
stricter among the Bété.

One would anticipate some correlation between the incidence of quarrels pertaining to adultery and the nature of the
particular code to which spouses subscribe concerning sexual
morality. Our data show that a high incidence of domestic
quarrels of a sexual nature is associated with an equalitarian
orientation with regard to sexual morality. Abouré women
challenge the validity of a differential treatment of either sex
in these matters and plead for a single standard of ethics. This
is particularly true of Abouré senior co-wives: *separate but
equal* is their motto—separate, because their loyalties and
those of their husbands diverge; equal, because this divergence
is not perceived as leading to an uneven distribution of domestic obligations. On the other hand, a high degree of social
absorption does not necessarily induce married women to recognize the validity of the preferential treatment that African
males are eager to obtain. If they do not believe in a single
standard rule of ethics, Bété married women are nevertheless
split in terms of which spouse should be subjected to the most
restrictive norms. One-third of the Bété respondents think that
male adultery is a worse domestic offense than female adultery, a position which is taken by less than 14 per cent of
Abouré married women. The contrast between the two peoples
is even sharper when only the responses of the senior co-wives
are taken into consideration; in general, the Bété senior co-
wife views plural marriage as a legitimation of the sexual

173

aspirations of her husband, but she also believes that this legitimation enhances his obligations. As mentioned earlier, polygyny is regarded by the Abouré co-wife as increasing equally the weight of each spouse's duties.

The lack of functionality of the Abouré family reduces the number of arenas where norms are necessary for regulating interaction between familial actors; simultaneously, this lack certainly accentuates the strict character of the normative prescriptions regarding sexual behavior. Conversely, among the Bété, both the greater social absorption of married women and the higher functionality of familial groups tend to make interaction among familial actors more diversified, which is in turn associated with a differentiation of the relevant individual value systems.

So far, we have seen how the influence of plural marriage on familial relations varies with cultural factors, but this influence is not always culture-bound. Polygyny exerts a uniform influence on certain patterns of attitudes and behavior. For example, even though the vast majority of married women are indifferent to the upward mobility of their husbands, slight differences do emerge when type of marriage is taken into consideration. Of all respondents, Bété single spouses are the most concerned with the upward mobility of their husbands, for their own welfare depends upon the resources of their husbands. Because of their economic independence, the anxieties of their Abouré counterparts in this regard are more limited, but women married into polygynous families tend to be the *least* concerned, for plural marriage characterizes all males who have already achieved a high status in their community. As a result, mobility ceases to be an important issue for their wives.

There is no difference either between the two cultures compared here as far as mealtime etiquette is concerned, but the extent of this particular institutionalized form of male preeminence varies with type of marriage.

174

Relations between Wives
and their Families of Origin

We have argued that low social absorption into affinal groups
should lead married women to maintain a high absorption
within their family of origin. This assumption is upheld. The
rights that Abouré children can claim are, for the most part,
materialized at the residence of their matrilineal descent
group. Furthermore, the exercise of such rights presupposes
that these children acquire a legitimate position in the descent
group to which they are naturally affiliated; accordingly, a
high proportion of Abouré women return to their mother's
residence for delivering their first child. By contrast, the most
essential rights of Bété children are claimed at the residence of
their patrilineal descent group, and a majority of Bété women
stay with their affines at the time of delivery.

Polygyny does not affect the relevant patterns of behavior
of Abouré and Bété mothers in the same way. Abouré senior
co-wives do not differ from their counterparts in monogamous
households, and the percentage who return to their maternal
residence for giving birth does not vary significantly. In contrast, less than 29 per cent of Bété monogamous wives have
delivered their first child at their husband's residence vis-à-vis
over 50 per cent of the senior co-wives. Seniority is a significant antecedent of familial status among this patrilineal people and particularly so within polygynous households, since it
increases the value of the rewards that senior co-wives can
obtain by conforming to the relevant traditional models.

Contrasts in type of descent are also associated with variations in the incidence of post-partum leaves. Again, the persistence of strong loyalties between Abouré women and their
family of origin enables them to return in large numbers to the
residence of their familial groups. This privilege is not shared

175

by Bété women, who, in addition, are usually living at quite a large distance from their kin groups. Although plural marriage affects many other aspects of the relations between Bété spouses, it neither encourages nor prevents married women from taking such a leave; there are no differences between monogamous and polygynous families along these lines.

The examination of these institutionalized forms of sociability yields significant contrasts between Abouré and Bété. Are these contrasts equally characteristic of the noninstitutionalized forms of sociability between married women and their families of origin? The responses to the dilemma story used in the survey show that Bété married women are more likely than their Abouré counterparts to save their mothers. This seems paradoxical, for one would have expected variaions in the social absorption of a married woman into her affinal group to be inversely associated with her propensity to overtly express her loyalties toward her own mother.

This observation leads us to tentatively revise our conceptions of the consequences attached to the integration of a married woman into the family of her husband. If a greater integration multiplies her obligations, it appears also to simultaneously increase some of her rights in proportion. Her marriage obliges her to perform a variety of tasks which are beneficial to her affines, but also entitles her to directly express her loyalties toward her mother. By contrast, the few obligations which accompany the marriage of an Abouré woman limit her choices under the circumstances described by the dilemma story. She is more likely to be suspected of disloyalty by her husband and his relatives; accordingly, she is less prone to expose her own relatives to the retaliations of her affines.

We have seen that the relative authority and power that husbands are able to exert on their wives differ between Abouré and Bété. We have also seen that plural marriage accentuates the relevant contrasts between these two peoples. In addition, we have seen that the women of the two cultures do not maintain a similar number of obligations toward their own relatives and that their differences in this respect tend to be, in part, accentuated by plural marriage. We could therefore anticipate that the responses of Abouré and Bété senior co-wives to the dilemma story would be more dissimilar than those offered by wives married into monogamous households. This is not so. Plural marriage neither enhances nor reduces the extent to which a married woman affirms her solidarity with her mother and gives her preeminence over her husband.

Relations among Co-wives

The degree of social absorption into her affinal group determines the extent to which a woman is subjected to the authority and power of her husband. In turn, the extent of her subordination seems to influence the relations that she entertains with the other women present in the family. The greater her subordination to her husband, the more she will compete with the other co-wives to gain or keep his favors and to receive a larger share of the rewards delivered by her affinal group. Her high social absorption increases her economic dependence upon her husband and limits, accordingly, her access to alternative sources of rewards. Conversely, among families characterized by a low degree of social absorption, an additional co-wife represents a decline in the domestic burden imposed upon each one of the women already present in the family; in turn, this decline facilitates their participation in activities other than those controlled by their husband. In summary, competition among co-wives is a negative function of the number of sources of various rewards to which they have access.

Further, the advantages that a married woman can claim depend not only upon her own behavior but also upon the status that her offspring can achieve within the familial group within which they are placed. Accordingly, competition should be keener among co-wives married into patrilineal descent

177

groups, and particularly so when the advantages attached to the seniority of the first co-wife are counterbalanced by differences between her social background and that of her co-wives. It is not surprising to note that Abouré senior co-wives are less likely than their Bété counterparts to report quarrels among co-wives as frequent; competition is more characteristic of Bété co-wives.

In addition, a low degree of social absorption does more than limit the authority and power that a husband is entitled to exert upon his wife. Influencing the *intensity* of competitive feelings among co-wives, variations in the form and intensity of conjugal interaction also affect the *object* of such competitive feelings. Among the Bété, quarrels among co-wives are most likely to result from reciprocal suspicions concerning the treatment that each one of them has been able to obtain from the head of the household. In contrast, Abouré co-wives are more concerned with the violations of the principles of solidarity which should constantly underlie their reciprocal relations. No less than 44 per cent of the Abouré senior co-wives consider that quarrels among the women of the household are predominantly produced by disagreements about the division of domestic chores; this view is shared by only 15 per cent of the corresponding Bété respondents. Similarly, whereas 20 per cent of Bété senior co-wives perceive quarrels among co-wives as being most frequently induced by the behavior of their respective children, this characterizes only 12 per cent of the Abouré senior co-wives.

We saw in the previous chapter that polygynous familial organizations are often perceived as matrifocal in character, that is, as characterized by a reinforcement of the bond interwoven between a mother and a child. The intensity of this particular dyad is, however, dependent upon the relations prevailing between husbands and wives on the one hand and between the co-wives themselves on the other. Thus, the relatively high degree of cooperation prevailing among Abouré co-wives enables them to share the tasks related to the socialization of their children. In this context, relations between mother and child are not particularly personalized. The social-ization of children involves the participation of many female adult members of the familial group. The situation is different among the Bété. Although her authority can be challenged, the Bété senior co-wife is entitled, due to her seniority, to control the socialization of all the children present in the household. Almost one-half of these senior co-wives indicate that they exert such a control, against only 12 per cent of their Abouré counterparts.

In short, differences in the relations between husbands and wives and between the co-wives themselves are associated with contrasts in the bonds which develop between mothers and children. Absence of competition among co-wives increases the number of adult females participating in the socialization of a particular child. In contrast, a marked competition among these co-wives, as in Bété familial organizations, either en-hances the significance of the mother-child dyad or, more fre-quently, induces inconsistencies in the demands of the mother and of the senior co-wife. It is, indeed, not unlikely that this duality of socializing influences imposed upon Bété children accounts for a part of the competitive climate which is said to characterize most of the interactions taking place between Bété adult actors.

Relations between Parents and Children

As plural marriage may, at least temporarily, lessen the do-mestic burden imposed upon each co-wife, one would expect polygynous mothers to display more initial warmth toward their newborn child than mothers in monogamous households.

However, the intensity of the tie between a mother and her child is also determined by cultural factors. Thus, among patri-lineal societies, paternal and maternal orientations toward children are likely to be consistent. The status of a father

179

within his extended family depends on the size of his own familial group. The status of the mother is influenced by the subjective views of her affines, but most of all by the significance of her contributions to the perpetuation of that group. These two factors induce both actors to adopt favorable attitudes toward children. Both of them unequivocally want their offspring to grow and constitute a new asset for the patrilineal descent group. As a result, Bété mothers tend to nurse their children for a long period of time. This is not so among the Abouré. First, the demands of the maternal role are not necessarily consistent with those attached to the exercise of an independent occupation. Second, maternal and paternal orientations toward children do not reinforce one another; the rewards that each of these actors can gain through their offspring are not alike and not delivered by the same descent groups.

Polygyny enables all senior co-wives to nurse their children for longer periods of time, but this is more evident among the Bété than among the Abouré. In the Bété case, the presence of other co-wives facilitates a greater dissociation throughout time between the maternal and the economic roles expected from a senior spouse. This dissociation is less characteristic of the Abouré. Plural marriage leads to a decrease in the amount of domestic chores discharged by Abouré senior co-wives, but it is also accompanied by an increase in their economic independence and hence in their individual economic responsibilities. These accentuated economic responsibilities tend to clash somewhat with the demands of the maternal role.

In the sample examined here, there seems to be a negative correlation between length of nursing period and length of the initial indulgence period. Abouré mothers wean their children early but tend to display indulgence toward them for a long period of time. The opposite pattern can be observed among the Bété. The dependence of a Bété mother upon the position that her children achieve in their patrilineal descent group induces her to socialize them as early as possible. The faster they meet the standards of behavior set up by her affines, the more she herself can hope to occupy a rewarding position in this particular group.

The effects of plural marriage upon the initial indulgence displayed by Abouré and Bété mothers are not alike. Plural marriage jeopardizes the chances of a Bété senior co-wife to acquire an unequivocally rewarding status. Competition with other co-wives requires her to stress the demands exerted upon her children and thus to begin their socialization earlier. In contrast, both the marked cooperation which characterizes interaction among Abouré co-wives and the very nature of the bond that each one establishes with her children leads them to be indulgent for a longer period of time. Thus, in this particular instance, plural marriage reinforces the distinctive traits of the two cultures compared here.

Since the expressive nature of the maternal role varies both with cultural factors and with type of marriage, one can expect similar contrasts in the instrumental nature of the paternal role. The examination of decision-making patterns pertaining to the formal schooling of children should yield particularly significant results in this context.

On the one hand, one could anticipate the participation of each conjugal partner in this specific decision to be a function of his or her own level of education. In general, Abouré have been more exposed to modernization. Because the level of school enrollments of Abouré males has been substantial for a relatively long period of time, the average level of education of their female counterparts is significantly higher than that of their Bété counterparts. In consequence, the participation of Abouré women in the decision to send children to school should be more manifest.

On the other hand, one could anticipate that this participation would be less influenced by individual levels of exposure to modernizing forces than by the rules underlying the division of

181

domestic roles along sex lines. The greater power and authority which Bété males exert vis-à-vis their wives should equally well characterize their relations with their offspring.

In fact, none of these hypotheses seems to hold true. Among monogamous families, Abouré fathers enjoy more visible authority than their Bété counterparts. In contrast, Bété single spouses have many incentives to exert instrumental authority and power over their children, particularly in areas such as formal schooling, which are deemed to yield high returns.

Such contrasts are less characteristic of polygynous families. The authority exerted by Abouré and Bété polygynous fathers are comparable, yet the competition prevailing among Bété co-wives reinforces the instrumental character of the relations that they entertain with their children.

Furthermore, the formal schooling of Abouré children is consistently jeopardized by the fact that modernization reinforces the tensions opposing affines to one another. Being held responsible for the socialization of their offspring, Abouré fathers and their relatives are expected to pay for all resulting expenses. Yet, because schooling is accompanied by a growing individualization of occupational slots, members of the patrilineal descent group are reluctant to pay for a more personalized investment, which in addition is not explicitly required of them by traditional norms. Specifically, they argue that the modernization of their obligations as agents of socialization initially requires a modernization, and hence a "bilateralization," of familial organizations. At the same time, the matrilineal kin group is not anxious to subsidize the child's schooling, first, because this obligation is not traditionally incumbent on them, and second, because the individualization of occupational roles produced by formal education is deemed to lead future generations to reject their traditional duties. Correspondingly, only the mothers have a vested interest in maximizing the educational level of their children: modernization makes their own status more vulnerable by weakening their ties with both their affines and their own relatives. As a result, their dependence upon their offspring increases, especially when they reach old age. Yet, the particular nature of their domestic position does not always entitle them to exert legitimate demands in this regard.

The tensions accompanying the equivocations pertaining to the definition of Abouré familial adult roles prevent an effective parental control on the academic behavior of children. In fact, half of Abouré monogamous respondents are unable to determine which familial actor should punish a child who fails to meet the requirements of the academic system. The patrilineal character of the Bété society is more consistent with the demands of modernization; individual obligations and duties are more clearly spelled out. Only 28 per cent of the Bété monogamous respondents fail to see who in the familial group should punish a child who does not behave properly by academic standards.

Polygyny sharpens this difference. Competition among Bété co-wives necessitates a strict definition of the domestic power which must be exerted on the children present in the household. We have seen that plural marriage reinforces in this people the superordinate position of both the husband and the senior co-wife vis-à-vis the other women present in the household. It reinforces as well their superordinate position vis-à-vis children and makes their disciplinary functions more evident. In contrast, plural marriage accentuates the loopholes characteristic of Abouré familial organizations; it limits the control that a father is expected to exert over his children, but it does not lead to a simultaneous increase in the authority that mothers can claim. In short, the inconsistencies between type of descent and plural marriage on the one hand and parental expectations with regard to formal schooling on the other are more evident among the Abouré than among the Bété.

This last observation is confirmed by an examination of the nature of the demands formulated by the mothers derived from the two peoples toward their children. In spite of their lower degree of involvement in educational structures, Bété mothers are more sensitive to the rewards attached to the formal education of their offspring than are their Abouré counterparts. At the same time, Abouré mothers are keener to see their children helping them in the performance of their domestic and economic activites, and 12 per cent of them place this item as their most important demand as against only 5 per cent of Bété respondents. There are, however, no differences between monogamous and polygynous families along these lines.

We have seen that the Abouré and Bété definitions of maternal roles are not comparable. Bété mothers appear to be more achievement-oriented and begin the socialization of their offspring at an earlier age than do their Abouré counterparts. This particular concern of Bété women has been attributed to the marked degree of competition which characterizes individual interaction within the culture. Insofar as a competitive climate leads to aggressive orientations, it is not surprising to note that the punishments most often used by Bété mothers are physical in nature.

In contrast, the Abouré seem to put a stronger emphasis on the expressive nature of the maternal role; thus the period of initial indulgence is longer; academic achievement is not regarded as the most important demand to be imposed upon children. In fact, the centrifugal pressures exerted on each individual adult actor in this type of familial context are numerous enough to induce them to use the child's need for affiliation as a socializing strategy. Thus 40 per cent of Abouré mothers use threats of love withdrawal and of isolation to cope with their deviant children. The corresponding proportion among the Bété is lower and does not exceed one-third.

The circumstances surrounding plural marriage among both peoples tend to reinforce the differences in the socializing techniques that they use. To a large extent, polygyny accentuates the centrifugal forces exerted on Abouré families. In consequence, the proportion of Abouré mothers using expressive techniques increases from 40 per cent among monogamous families to 53 per cent among polygynous households.

The nature of the maternal role, however, depends also upon the number of socialization agents. Expressive and instrumental demands cannot have the same meaning when the bond between a mother and her offspring is privileged as when it is not distinguishable in frequency from the interactions which develop between the child and other adult actors.[1] On the whole, Abouré nuclear families are more functional with regard to child rearing than their Bété counterparts. That is, Abouré children are more likely to be exclusively brought up within the household of their immediate parents—first, because the average distance between affines is smaller and the maintenance of loyalties between a child and his matrilineal descent group does not require his physically moving to their residence; second, because of the greater participation of this culture in the modernization process and because of the ensuing individualization of residential patterns.

We could anticipate differences between the two groups along these lines to decline in intensity with plural marriage. Because this form of marriage is the privilege of male individuals who have already achieved a certain seniority and a rewarding status both in their communities and their kin groups, we could expect them to play a more crucial role in the upbringing of their children than their monogamous counterparts would. Indeed, the position of the latter in the power structure of the extended kin group is more marginal, and their socializing influences should thus be minimal. However, our data do not support such a hypothesis. There are no differences between monogamous and polygynous Abouré families in this regard; conversely, among the Bété, plural mar-

---

1. For a full discussion of this problem, see M. Zelditch, "Family, Marriage, and Kinship," in *Handbook of Modern Sociology,* ed. R. E. L. Faris (Chicago: Rand McNally, 1964), pp. 680–773.

riage is slightly associated with an increase in the mobility of children. In fact, the children of Bété senior co-wives appear to be more frequently claimed by their maternal relatives than the offspring of women married into monogamous families. It is not unlikely that the competition which develops among the various wives of this culture leads each one of them to transfer socialization functions to her own family.

We have noted that the relative power and authority exerted by husbands vary both with cultural factors and with type of marriage. We have also noted that some of the characteristics of maternal and paternal roles are influenced by these two variables. We may ask ourselves whether the contrasts which we observe are perceived as such by familial actors and whether such contrasts are accompanied by differing aspirations on the part of the respondents. More specifically, does a low degree of absorption lead married women to have strong desires to cooperate with their husbands in the upbringing of their common offspring? On the whole, Abouré women are more inclined to promote cooperation across sex lines in this particular area. There are two competing arguments likely to account for such a difference between the two peoples compared here. One can assume that aspirations toward cooperation between conjugal partners is determined by level of exposure to European norms and practices; the Abouré have been more "acculturated" than the Bété. On the other hand, one can also suppose that there is a negative correlation between such aspirations and social absorption. A higher degree of social absorption is associated with an accentuation of the distinctions of individual roles along sex lines. In turn, this accentuation is accompanied by an increase in the relative domestic power held by women, at least in certain specific areas such as child-rearing practices. In this context, then, an increased domestic cooperation is perceived as leading to a decline in the specific form of power currently held by Bété women over their offspring.

Plural marriage is accompanied by a uniform, although

moderate, decline in the cooperative aspirations of women. The extent of this decline is, however, more manifest among the Bété.

Conclusions

In the previous chapter we noted the absence of significant differences between the styles of familial interaction prevailing in monogamous and polygynous families. The present chapter has enabled us to observe that cultural contrasts override differences due to marriage types, and that the meaning and manifestations of polygyny vary with the cultural context in which it takes place. Differences between Abouré and Bété mainly concern the degree of social absorption of married women into their affinal group. The higher this social absorption, the more evident the authority and the power invested in husbands, the greater the degree of interaction between spouses, and the less suspicious both partners are of their respective sexual behavior. In addition, a higher degree of social absorption reinforces competition between co-wives and makes their relations dependent upon their respective dealings with the head of the household. Furthermore, it reduces the obligations of married women toward their family of origin although it does not necessarily reduce their loyalties toward the individual members of such groups. Lastly, a higher degree of social absorption seems to minimize the social-emotional aspects of maternal roles, and to accentuate the lines of authority and power exerted over the children in the household. In summary, we can now verify certain of the hypotheses formulated in Chapters 3 and 4 and ascertain how variations in social absorption affect domestic relations. Whereas the ethnographic method summarized in Chapter 4 only suggests the presence or absence of contrasts between familial organizations, the survey method used here leads to an evaluation of the amplitude and significance of such contrasts.

187

In Chapter 4, however, we also indicated a certain number of competing assumptions about the variability of the patterns of familial relations prevailing among Abouré and Bété. The present chapter has enabled us to demonstrate that apparently none of these assumptions is upheld. The most important factor likely to account for the variance of the distribution of a particular form of familial relations concerns the degree of consistency between the demands associated with the general principles derived from male preeminence on the one hand and type of descent on the other.

In different cultural environments, polygyny cannot have a uniform meaning. The direction and the intensity of its effects vary both between and within cultures. In fact, it is possible to isolate four distinct types of influence exerted by this institution on the various familial relations analyzed in the context of the present study.

First, it may accentuate differences which are already visible between monogamous households characterized by differing types of descent and degrees of social absorption. Thus, polygyny is associated with an increase in the extent to which Bété husbands exert an absolute control over the handling of familial resources and Abouré spouses have distinct, autonomous budgets. In this perspective, polygynous families can be regarded as prototypes of the two cultural systems compared. Plural marriage is still normative, that is, a type of familial arrangement to which all individuals aspire. For this very reason we can suspect that it more accurately reflects traditional models of familial interaction.

Second, polygyny may also be associated with a decline in the contrast between Abouré and Bété familial organizations. In certain instances, type of marriage seems to be a more powerful indicator of women's patterns of attitudes and behaviors than type of descent or degree of social absorption. This effect of polygyny is illustrated by the differential reactions of the respondents toward the upward mobility of their husbands. Whereas there are significant differences between the reactions of Abouré and Bété monogamous wives in this respect, the senior co-wives of the two groups react similarly. This is apparently due to the fact that plural marriage requires males to have achieved a minimal level of economic success, which reduces the economic anxieties of their wives proportionately.

Third, polygyny may not modify the contrast between families characterized by differing types of descent and degree of social absorption. Thus, the stress put by mothers upon academic achievement as the most important thing that they expect from their children varies between the two cultures compared here, but the intensity of the contrast is alike for both monogamous and polygynous families.

Fourth, in a limited number of instances, variations in type of marriage introduce a differentiation of individual patterns and behavior which does not emerge when variations in type of descent or in degree of social absorption are taken into consideration. Thus, mealtime etiquette shows that distance between spouses is more institutionalized among polygynous than among monogamous households but is alike for Abouré and Bété families.

In summary, this chapter has enabled us to conclude that the effects of polygyny are differentiated. That is, they vary with both the particular pattern of behavior investigated and the particular culture in which polygyny takes place. Once more we are confronted with the notion that the significance of an institution cannot be apprehended without reference to the basic properties of the entire cultural system of which it is a part. Our next step shall be to ascertain which components of these systems must be taken into consideration. Thus, we may decide that systems differ when there are inequalities in the relative participation of various individual actors in crucial forms of communication. For example, we may posit that there are differences between Abouré and Bété social organizations by observing for example that the incidence of polygyny is not alike among these two peoples. Alternatively, we may

189

see cultures as models linking together not only differentiated forms of communication but also the rules pertaining to such forms.[2] We shall now analyze the relative validity of these two definitions of culture.

2. For a full treatment, see Claude Leví-Strauss, *Anthropologie structurale* (Paris: Plon, 1958), chap. 15.

CHAPTER 7

The Influence
of Variations
in the Definition
of Domestic Roles

We have noted that the polygynous and monogamous families compared here have similar organizations but that familial relations prevailing among the Bété differ markedly from those characteristic of the Abouré. In other words, we have indirectly demonstrated that contrasts in the functioning of families with different types of marriage, far from being universal, are markedly influenced by the properties of each ethnic group investigated.

At this point we must go one step further and explore more thoroughly the concept of ethnicity. This concept is subject to two sorts of equivocations. First, the concept refers to differences in the geographic locations of various human settlements and hence to differing levels of exposure to modern norms and practices or to differing patterns of economic exploitation. It also refers to variations in types of social organizations, and it is with this second aspect of ethnicity that we are now concerned.

At the same time, however, contrasts between ethnic groups can reflect the differential emergence of selected forms of social participation as well as contrasts in the overall nature of the global models underlying these various forms of social participation.[1] In this chapter, we will evaluate the relative validity of these alternative definitions of ethnicity.

When we posit that two ethnic groups can be isolated from one another because of significant differences in the incidence of certain crucial forms of social participation among their respective members, we must also determine which of these forms we should analyze. Can we say, for example, that two peoples have distinctive forms of organization because of disparities in their respective distributions of polygynous families? Obviously, plural marriage is not an unequivocal determinant of culture. Differences in the relations that Abouré and Bété women maintain with their husbands, their family of origin, their co-wives, and their own children cannot be entirely explained in terms of the uneven incidence of plural marriage within each of these peoples. Had this been the case, the two distributions of familial relations, one by ethnic group and the other by type of marriage, would have been alike. Can we infer then that the contrast between monogamy and polygyny is meaningless and that variations in the number of wives do not exert any influence on patterns of interaction? We are not sure; type of marriage may still act as an intervening variable in this context.

We have noted that there are marked variations in the degree of social absorption of Abouré and Bété women and that there are significant contrasts both in the functionality of their domestic role and in the amount of economic independence that they are entitled to exert. Insofar as these differences are fundamental determinants of forms of social organization, one could expect that Abouré and Bété women characterized by an identical degree of social absorption will hold a similar amount of power and authority over their husbands and will retain an identical amount of obligation toward their family of origin. The question remains, however, to determine whether

1. For a discussion of the concept of culture, see Claude Lévi-Strauss, *Anthropologie structurale* (Paris: Plon, 1958), pp. 325–59.

the effects of variations in the degree of social absorption within a single ethnic group are independent of the number of incumbents in the role of wife-mother. Are these effects alike in both monogamous and polygynous families? Are there, for example, greater contrasts between senior co-wives characterized by differing degrees of social absorption than between co-wives and single spouses characterized by an identical degree of social absorption?

Nevertheless, this first definition of ethnicity is not necessarily acceptable. Indeed, cultures are encompassing, and there are necessarily linkages among the various demands imposed upon individuals. First, cultural integration requires the use of a common set of symbols; second, this integration necessitates coordination between the activities of individuals and groups; finally, certain forms of social participation reinforce others.[2] In short, the definition of culture cannot only rely upon the differential emergence of a variety of forms of social participation. It must also refer to the models that all peoples elaborate, in order to perpetuate their present overall organization and to introduce consistency in the various requirements that they impose upon individuals and groups.[3] For this very reason, we cannot expect identical forms of social participation to have similar implications, when they take place in distinctive cultural contexts. These similar forms of social participation are not integrated into similar models.

The first notion of culture minimizes the significance of linkages among cultural demands, while the second notion maximizes this significance. To evaluate the limits of these

2. This second definition of culture is exhaustively presented in E. Spicer, "Portam: A Yaqui Village in Sonora," *American Anthropologist*, 1956, Memoir no. 67, particularly in chapter 9.

3. The very nature of the over-all models underlying social relations increases the difficulties of cross-cultural analyses; see, for instance, S. F. Nadel, *The Foundations of Social Anthropology* (London: Cohen, 1951), esp. chaps. 8 and 9. See also Remi Clignet, "The Method of Concomitant Variations: A Critical Evaluation," in *A Handbook of Anthropological Methodology*, ed. R. Cohen and R. Naroll (forthcoming).

competing definitions requires the following comparisons: (a) between monogamous and polygynous families derived from the same ethnic background, in order to examine the conditions under which contrasts between types of marriages vary in direction and in intensity; (b) between polygynous families of different ethnic backgrounds, in order to measure the extent to which variations in the demands imposed upon married women or variations in their social status are associated with a persistence, an accentuation, or a decline of ethnic contrasts.

Each comparison involves, in effect, two complementary types of evaluation. First we must isolate the intensity and direction of the responses of families characterized by differing types of descent and marriage to variations in each one of our independent variables. We are here mainly interested in *processes.* However, differing processes may result in the emergence of either distinctive or uniform styles of familial interaction, so we must also examine the *products* of variations in our independent variables—that is, evaluate the degree to which these variations lead to the emergence of uniform styles of interaction among Abouré and Bété monogamous and polygynous families.

To begin with, we will analyze the influence exerted by increases in the number of co-wives. In other words, we will measure the degree to which the influence exerted by variations in the *intensity* of polygyny remains independent of ethnic factors.

Next we will investigate whether variations in the economic and social roles performed by Abouré and Bété married women have similar consequences on the functioning of monogamous and polygynous families and whether these consequences depend upon ethnic factors. In brief, we will assess the degree to which the consequences attached to the functionality of the domestic role of married women are independent of type of marriage and of ethnicity.

Last, we will determine whether differences in the social background of these women affect similarly the functioning of

194

Table 36

Scheme of Analysis of Contrasts between Polygynous and Monogamous Families

Independent Variables	Comparisons	Dependent Variables
Type of descent (7)	1. Monogamy versus polygyny (processes and products)	*Conjugal relations* 1. Financial integration 2. Domestic power 3. Emotional power 4. Institutionalization of male preeminence
Intensity of polygyny (7)		
Functionality: a. Reproductive (fertility)(7) b. Economic (7)		
		Solidarity with group of origin
Economic independence (7)	2. Polygyny among different ethnic groups (processes and products)	*Solidarity with co-wives*
Social background of the wife a. Age at marriage (7) b. Brideprice (7) c. Gift from bridegroom (7) d. Previous matrimonial experience (7)		*Child-rearing practices* 1. Early childhood training
		2. Importance and nature of parental roles
Degree of exposure to modernization: a. Urban-rural differential (8) b. Occupational differentiation (8) c. Scale of employment (8)		3. Attitudes toward schooling

NOTE: Numbers in parentheses refer to the chapters in which these variables are analyzed.

the monogamous and polygynous families compared in the context of the present study.

The terms of the comparisons that we intend to make are presented and summarized in Table 36.

The Intensity of Polygyny

According to the first definition of ethnicity, differences between Abouré and Bété patterns of familial interaction should reflect the uneven incidence of plural marriage among these two peoples. We have already seen that this assumption is not borne out; contrasts between monogamy and polygyny are not universal. The intensity of plural marriage must also be investigated. Whereas only 14 per cent of the Abouré polygynist males have more than two wives, almost one-third of their Bété counterparts do.[4] It may very well be that among these two peoples the dominant traits of large-sized polygynous households are analogous.

According to the second definition of ethnicity, however, the effects of plural marriage can be assessed only within a single people. The direction and intensity of the effects of plural marriage on familial relations depend upon the distribution of this institution within *each* of the two cultures investigated. Thus, one can argue that when the incidence of plural marriage among a particular people is low, polygynous families are marginal and differ most markedly from their monogamous counterparts. Similarly, the lower the intensity of polygyny, the more marginal the three-wife household should be, and the more its internal organization should present distinctive features. As a consequence, one can expect differences

4. The figures given here differ somewhat from those observed in our sample. We have used here the figures of the census report for the entire Ivory Coast. See *Supplement mensuel au bulletin trimestriel de statistiques*, vol. VIII (Abidjan: Ministere des Affaires Economiques, des Finances et du Plan, 1966).

between monogamous and polygynous families to be more sizable among the Abouré than among the Bété. Similarly, one can predict that the Abouré three-wife households will present more distinctive profiles than the corresponding Bété familial units. Yet, one can also argue that both a high incidence and a high intensity in the distribution of plural marriage indicate that this institution serves a variety of significant purposes; one would expect, therefore, that the contrast between monogamy and polygyny or between various types of polygyny will be maximal among the Bété. In brief, our intention here is to test whether the properties of a familial group vary with its size, and whether such variations are different for different ethnic groups.

On the whole, differences between households with two co-wives and those with more than two are hardly significant. (See Table 37.) Increases in the size of polygynous households do not affect the importance of contrasts between differing types of marriages, nor do they affect the size of ethnic cleavages.

These are, of course, certain exceptions to these general principles. An increase in the number of co-wives appears, for example, to be associated with a greater segregation of familial roles and, more specifically, with a greater isolation of the mother-child dyad. Regardless of their ethnic background, the senior co-wives of the largest polygynous households tend to nurse their children for a longer period of time than those who have only one co-wife or, a fortiori, than women married to monogamous males.

Similarly, an increase in the number of co-wives is uniformly associated with an accentuated differentiation of disciplinary functions along sex lines. The more co-wives they have, the more all senior co-wives are reluctant to cooperate with their husbands in the rearing of their common offspring. However, this common property of Abouré and Bété senior co-wives reflects different processes. The *intensity* of the responses of

197

Table 37

Relationship between Number of Wives and Family Life (Percentages)

	Abouré			Bété		
	1 Wife	2 Wives	3 Wives	1 Wife	2 Wives	3 Wives
Conjugal Relations						
Incidence of women reporting:						
1. Exclusive control of family budget by husband	22.4	7.7	19.0	50.5	59.1	58.6
2. Exclusive control of clothing expenditures by husband	34.9	24.4	28.0	56.6	62.9	67.5
3. Domestic quarrels mainly caused by adultery	50.9	60.5	58.0	21.7	18.5	20.4
4. Exclusive dominance of husband in domestic quarrels	25.0	21.1	23.0	58.0	52.8	69.1
5. Single standard on conjugal morality	62.5	67.2	68.0	32.5	29.7	24.6
6. High concern with upward mobility of their husbands	10.8	15.0	9.2	11.4	15.0	12.5
7. Patterned segregation at mealtime	83.0	89.1	89.0	84.5	90.0	93.7
Relations between Wives and their Families						
Incidence of women reporting:						
8. Preeminent status of their mothers	18.8	20.0	24.0	30.3	29.3	16.2

	Abouré			Bété		
	1 Wife	2 Wives	3 Wives	1 Wife	2 Wives	3 Wives
9. Their mother's residence as the place where they delivered their first child	42.9	52.8	31.0	6.6	3.8	3.1
10. Post-partum leaves from their husbands	59.1	58.3	59.0	49.3	47.1	50.2
Relations among Co-wives						
Incidence of women reporting:						
11. Cooperative practices in raising children	—	58.3	55.0	—	25.5	11.5
12. "Frequent" quarrels among co-wives	—	13.5	18.9	—	28.8	33.6
13. Quarrels mainly caused by jealousy toward husband	—	38.9	16.2	—	47.8	30.2
Relations between Women and Children						
Incidence of women reporting:						
14. Nursing period of last-born child less than two years	53.4	53.9	47.0	40.6	36.0	32.5
15. Initial indulgence period ceasing with talking	68.8	77.7	75.0	58.5	56.6	56.5

Table 37—(Continued)

	Abouré			Bété		
	1 Wife	2 Wives	3 Wives	1 Wife	2 Wives	3 Wives
16. Exclusive control of father over schooling of children	64.2	64.4	66.0	53.8	61.5	63.3
17. Exclusive control of father over academic behavior of children	35.1	29.4	37.0	39.6	44.7	48.1
18. Exclusive use of physical punishment	26.5	23.1	31.0	41.4	41.2	36.1
19. Academic achievement as the most important parental demand	44.4	41.4	49.0	51.5	51.4	53.8
20. Socialization of children carried out exclusively by the nuclear family	53.4	53.3	55.0	41.1	40.0	38.9
21. Preferences for joint parental control over children	77.8	79.8	67.0	65.1	59.7	58.6
N	464	180	100	547	286	191

Abouré senior co-wives to an increase in the size of their households differs from that of their Bété counterparts.

The greater isolation of all senior co-wives married into large-sized households uniformly accentuates the instrumental nature of their roles as agents of socialization. Both Abouré and Bété senior co-wives in three-wife households attach the same amount of importance to the educational achievement of their respective offspring. Yet, an inspection of Table 37 shows that this similarity also results from the fact that the reactions of Abouré and Bété senior co-wives to the addition of a co-wife have the same direction but an uneven intensity. Lastly, the proportions of Abouré and Bété senior co-wives of large-sized polygynous households using physical punishments are alike, but this similarity is the product of *diverging* responses to the presence of an additional co-wife.

An increase in the size of familial groups has also effects which vary along ethnic lines. Although conducive to a greater isolation of the Bété senior co-wife, this increase nevertheless reinforces her social absorption into her affinal group. The more co-wives she has, the more frequently the senior co-wife yields to her husband in domestic quarrels, and the more fearful she is to express her ties with her own mother. In turn, her greater absorption in her affinal group reinforces the preeminent character of the position that she occupies vis-à-vis the other women present in the household. Indeed, the more co-wives she has, the more a Bété senior co-wife is expected to control the socialization of all the children who are under her husband's authority. Only 38 per cent of the senior co-wives of bigamous families claim to have this privilege, as against 53 per cent of those who have at least two other co-wives.

An additional co-wife among the Abouré does not reinforce the preeminent character of the senior co-wife's position. Neither does it modify the incidence of quarrels between co-wives. It does alter, however, the object of such quarrels, which are increasingly likely to result from disagreements about the division of the domestic tasks that the wives must perform.

In summary, most of the indicators of familial relations used in the present study show that variations in the size of polygynous households have few uniform implications for the status of senior co-wives. To such variations, there does correspond a persistence or an accentuation of the contrasts between Abouré and Bété familial organizations. In short, most of the demands resulting from an increase in the size of polygynous families are culture-bound.

Such demands are partially determined by the characteristics of the distribution of plural marriage within each one of the two peoples investigated here. According to the first hypothesis, we had expected differences between Abouré three-wife and one-wife families to be larger than differences between one-wife and two-wife families of this particular people, and we had expected both differences to be greater than those found between corresponding Bété familial units. This assumption is not borne out. In most cases the addition of a co-wife accentuates contrasts between Bété monogamous and polygynous families but does not affect cleavages between the corresponding Abouré familial groups. In fact, variations in the intensity of polygyny have asymmetric effects.

Not only does plural marriage increase the degree of social absorption of each Bété woman in her affinal group, but the extent of this increase also seems to be often proportional to the number of her co-wives. It is because of the large number of significant contributions that women make to their affinal group that Bété males want to be polygynist; it is also because they have more than one wife that they can correspondingly enhance the demands that they impose upon each of their spouses.

In contrast, although polygyny is associated with a decline in the degree of social absorption of each Abouré married woman, the extent of this decline is not proportional to the number of her co-wives. Differences in the organization of Abouré three-wife households and monogamous families are often more limited than contrasts between bigamous and monogamous units. Indeed, it cannot be argued that Abouré males are polygynist either in spite of or because of the limited contributions of their wives. Neither can it be said that polygyny accounts for the limited degree of social absorption of Abouré married women.

In brief, polygyny belongs to the core of the Bété cultural system, because it is consistent with the patterns by which male preeminence manifests itself. Plural marriage is a marginal element of the Abouré culture because it accentuates the inconsistencies between the principles derived from male preeminence and those associated with a matrilineal organization.

Fertility

The survival of most African cultures has depended for a long time upon the size of their familial groups. Accordingly, fertility has always been a crucial determinant of the status occupied by women—both in familial and in larger social structures. Women can easily be divorced when they do not bear as many children as deemed desirable; their sterility often leads them to believe that they have been the victims of witchcraft. In a parallel manner, the rewards to which they aspire when they have met the relevant requirements of their affinal group are usually clearly spelled out.[5]

Under such conditions, one can assume that (1) the sanctions attached to sterility will be universal, (2) the rewards derived from participation in large-sized families will be alike for familial actors from differing cultural backgrounds, and

5. The importance of the rewards attached to the fulfillment of her domestic role by a married woman is underlined by E. and M. C. Ortigues, *Oedipe africain* (Paris: Plon, 1967), pp. 276–83, who show the psychological disturbances experienced by a woman who, after having given birth to a child, feels that she has not been sufficiently rewarded by her husband.

(3) the presence of the same number of children in different family groups will be associated with the emergence of the same types of strains and tensions.

The definition of the ideal number of children varies however from culture to culture, and depends upon, other factors, for example upon rules of descent. The rewards that a male individual derives from a numerous offspring are not alike among matrilineal and patrilineal cultures. Also, the rewards which can be claimed by his wife or wives are not the same. These rewards are interdependent among patrilineal peoples but are more or less independent of one another among matrilineal cultures.[6] One can anticipate, therefore, that the effects of variations in the number of children will not have the same direction or the same intensity in the Bété and Abouré families compared here.

The negative sanctions attached to sterility and the rewards attached to fertility should also vary with type of marriage. Strategies available to familial actors are certainly not alike when the head of the household has a single spouse and when he has at least two wives, between whom he can stimulate competitive feelings.

In short, this section is devoted to an examination of the following questions: (1) Are the consequences of an increase in the number of children universal? (2) If not universal, how are these consequences modified by ethnicity and type of marriage?

Initially, it should be noted that fertility and the exercise of an independent occupation by married women are positively correlated. Among Abouré monogamous families, 77 per cent of the women engaged in the labor force have more than two children, as against 68 per cent of those wives who do not

6. These rewards are interdependent among the Bété insofar as the gains in status acquired by Bété husbands result from the large size of his own family and hence depend upon the fertility of his wife or wives. In contrast, the rewards obtained by Abouré women are delivered by their matriclan.

work. Among Abouré polygynous families, the corresponding proportions are 83 and 72 per cent, respectively. As far as the Bété are concerned, 85 per cent of monogamous women who have an independent occupation have more than two children, compared with 62 per cent for those who remain housewives. Similarly, 70 per cent of the senior co-wives derived from this people who participate in the labor force have more than two children, against 63 per cent of those who do not work. Thus, the association between fertility and participation of women in the labor market seems to be independent both of ethnicity and of type of marriage. This observation is parallel to that made by McElrath on a sample of female residents of Accra, Ghana, and it suggests that economic independence and fertility do not necessarily represent conflicting alternatives which are available to married women.[7] Rather, under certain conditions one can be a prerequisite to the other. It is only after a woman has performed her basic familial function—that of reproduction—that she is entitled to claim the rewards to which she aspires. Economic independence is a particularly appealing reward, because of both the marked differentiation of roles along sex lines and the increasing insecurity of the position occupied by married women in their affinal groups and in their own families of origin.

The most significant influence of variations in the number of children on the power structure of the families investigated here is summarized in Table 38.

7. D. McElrath, "Migrant Status in Accra," mimeo. (Northwestern University, 1965). Both fertility and participation in the labor force depend on migratory experiences. Indeed, the women who have lived for a long time in urban centers are usually affiliated with large-sized households which include many other women. The presence of such women solves the contradictions between the desires for gainful employment and fertility. Among traditional societies, on the whole, incompatibilities between the reproductive and productive roles of women are more limited than those observable in highly industrial nations.

Table 38

Relationship between Number of Children and Family Life (Percentages)

Abouré

No. Children:	Monogamous Families				Polygynous Families			
	0	1	2	3 and more	0	1	2	3 and more
Conjugal Relations								
Incidence of women reporting:								
1. Exclusive control of family budget by husband	18.0	24.3	24.5	20.5	19.2	16.7	8.2	11.5
2. Exclusive control of clothing expenditures by husband	44.0	37.8	33.7	32.1	23.1	40.0	27.7	20.4
3. Domestic quarrels mainly caused by adultery	56.0	50.0	51.1	49.4	57.7	46.7	55.4	68.1
4. Exclusive dominance of husband in domestic quarrels	26.0	23.0	23.4	27.6	11.5	10.0	21.4	27.4
5. Single standard on conjugal morality	44.0	59.5	65.8	66.0	69.2	56.7	66.1	71.7
6. High concern with upward mobility of their husbands	12.0	8.2	10.9	11.6	3.8	20.0	10.7	11.5
7. Patterned segregation at mealtime	78.0	79.7	82.0	89.1	100.0	83.4	85.7	91.9

No. Children:	0	1	2	3 and more	0	1	2	3 and more
Relations between Wives and their Families								
Incidence of women reporting:								
8. Preeminent status of their mothers	32.0	16.2	21.2	12.8	23.0	20.0	21.4	21.2
9. Their mother's residence as the place where they delivered their first child	—	39.2	45.7	57.4	—	46.7	49.1	51.3
10. Port-partum leaves from their husbands	—	73.0	65.7	61.5	—	70.0	63.4	63.7
Relations among Co-wives								
Incidence of women reporting:								
11. Cooperative practices in raising children	—	—	—	—	46.6	53.3	56.3	61.1
12. "Frequent" quarrels among co-wives	—	—	—	—	(75.0)	(12.5)	2.6	10.8
13. Quarrels mainly caused by jealousy toward husband	—	—	—	—	(25.0)	(75.0)	31.5	21.7

Table 38—(Continued)

Abouré

No. Children:	Monogamous Families				Polygynous Families			
	0	1	2	3 and more	0	1	2	3 and more
Relations between Women and Children								
Incidence of women reporting:								
14. Nursing period of last-born child less than two years	—	53.8	66.8	51.2	—	50.0	59.8	54.9
15. Initial indulgence period ceasing with talking	—	64.9	67.4	75.0	—	80.0	77.7	72.6
16. Exclusive control of father over schooling of children	—	59.5	65.8	63.5	—	66.7	63.3	69.9
17. Exclusive control of father over academic behavior of children	—	18.9	34.8	53.8	—	23.1	31.4	42.5
18. Exclusive use of physical punishment	—	14.9	31.0	34.0	—	36.7	30.4	24.8
19. Academic achievement as the most important parental demand	—	36.5	48.4	47.4	—	43.3	42.9	47.8
20. Socialization of children carried out exclusively by the nuclear family	—	56.8	50.5	57.7	—	46.7	51.6	59.3
21. Preferences for joint parental control over children	—	81.1	75.5	80.8	—	50.0	71.4	84.1
N	50	74	184	156	26	30	112	113

Bété

No. Children:	Monogamous Families				Polygynous Families			
	0	1	2	3 and more	0	1	2	3 and more
Conjugal Relations								
Incidence of women reporting:								
1. Exclusive control of family budget by husband	55.0	53.1	48.8	47.9	63.4	64.1	57.5	51.8
2. Exclusive control of clothing expenditures by husband	59.0	56.1	54.3	60.6	68.3	67.4	63.5	61.2
3. Domestic quarrels mainly caused by adultery	24.0	27.6	18.5	21.3	31.7	19.6	21.0	14.1
4. Exclusive dominance of husband in domestic quarrels	61.0	55.1	58.2	57.4	59.8	64.1	61.6	71.8
5. Single standard on conjugal morality	34.0	33.7	32.4	29.8	32.9	33.7	22.4	30.6
6. High concern with upward mobility of their husbands	22.0	19.4	23.1	19.1	9.8	18.5	13.2	15.3
7. Patterned segregation at mealtime	80.0	82.7	84.7	90.5	90.2	90.2	83.6	90.6
Relations between Wives and their Families								
Incidence of women reporting:								
8. Preeminent status of their mothers	35.0	29.6	32.0	21.3	22.0	37.0	25.1	25.1

Table 38—(Continued)

Bété

No. Children:	Monogamous Families				Polygynous Families			
	0	1	2	3 and more	0	1	2	3 and more
9. Their mother's residence as the place where they delivered their first child	—	7.1	7.4	7.4	—	4.3	5.0	2.4
10. Post-partum leaves from their husbands	—	65.3	62.9	41.5	—	58.7	58.5	50.6
Relations among Co-wives								
Incidence of women reporting:								
11. Cooperative practices in raising children	—	—	—	—	13.4	26.1	20.1	20.0
12. "Frequent" quarrels among co-wives	—	—	—	—	40.4	25.9	32.1	24.1
13. Quarrels mainly caused by jealousy toward husband	—	—	—	—	40.5	42.6	49.1	39.6
Relations between Women and Children								
Incidence of women reporting:								
14. Nursing period of last-born child less than two years	—	46.9	54.3	40.4	—	43.4	37.4	50.6
15. Initial indulgence period ceasing with talking	—	59.2	59.0	59.5	—	53.3	59.8	60.2

No. Children:	0	1	2	3 and more	0	1	2	3 and more
16. Exclusive control of father over schooling of children	—	55.1	53.1	58.5	—	58.7	65.8	67.1
17. Exclusive control of father over academic behavior of children	—	33.7	47.7	48.9	—	39.1	56.2	50.2
18. Exclusive use of physical punishment	—	36.7	51.2	44.7	—	43.5	42.0	45.9
19. Academic achievement as the most important parental demand	—	51.0	57.4	56.4	—	57.6	53.4	60.0
20. Socialization of children carried out exclusively by the nuclear family	—	31.6	45.3	33.0	—	30.4	39.3	38.3
21. Preferences for joint parental control over children	—	68.5	64.5	67.0	—	59.8	60.3	60.0
N	100	98	256	94	82	92	219	85

NOTE: Figures given in parentheses are derived from less than 10 respondents.

Relations between Husbands and Wives

Let us consider first how variations in the fertility of married women affect their relations with their husbands, and let us examine initially the nature of the sanctions exerted upon childless women.

EFFECTS OF STERILITY. Regardless of their ethnic backgrounds, childless senior co-wives are more frequently obliged to observe forms of deference toward their husbands than are their monogamous counterparts. Mealtime etiquette is more strictly followed in the former case than in the latter. The observance of such an etiquette probably limits the frequency of domestic quarrels resulting from invidious comparisons between the reproductive roles of senior and junior co-wives.

On the other hand, childless single spouses are uniformly more concerned than senior co-wives with the upward mobility of their husbands. The absence of children among monogamous households may reflect a deliberate choice and such families may have decided to use their surplus resources for moving up in the social structure. However, the presence of children tends to be uniformly perceived in Africa as an alternate mechanism of upward mobility; the presence of junior co-wives facilitates the eventual use of this particular mechanism by polygynous families, but sterile monogamous spouses have to rely solely upon the achievements of their husbands in order to reach a higher social station.

On the whole, sanctions imposed upon childless Bété senior co-wives and single spouses are comparable, but there are marked differences in this regard between their Abouré counterparts. Her sterility obliges an Abouré single spouse to be more subservient toward her husband, that is, to yield more often in domestic quarrels, to emphasize more the significance of the unilateral loyalty that she owes him, and to depend more frequently upon his initiatives concerning the purchase of her clothes. The relative subordination of childless monogamous Abouré spouses probably results from the low incidence of plural marriage prevailing among this particular people. Whereas a Bété husband whose wife is sterile is legitimately expected to marry a second woman, this solution is less normative among the Abouré. In addition, we have seen that the domestic role of Abouré wives has a low level of functionality. As a result, the inability of an Abouré monogamous wife to fulfill the limited obligations expected from her is more strictly sanctioned.

EFFECTS OF FERTILITY. Regardless of their ethnic background, all married women with three or more children present certain common characteristics. More likely to be gainfully employed, they are also less frequently subject to the exclusive budgetary control of their husbands. Only 73 per cent of the Abouré childless senior co-wives have an autonomous budget, as against 86 per cent of those with three or more children. Among the Bété, the relevant figures are 1 and 7 per cent, respectively. The corresponding effects of an increase in the number of children born to monogamous spouses are more limited.

Variations in the number of children are not associated with significant changes in the attitudes held by monogamous wives toward the upward mobility of their husbands. Such changes are, however, characteristic of senior co-wives. The gains that senior co-wives derive from their participation in the labor force are apparently eroded by the additional expenses accompanying an increase in the number of children. Among both peoples, the relationship between number of children and concern with upward mobility is, however, curvilinear. This concern is less apparent among the senior co-wives who have three or more children than among those who have only two children. This seems to suggest that the degree to which African families consider a large number of offspring to be an asset rather than a liability varies with the existing size of the

213

family. This influence of family size probably reflects the impact of aging on economic status. The more children a woman has borne, the older she and her husband tend to be, and the more likely they are to be economically well-off. Rewards attached to age happen to be more significant than the costs attached to an increase in the number of dependents.

Thus, variations in the number of children uniformly modify certain aspects of the contrasts between monogamous and polygynous families. Yet, the extent and the form of such modifications also tend to vary along ethnic lines. These variations reflect differences in the degree to which additional children are regarded as assets or liabilities.

Among the Bété, an additional child is an asset both for the husband (since the child represents a new source of labor as well as an increase in the number of persons subjected to his authority) and for the wife (since the child helps her to attain a higher status in her affinal group). As a result, the effects of fertility reinforce those of plural marriage, and both factors accentuate the dominant traits of this particular ethnic group. Thus, an increase in the number of children reinforces the domestic power of Bété polygynous husbands, but does not affect that of their monogamous counterparts nearly as much. Alternatively, it is associated with a decline in the differential degree of social absorption of single spouses and of senior co-wives. Whereas the financial authority of polygynous husbands is particularly evident among small-sized families, his relative preeminence declines among families with three or more children. Similarly, additional children enhance the security of the status allocated to senior co-wives and the incidence of domestic quarrels pertaining to adultery declines sharply, to become inferior to that among corresponding monogamous households.

In summary, with the exception of domestic power, additional children limit the contrasts between the types of conjugal relations prevailing among Bété monogamous and polygynous families. The resulting similarity reflects, however, the fact that the responses of single spouses and of senior co-wives differ in intensity, in direction, or in both.

Among the Abouré, children are both assets and liabilities. Plural marriage accentuates the equivocal nature of the status ascribed to children by increasing the centrifugal forces exerted on familial groups and by multiplying the number of potential strains between husbands and their various brothers-in-law. As a result, an increase in the number of children has distinct effects upon the status of Abouré single spouses and senior co-wives. Senior co-wives with three or more children are less often financially dependent upon their husbands than are single spouses with a similar number of children. The lower degree of absorption of such senior co-wives is not only financial but emotional as well: their quarrels with their husbands are more likely to pertain to adultery. Yet, with an additional child, the proportion of senior co-wives who yield most frequently to their husbands increases, whereas there is no change in the domestic power structure of monogamous families.

To sum up this description of conjugal relations: (1) The direction and degree of contrasts between the conjugal status of Abouré and Bété senior co-wives are independent of the number of children that they have borne. (2) The more numerous their children, the more alike are the financial and emotional statuses of Bété single spouses and of senior co-wives, and this similarity reflects the complementary nature of the influences exerted by the addition of a co-wife and of a child. (3) The more numerous their respective children, the more distinctive are the responses of Abouré single spouses and senior co-wives, and this dissimilarity results from the fact that additional children exacerbate the strains and tensions between plural marriage and matrilineal type of descent.

Relations among Co-wives

In Chapters 3 and 4 we saw that plural marriage often results from the sterility of the senior co-wife. Under such conditions,

215

it could be predicted that quarrels among co-wives will be more frequent when the senior co-wife is childless than when she has many children herself. In the first instance she is more likely to regard an additional spouse as a competitor; in the second, junior co-wife is not necessarily a threat. This hypothesis is upheld. All senior co-wives with three or more children perceive fewer such tensions than do their childless counterparts. Fertility is associated with a decline in the incidence of domestic quarrels among co-wives, but with an increased specificity in the objects of these disputes. Only 13 per cent of Abouré childless senior co-wives—as opposed to 40 per cent of those with three or more children—are able to indicate clearly the nature of their quarrels with the other spouses of their husbands. Among the Bété, the corresponding figures are 48 and 60 per cent.

However, the consequences of fertility on the types of relations developed among co-wives are not systematically alike on the two peoples compared here. Her fertility enables a Bété senior co-wife to claim all the privileges attached to her rank and thus to exert control over all the children in the household. Thus, 60 per cent of the Bété senior co-wives with three or more children indicate that the rearing of these children is subject to their authority, as against only 42 per cent of those who have no children.

Among the Abouré, the rewards gained by a woman through her fertility are not exclusively controlled by her affinal group. In consequence, quarrels among co-wives are less likely to result from the differential treatment meted out by their husband to each of them. Further, the incidence of this type of quarrel declines with the number of children borne by the senior co-wife. Lessening both the level of over-all competition among co-wives and their competitive feelings vis-à-vis the head of the household, the fertility of the senior co-wife facilitates the emergence of cooperative patterns of behavior among all the women present in the household; the degree to which Abouré co-wives raise their children jointly seems to be a function of the number of children that the senior co-wife has borne.

Relations between Wives and their Families of Origin

First, it should be noted that the degree to which all women comply with norms pertaining to social affiliation varies with the number of their offspring. The Abouré women who report that they returned to their village of origin to deliver their first baby tend to be the most fertile. So are the Bété women who indicate that they stayed with their affines to have their first-born. Thus, 58 per cent of Bété senior co-wives with three or more children report that they gave birth to their first child at their husband's residence, as against only 36 per cent of those who have only one child. Among monogamous respondents, the proportions are 44 and 32 per cent, respectively. It is quite clear that the implications of differing types of descent vary with family size; the larger the family, the more it tends to conform to traditional norms. It is also apparent that competition among Bété co-wives reinforces their desire to endow their children with a proper social affiliation. Bété senior co-wives with a large family are more prone to follow the traditional rules in this respect than single spouses with a similar number of children.

However, fertility seems to reduce the intensity of the relations that all the women interviewed are able to maintain with their family of origin. For example, regardless of both type of marriage and ethnicity, women with many children are less prone than those who have only one child to take post-partum leaves from their husbands. The decline of such loyalties is, however, more characteristic of single spouses, who are also less willing to express their solidarity toward their mothers when they have many children than when they have none. In short, regardless of ethnicity, women with differing matri-

217

monial status do not respond with the same *intensity* to an additional child. Fertility increases the domestic burden of single spouses to a larger extent than that of senior co-wives.

Child-Rearing Practices

Given the equivocal status of children among matrilineal peoples, one could expect contrasts in the child-rearing practices of Abouré single spouses and senior co-wives to increase as a direct function of the number of children they have respectively borne. This assumption is not verified.

In fact, an increase in the number of children enhances the significance of the socialization functions carried out by Abouré senior co-wives, who are less prone to send their offspring away to the compounds of their own relatives or of their affines. Thus it is not universally true that children born in polygynous households cannot develop strong identifications with adult models because of the variety of socialization agents to which they are exposed.[8] Among the Abouré, the number of such agents probably declines as the number of children increases, and there are ultimately no differences between monogamous and polygynous large-sized families in this respect.

The decline of this particular contrast presents a variety of implications. First, additional children lead senior co-wives to cooperate with their husbands as frequently as single spouses. Second, this cooperation leads them to be as much preoccupied by the academic achievement of their offspring. Thirdly, both types of women display a similar amount of initial indulgence toward their children and use comparable techniques of control. This similarity, however, involves different processes; additional children lead senior co-wives to use less frequently

8. For a discussion of this theme, see G. P. Murdock and J. Whiting, Cultural Determination of Parental Attitudes, in M. J. N. Senn, *Problems of Infancy and Childhood: Transactions of the Fourth Conference* (New York: Joshua Macy Foundation, 1950), pp. 13–14.

sanctions of a physical nature and to observe a shorter period of initial indulgence. Conversely, single spouses with many children are more likely than are their counterparts with only one child to use physical punishments and to associate the end of the initial indulgence with the acquisition of language. Finally, cooperation between the parents of all large-sized families enhances the visibility of the disciplinary structure of such groups. Thus, no less than 70 per cent of Abouré senior co-wives with one child ignore the problem of which parent should punish a child who does not meet academic standards, as against only 43 per cent of their counterparts with three or more children, a proportion comparable to that observed among monogamous families of the same size. Additional children, however, reinforce the disciplinary role of monogamous fathers to a larger extent than that of their polygynous counterparts.

By contrast, variations in the number of children do not affect differences in the child-rearing practices of Bété single spouses and senior co-wives, with one notable exception: additional children enable senior co-wives to nurse their children for a longer period of time.

After having assessed the degree to which contrasts between monogamous and polygynous families are independent of their size, we must also examine the extent to which additional children lead to a persistence, an accentuation, or a decline of the cleavages between polygynous families of distinctive ethnic backgrounds. If differences in the roles held by polygynous fathers decrease in size, contrasts in the definition of maternal roles tend to persist, or even to increase.

Some Concluding Remarks

Our purpose was to test the universality of the effects of fertility on the domestic status of women married in differing types of families and in differing types of cultural environments. We have demonstrated that such effects are not universal. Large-sized polygynous families are not characterized by similar features, even though their responses to fertility might be parallel.

We have also demonstrated not only that fertility modifies the extent and the direction of differences in the conjugal relations and the child-rearing practices of monogamous and polygynous families, but also that these modifications vary along ethnic lines.

On the whole, both Abouré and Bété polygynous families are more responsive to an additional child than their monogamous counterparts are. This results from the fact that, although participation in large-sized families requires marked interdependence and hence marked interaction between familial actors, polygyny multiplies sources of potential strains and tensions between the same actors. We suggest, then, that the extent of changes in familial organizations is determined by the inconsistencies of the principles underlying the functioning of such groups. Such inconsistencies are particularly evident among matrilineal polygynous families, and this explains why variations in fertility affect the contrasts between monogamous and polygynous households more extensively among the Abouré than among the Bété.

Economic Functionality of Women

In Chapter 3 we saw that the functionality of the domestic role of a woman depends on the number of familial activities that she performs. For this reason, the functionality of rural housewives is greater than that of their urban counterparts. There are fewer alternative solutions for the gratification of basic familial needs in the rural environment; sources of water, food, and wood are both less numerous and more distant. In addition, rural housewives are frequently expected to participate in the economic enterprises of their husbands. Thus, the value of the chores performed by women is higher in a rural than in an urban environment.

According to the hypotheses formulated in Chapter 3, high

functionality should enable married women (1) to hold an enhanced power and authority over their partners, (2) to have more friendly relations with the other spouses of their husbands, and/or (3) to be more severe and unstable in their attitudes toward children. The effects of functionality should depend, however, upon the number of incumbents in uxorial roles. Since the value of the domestic contributions of a woman varies as a negative function of the number of alternative sources of rewards available to married males, the consequences of variations in functionality should be more significant upon the status of monogamous spouses than upon that of senior co-wives.

Yet, it may also be argued that the effects of functionality along these lines vary from culture to culture. Thus, a low functionality has not the same significance among the Abouré and among the Bété. Insofar as there is a certain amount of overlapping in the implications of functionality and social absorption, a high functionality seems to be normative among the latter people, whereas it departs markedly from the expectations surrounding the domestic role of Abouré women. In this context, one could expect variations in the functionality of the female role to have opposite effects on the familial organization of the two peoples compared here. Our results are presented in Table 39.

Conjugal Relations

Obviously, a low functionality in the role of married women has some uniform implications on the organization of the domestic groups investigated here. As we could have anticipated, the less functional her role, the more a woman is dependent upon the resources of her husband, and the more she is naturally concerned with his upward mobility. This increased dependence of women with a low functionality does not oblige them, however, to occupy a more subordinate position vis-à-vis their husbands. In fact, regardless of ethnicity and type of marriage these women are more prone to claim

Table 39

Relationship between Functionality of the Domestic Role of Wife-Mother and Family Life (Percentages)

Functionality:	Abouré				Bété			
	Monogamous		Polygynous		Monogamous		Polygynous	
	High	Low	High	Low	High	Low	High	Low
Conjugal Relations								
Incidence of women reporting:								
1. Exclusive control of family budget by husband	22.1	45.1	13.0	27.3	43.4	65.4	53.5	72.9
2. Exclusive control of clothing expenditures by husband	54.4	48.1	39.1	36.4	67.1	51.4	73.3	48.9
3. Domestic quarrels mainly caused by adultery	48.5	46.2	73.9	56.8	21.0	19.5	20.4	24.1
4. Exclusive dominance of husband in domestic quarrels	23.5	26.4	21.7	11.4	62.7	52.4	68.6	55.6
5. Single standard on conjugal morality	73.5	51.9	73.9	54.5	31.9	31.9	26.4	30.8
6. High concern with upward mobility of their husbands	8.9	16.1	8.7	18.2	9.1	34.1	11.7	18.0
7. Patterned segregation at mealtime	91.2	74.5	87.0	86.4	92.6	77.8	93.4	91.7
Relations between Wives and their Families								
Incidence of women reporting:								
8. Preeminent status of their mothers	7.4	29.4	4.3	31.8	22.7	41.1	14.8	42.1

9. Their mother's residence as the place where they delivered their first child	38.2	21.7	56.5	22.7	4.4	8.1	2.5	6.0
10. Post-partum leaves from their husbands	42.7	64.2	52.2	59.0	43.1	55.7	42.4	60.2

Relations among Co-wives

Incidence of women reporting:

11. Cooperative practices in raising children	—	—	82.6	52.3	—	—	15.1	30.8
12. "Frequent" quarrels among co-wives	—	—	57.6	46.1	—	—	41.8	57.0
13. Quarrels mainly caused by jealousy toward husband	—	—	57.1	46.1	—	—	45.1	45.6

Relations between Women and Children

Incidence of women reporting:

14. Nursing period of last-born child less than two years	45.6	67.9	69.6	47.8	32.9	47.6	29.3	46.6

Table 39—(Continued)

Functionality:	Abouré Monogamous High	Abouré Monogamous Low	Abouré Polygynous High	Abouré Polygynous Low	Bété Monogamous High	Bété Monogamous Low	Bété Polygynous High	Bété Polygynous Low
15. Initial indulgence period ceasing with talking	64.7	66.0	91.3	65.9	53.9	68.6	53.5	65.4
16. Exclusive control of father over schooling of children	73.5	63.6	57.5	63.6	57.3	50.8	62.3	66.9
17. Exclusive control of father over academic behavior of children	25.0	48.1	39.1	38.6	47.2	47.4	47.2	47.4
18. Exclusive use of physical punishment	20.6	34.9	34.8	43.2	40.0	44.9	35.5	48.1
19. Academic achievement as the most important parental demand	30.9	65.1	17.4	63.6	51.5	52.4	53.5	52.6
20. Socialization of children carried out exclusively by the nuclear family	48.1	61.3	52.2	61.4	38.3	45.9	53.5	40.6
21. Preferences for joint parental control over children	64.7	80.2	78.3	65.9	69.8	61.3	61.3	53.4
N	68	106	23	44	295	185	318	133

that their husbands do not exert an exclusive control on the purchase of clothing. They are also more likely to claim a greater share of domestic power than married women with a functional role.

Variations in the functionality of the domestic role of Abouré women affect the importance of the contrasts opposing some aspects of the conjugal relations prevailing among monogamous and polygynous families. Thus, when this functionality is high, monogamous and polygynous husbands claim a similar amount of domestic power and an identical amount of control over familial resources. Further, high functionality also minimizes differences in the mealtime etiquettes followed by the two types of familial groups. Institutionalization of male preeminence ceases to be an exclusive characteristic of polygynous families. At the same time, high functionality is associated with an increase in the incidence of conjugal quarrels pertaining to adultery among polygynous families, and the corresponding contrast between families with differing type of marriage is more evident.

Variations in functionality hardly affect the significance of any contrast between Bété monogamous and polygynous families. Their responses to a decline in this functionality usually have the same intensity and the same direction. There are, however, two exceptions to this general principle. As in the case of the Abouré, a low functionality obliges senior co-wives to observe more frequent acts of deference toward their husbands than it does their monogamous counterparts. In addition, a low functionality leads single spouses to be more concerned with the upward mobility of their husbands.

Finally, differences between Abouré and Bété polygynous households are maximal when the domestic roles of senior co-wives are highly functional. The financial and social rewards obtained by the two types of senior co-wives with such characteristics are highly distinctive. In fact, Bété women have relatively less initiative in financial matters; they are also less demanding of their husbands in terms of conjugal morality.

225

This could have been anticipated: Bété senior co-wives, in this context, are only conforming with the cultural norms of their affinal group. In contrast, Abouré women are doing more than is expected from them and are therefore differently rewarded.

Relations between Wives and their Families of Origin

A low functionality implies a decline in the significance of the domestic contributions of married women to their affinal group. Correspondingly, it should make them more available to the demands of their own family of origin. This is in fact the case, and regardless of type of marriage or ethnic background, all married women whose contributions are minimal tend to return more frequently to their own village of origin after the birth of their last-born child. They are also more eager to express their solidarity and affection toward their mothers. Variations in functionality do not affect contrasts between Bété monogamous and polygynous families in this respect. Conversely, high functionality is more rewarding for Abouré senior co-wives than for single spouses. They are more likely to return to their mother's residence for giving birth to their first child; they also tend to take more frequent post-partum leaves.

Finally, low functionality is associated with a decline of the differences between Abouré and Bété senior co-wives.

Relations among Co-wives

The direction of the effects of variations in functionality depends upon ethnic factors. Thus, Bété senior co-wives whose functionality is low quarrel less frequently with the other spouses of their husbands than do their counterparts whose functionality is high. The superordinate position of the former is also less apparent than that of the latter. No less than 54 per cent of Bété senior co-wives whose domestic contributions are maximal claim to control the socialization of all the children placed under the authority of their husbands. This characterizes only 22 per cent of those senior co-wives whose domestic contributions are minimal. To this decline in the authority held by such senior co-wives corresponds the emergence of an equalitarian climate; all co-wives tend to raise their children jointly. Alternatively, high functionality diminishes strains among Abouré co-wives; it is correspondingly associated with an increase in their propensity to cooperate with one another. This high functionality, however, makes these women more dependent upon their husbands, and quarrels among Abouré co-wives in this context are more likely to originate from competition about the rewards distributed by the heads of their households.

In short, the responses of Abouré and Bété co-wives to a decline in the functionality of their role run in opposite directions. Given these divergences, a low functionality is still characterized by the emergence of a uniform pattern of interaction between the female actors of polygynous families of distinctive ethnic backgrounds.

Child-Rearing Practices

Among the Abouré, the traditional definition of domestic roles limits the number of demands imposed upon married women. As a result, there are few differences in the child-rearing practices of senior co-wives and single spouses. To be sure, single spouses are more likely to cooperate with their husbands in the rearing of their children, and this results from their relatively higher integration in their affinal group. Correspondingly, senior co-wives wean their children at a later date, and this reflects the fact that, in proportion, their domestic burden is even more limited than the obligations that single spouses are expected to perform.

An increase in the functionality of their respective roles has not therefore similar implications on the socialization techniques of these two types of Abouré women. Indeed, a high functionality leads them to experience quite distinct tensions. Thus, a high functionality reinforces parental cooperation

227

among polygynous households but has an opposite effect on monogamous families. It modifies the nature of the socializing functions exerted by monogamous fathers but leaves that of their polygynous counterparts unchanged. It is associated with a late weaning among monogamous wives but with a shortening of the nursing period among senior co-wives. Alternatively, Abouré co-wives whose domestic role is highly functional tend to observe a longer period of initial indulgence, whereas variations in functionality have no effect on the relevant behavior of their monogamous counterparts. Lastly, an increase in functionality is accompanied by increased divergences both in the relative importance that single spouses and senior co-wives attach to academic achievement and in their respective techniques of control.

The effects of variations in functionality are far more moderate among the Bété. A low functionality maximizes the differences in the authority exerted by monogamous and polygynous fathers. The latter are more likely to make alone the decision to send their children to school. It also reinforces the severity of senior co-wives who tend to use more systematically physical sanctions.

Last, it should be noted that a decrease in the functionality of the role held by Abouré and Bété senior co-wives is accompanied by a partial decline of the contrast between their respective child-rearing practices. Their attitudes toward young children are more comparable, their perceptions of formal schooling are analogous, and their attitudes about the optimal division of roles along sex lines do not differ.

Summary and Conclusions

Our first hypothesis stated that the domestic power and authority of a married woman over her husband would be a function of her contributions to the economic welfare of her household. This hypothesis is not supported. Neither is it tenable that an increased functionality increases the degree to which co-wives are able to cooperate with one another.

We also predicted that variations in functionality would have more powerful effects on the status of single spouses than on that of senior co-wives. This hypothesis, too, is not warranted. The intensity and the direction of responses of monogamous and polygynous families to such variations are not systematically different.

Our last task was to determine whether the influence of variations in functionality on the contrast between polygyny and monogamy is independent of cultural factors. Such variations affect the direction and the extent of the differences in the conjugal relations and child-rearing practices of Abouré single spouses and senior co-wives, but are less operative among the Bété. Thus, the influence of functionality seems to be maximal when this factor is not highly normative, as is the case among the Abouré. In other words, an increase in the number of wife-mothers makes a difference in the domestic status achieved by each female adult actor through her functionality only when the cultural demands imposed upon her are limited in scope.

Furthermore, although a low functionality is associated with the emergence of more uniform styles of interaction among Abouré and Bété polygynous families, this emergence still results from strains and pressures which are culturally specific. In fact, Abouré senior co-wives whose domestic contributions are maximal tend to differ markedly from the population at large, in contrast to those with a low functionality. Symmetrically, the domestic status of Bété senior co-wives with a low functionality departs more from the average than that of their counterparts whose role is highly functional and meets, therefore, the requirements of this particular culture.

Economic Independence

African domestic power structures are, however, not only influenced by the functionality of the role held by married women but also by the extent to which these women have

229

access to economic rewards outside of the family.[9] Such an access reduces their dependence upon the head of their household and should modify their domestic role accordingly. In Chapter 3 we made the assumptions that participation of married women in the labor force would (1) accentuate the segregation of domestic roles along sex lines, (2) increase the domestic power exerted by these women, (3) facilitate their cooperation with the other spouses of their husbands, and (4) accentuate their severity toward their children.

There are, however, two competing hypotheses to be discussed in this regard. On the one hand it can be proposed that the rewards and the costs attached to this participation are universal. The organization of families whose wives have independent resources should be alike in a variety of cultural environments.

On the other hand, it can be posited that participation of women in the labor force depends on the stereotypes prevailing in the culture of which they are members. The entry of women into a variety of occupations is not equally prescribed, forbidden, or tolerated by a variety of human societies. The number of jobs in which they participate varies along ethnic lines; patterns of recruitment into a single occupation are not constant across geographic, cultural, or ethnic boundaries.[10] Further, the extent of this participation is affected by the cultural stereotypes regarding the domestic position of married women; opposition to their participation in the labor market should vary as a direct function of the degree of their social absorption into their affinal group. The domestic strains

9. Of course, the nature of the occupations of the women sampled would have been a relevant dimension to explore. The small number of Bété women engaged in independent agricultural activities and the small number of senior co-wives participating in salaried employment have prevented us from introducing occupational distinctions.

10. For a full discussion and presentation of concrete evidence see P. H. Chombart de Lauwe, ed., *Images de la femme dans la société* (Paris: Editions Ouvrieres, 1964).

associated with the gainful employment of married women should be accordingly more numerous among the Bété than among the Abouré. Such strains, furthermore, should be more characteristic of the polygynous families of the former people insofar as plural marriage enhances the domestic demands imposed upon each Bété co-wife. In contrast, since plural marriage increases the availability of Abouré co-wives to the demands of the labor market, the gainful employment of such women should have few consequences on the organization of their family.

Further, the geographic distributions of women gainfully employed is not alike for the two ethnic groups compared here. Among the Abouré, participation in the labor force is maximal for rural women; among the Bété, this participation is maximal for urbanized wives. Thus, only 14 per cent of the Abouré respondents who have an occupation independent of that of their husbands are derived from an urban environment, against 81 per cent of their Bété counterparts. The influence exerted by the socioeconomic status of husbands along these lines is not alike either for these two peoples. For example, 86 per cent of the women married to Abouré polygynous farmers have independent sources of income, against only 3 per cent of the Bété. About one-third of the Abouré women married to polygynous manual and clerical workers are gainfully employed, against only one-tenth of the Bété women in the same environment.

In conclusion, participation of Abouré women in the labor force is more frequent than that of their Bété counterparts. This difference results from the conjunction of two factors: the economic autonomy of Abouré women results not only from their low degree of social absorption but also from the limited distance between the natural habitat of the Abouré and the capital city. This proximity facilitates the over-all involvement of this people in the modern sector of the economy and enhances correspondingly the chances of the Abouré women to acquire access to economic independence.[11] Yet, in relative terms, urbanization is associated with a decrease in the gainful employment of Abouré women, but with an increase in that of Bété respondents. We can infer that economically independent Bété women will be more "innovative" than their Abouré counterparts.

The influences of the gainful employment of married women on the domestic power structure of their familial group are summarized in Table 40.

Conjugal Relations

This gainful employment has uniform effects on the financial autonomy enjoyed by the respondents vis-à-vis their husbands.[12] Only one-half of the Abouré monogamous wives who do not participate in the labor force have a budget which is independent of that of their husbands, as against three-fourths of those who work.[13] Among the Abouré polygynous households, the corresponding figures are 75 and 85 per cent, respectively. These effects of gainful employment are identical among the Bété. Only 6 per cent of the monogamous women and 4 per cent of the senior co-wives who are not gainfully employed indicate that they have autonomous resources. Such a privilege characterizes 19 and 23 per cent, respectively, of their counterparts who participate in the labor force.

Yet, the effects of the participation of women in the labor

11. See Chapter 4.

12. Of course, the significance of this discussion extends far beyond the limits of the present sample. In fact, the whole question is the problem of determining whether occupational success is accompanied by variations in the domestic power structure. For a discussion of this problem in the United States see, for example, Robert Blood and Robert Hamblin, "The Effects of the Wife's Employment on the Family Power Structure," *Social Forces*, XXXV (1958), 347–52; and David Heer, "Dominance and the Working Wife," *Ibid.*, pp. 341–47.

13. In the cases where the wife is not gainfully employed, one can speculate about the origin of her independent resources. The fact remains that women derived from matrilineal peoples are entitled to manage by themselves a certain amount of resources.

Table 40

Relationship between Participation of Wives in Labor Force and Family Life (Percentages)

	Abouré				Bété			
	Monogamous		Polygynous		Monogamous		Polygynous	
	Active	Inactive	Active	Inactive	Active	Inactive	Active	Inactive
Conjugal Relations								
Incidence of women reporting:								
1. Exclusive control of family budget by husband	12.8	38.5	8.4	22.4	41.8	51.8	53.8	59.1
2. Exclusive control of clothing expenditures by husband	25.5	50.6	22.0	37.3	25.4	60.9	42.3	65.9
3. Domestic quarrels mainly caused by adultery	53.1	47.1	58.9	62.7	31.3	20.4	19.2	21.5
4. Exclusive dominance of husband in domestic quarrels	24.8	25.3	23.8	14.9	53.7	58.6	42.3	64.8
5. Single standard on conjugal morality	63.8	60.3	69.6	61.2	37.3	31.8	26.9	27.9
6. High concern with upward mobility of their husbands	9.3	13.2	10.3	14.9	40.3	18.9	23.0	13.5
7. Patterned segregation at mealtime	85.5	81.0	89.7	86.6	68.6	86.7	73.0	92.9
Relations between Wives and their Families								
Incidence of women reporting:								
8. Preeminent status of their mothers	17.6	20.7	21.0	22.4	34.3	29.7	50.0	22.6

Table 40—(Continued)

	Abouré				Bété			
	Monogamous		Polygynous		Monogamous		Polygynous	
	Active	Inactive	Active	Inactive	Active	Inactive	Active	Inactive
9. Their mother's residence as the place where they delivered their first child	51.7	28.2	48.6	34.3	11.3	5.8	3.8	3.5
10. Post-partum leaves from their husbands	61.1	55.7	58.9	56.7	55.2	48.5	61.5	47.6
Relations among Co-wives								
Incidence of women reporting:								
11. Cooperative practices in raising children	—	—	55.6	62.7	—	—	26.9	19.7
12. "Frequent" quarrels among co-wives	—	—	18.3	5.0	—	—	40.0	30.0
13. Quarrels mainly caused by jealousy toward husband	—	—	25.0	50.0	—	—	45.0	45.1
Relations between Women and Children								
Incidence of women reporting:								
14. Nursing period of last-born child less than two years	49.3	59.2	50.0	55.3	56.7	38.5	42.4	34.3

15. Initial indulgence period ceasing with talking	70.7	65.9	77.1	74.6	52.2	59.5	50.0	56.9
16. Exclusive control of father over schooling of children	64.5	63.8	65.9	63.6	47.8	54.5	38.5	63.7
17. Exclusive control of father over academic behavior of children	32.8	39.1	30.4	38.8	40.3	39.5	26.9	47.7
18. Exclusive use of physical punishment	24.8	29.3	22.4	40.3	40.3	41.6	38.5	39.2
19. Academic achievement as the most important parental demand	40.0	51.7	42.5	47.8	49.3	51.8	34.6	53.5
20. Socialization of children carried out exclusively by the nuclear family	51.7	56.3	52.8	58.2	40.3	41.2	23.1	37.4
21. Preferences for joint parental control over children	80.0	74.1	75.7	70.1	55.2	66.5	61.5	59.3
N	290	174	214	67	67	484	26	452

force on the contrasts between differing types of marriage vary along ethnic lines. Among the Abouré, this participation *minimizes* differences in the conjugal relations characteristic of monogamous and polygynous families. Inactive Abouré senior co-wives are less frequently subject to the financial authority of their husbands than are the spouses of monogamous males. They are also less prone to yield first in domestic quarrels and are more inclined to be involved in feuds pertaining to adultery.

Among the Bété, the gainful employment of single spouses and of senior co-wives *maximizes* the differences between their respective styles of conjugal interaction. Thus, a single spouse is less frequently financially dependent upon her husband than is her counterpart married to a polygynist. In addition, she has more equalitarian orientations as far as conjugal morality is concerned, and this leads her to be more frequently engaged in quarrels pertaining to adultery. Yet she is also more prone to yield first in domestic feuds and has, accordingly, a smaller amount of domestic power.

Finally, the gainful employment of Abouré and Bété senior co-wives does not modify the terms of the contrasts between their respective styles of conjugal interaction. The rewards that they may obtain are not identical, but neither are their aspirations similar.

Relations between Wives and their Families of Origin

Participation in the labor force does not affect the size or the direction of the contrasts in the relations that Abouré senior co-wives and single spouses maintain with their family of origin. This participation reinforces for both types of wife the significance that they attach to the social affiliation of their children and both senior co-wives and single spouses are more likely to return to their own village to give birth to their first child.

In contrast, the enhanced domestic power acquired by Bété

married women through their employment can be equated with a decline of their absorption into their affinal group. This decline is most apparent among senior co-wives who are not only more often in a position to express their affection toward their mothers and to take post-partum leaves but are also less concerned with the social affiliation of their children. Thus only 7 per cent of the active senior co-wives have delivered their first child at their husband's residence against no less than 37 per cent of those who are unemployed. Differences between active and inactive single spouses are slightly less sharp and the corresponding proportions are 11 and 32 per cent respectively.

Relations among Co-wives

The gainful employment of Abouré and Bété senior co-wives modifies differences in the relations that they establish with the junior spouses of their husbands.

The gainful employment of Bété senior co-wives is associated with a decline in their dependence upon the head of their household and with a corresponding increase in the solidarity that they can manifest toward their family of origin. One would expect them to maintain more friendly relations with the other spouses of their husbands. Indeed, potential sources of strains have been removed. Such assumptions are, nevertheless, unwarranted. Participation in the labor force is uniformly accompanied by an increase in the quarrels which oppose co-wives to one another. Regardless of ethnic origin, the gainful employment of senior co-wives seems to accentuate differences in the social position that each married woman achieves both in her affinal group and in the society at large.

Participation in the labor market does not, however, modify the nature of the quarrels among Bété co-wives. By contrast, among the Abouré there is an increase in the incidence of tensions about the division of domestic chores. No less than one-half of the quarrels in Abouré households whose senior co-wife is gainfully employed have such a basis, as against only one-fourth of the conflicts among families whose senior co-wife is inactive. The increase of such quarrels limits, in turn, the extent to which these women cooperate with one another in the rearing of their children.

Child-Rearing Practices

Differences in the child-rearing practices of Abouré senior co-wives and single spouses are hardly affected by variations in the occupational status of these women. Participation in the labor force does alter, however, contrasts in the types of control used by women of different family types. Inactive Abouré senior co-wives are more likely than are single spouses to use physical punishments. Conversely, two-thirds of the active senior co-wives use sanctions of an emotional nature, as against less than half of their monogamous counterparts.

On the other hand, the gainful employment of Bété women is associated with an accentuation of the contrasts opposing the child-rearing practices of single spouses and of senior co-wives. First, monogamous families whose wives are gainfully employed play a more significant role in the socialization of children. In contrast, active Bété senior co-wives are more likely to send their children to their village of origin or to the compounds of their relatives.[14] This difference in turn leads to contrasts in the definition of parental roles. Active single spouses nurse their children for a shorter period of time, and this probably results from the sharp incompatibilities between their domestic and economic roles. Further, monogamous husbands follow more closely all the problems pertaining to the formal schooling of their children, and participation of women in the labor market is therefore associated with a reversal of the difference between monogamous and polygynous families

14. Thus only 14 per cent of inactive single spouses and senior co-wives indicate that the education of their children is the chief concern of their own relatives. This answer is given by 31 per cent of active senior co-wives, but only by 12 per cent of active single spouses.

in this respect. Finally, active single spouses attach more importance to the academic achievement of their children.

The gainful employment of Abouré and Bété senior co-wives is also associated with a modification of the extent and the direction of the differences between their respective child-rearing practices. Active Abouré senior co-wives and their husbands participate more extensively in the socialization of their children than do their Bété counterparts. In addition, participation of Bété senior co-wives in the labor force is associated with a decline in the length of their nursing period, and differences between Abouré and Bété in this respect become negligible. Active Bété senior co-wives display significantly less mothering than Abouré women with similar characteristics; the Bété's initial indulgence period is shorter, and they are more prone to use physical punishments. Furthermore, the decision to give a formal education to a child is more often an exclusive privilege of Abouré than of Bété husbands, and this privilege leads them to control more frequently the academic behavior of their offspring. Correspondingly active Abouré senior co-wives attach more importance to the academic achievement of their children than do Bété women of similar matrimonial and occupational status. In brief, incompatibilities between the maternal and the economic functions of senior co-wives seem to be sharper among the Bété than among the Abouré. The gainful employment of Bété senior co-wives limits the importance of the socialization functions carried by their immediate familial group. It limits as well the disciplinary role exerted by their husbands, and it makes the women themselves less likely to maintain social, expressive relations with their children.

Summary and Conclusions

We argued that the gainful employment of African married women would be associated with a decline of their financial and social dependence upon their husbands and with the emergence of more equaliterian relationships between them. Our data support this assumption. We also anticipated that active women would be more available to the demands of their own familial group, and our analysis has shown this to be the case. Evidence concerning the influence of participation of senior co-wives in the labor force on the relations that they maintain with junior spouses are less convincing. Similarly, it is impossible to draw generalized propositions about the effects of gainful employment on the child-rearing practices of the women interviewed here.

On the whole, variations in occupational status modify the extent and the direction of the contrasts between the organization of Bété monogamous and polygynous groups, but are less operative among the Abouré. The economic independence of married women is less normative among the first than among the second people, and we may suggest here that it is only in the absence of relevant norms that variations in the number of wives modify the intensity and the extent of the strains resulting from incompatibilities between the domestic and economic roles of married women.

To be sure, the entry of Bété women in the labor market could be regarded as symbolically equivalent to their participation in the economic enterprises of their husbands. Given the fact that social absorption induces married women to contribute to the economic resources of their affinal group, this obligation can be fulfilled in a variety of ways. In fact, the controls exerted upon the routines and the resources of a woman gainfully employed are not comparable to those exerted upon the routines and resources of a woman participating in the agricultural or commercial activities of her husband. Both the agents of control and the mechanisms that they use are distinctive. Accordingly, the entry of Bété women, particularly the senior co-wives, into the labor market makes them marginal; there are necessarily significant inconsistencies in their new status. This marginality, as we have seen, enables a large number of

Bété women to share a larger part of the domestic authority and power with their husbands. At the same time, since their position in their affinal group has never been a particularly gratifying experience, these women tend to use the new *means* at their disposal to get an easier access to the *rewards* they desire. Many of these rewards are to be found in their place and village of origin. There is, accordingly, an increasing matrifocalization and matrilinearization of the Bété polygynous families whose senior co-wife works.

Our data, however have shown not only that Bété respond more intensely than Abouré to variations in the economic status of married women, but also that the direction of their respective responses are different. Contrasts between monogamous and polygynous families are maximal among the Abouré when the wives are not active and do not therefore conform with the relevant cultural prescriptions; in contrast, we have seen that the trend is just the reverse among the Bété, that cleavages between differing types of marriages are maximal among families in which wives do participate in the labor force, thereby deviating from traditional norms.

Finally, participation in the labor market is associated with a persistence, even an accentuation, of the differences in the conjugal relations, the child-rearing practices, and the general organization of Abouré and Bété, polygynous families and this suggests that the strains associated with the gainful employment of married women are not universal but are rather determined by the social stereotypes regarding this phenomenon in each specific cultural environment.

The Social Background of Married Women

Thus far, we have examined the implications of the participation of married women in familial and other organizations on the domestic position that they hold. Above all, we have analyzed how such implications vary with type of marriage, that is, with the number of incumbents in the role of wife-mother. Yet, the domestic status of married women is also determined by their background—more specifically, by the relative position that they occupied, before marriage, in the field of eligibles in their own culture. It can be hypothesized that the authority and power that a woman can obtain in her affinal group is higher when she has socially valuable characteristics.

The importance of the social background of a married woman in this respect should vary, however, with the intensity of the competition prevailing in the field of eligibles to which she belongs. This background should have more consequences for the functioning of polygynous families than for that of monogamous households, because plural marriage enhances the visibility of each familial actor and facilitates comparisons between their respective origins.

Further, the consequences attached to these social antecedents should be maximal among peoples where plural marriage is a privilege attached to seniority. In this case, older individuals are in a position to preempt the most valuable brides from the field of eligibles; younger males are accordingly obliged to marry women who are not particularly attractive. These women are therefore more likely to become senior co-wives, and there should be numerous inconsistencies between the rights that they acquire through their seniority and the demands that their junior counterparts can exert because of their greater social value.

Finally, the consequences of these inconsistencies should vary as a direct function of degree of social absorption. When this degree is high, the husband's family controls all the rewards to which married women may aspire. These factors lead us to believe that the effects of variations in the social characteristics of senior co-wives on the status that they achieve in their affinal group will be more powerful among the Bété than among the Abouré.

The problem remains to measure the social attractiveness of our respondents. We have used in the context of the present study the following indicators: (a) age at marriage;[15] (b) the matrimonial compensation or brideprice payed by the bridegroom or his family at the time of marriage, (c) the presents offered by the bridegroom to his spouse at the time of marriage, and (d) the previous matrimonial status of our respondents.

Age at Marriage

Among the many African peoples where the two main familial functions of women are reproduction and participation in the economic enterprises of their husbands, a young bride is more attractive than an old one. The former will have more children and will remain active for a longer period of time. In fact, there is some evidence in the literature to suggest that age is an adequate indicator of the social value of a potential bride: young African males are often obliged to marry relatively older women, since the young brides have already been chosen by older males who have more economic and social resources at their disposal. In this sense we can assume that a late marriage will increase the subordination of a senior co-wife to her husband and will limit, accordingly, the number of contacts that she will maintain with her family of origin.

15. The use of this variable raises the whole problem of the measures of age in Africa. For this particular item, we have used as a point of reference the appearance of the first menstrual period. The questions pertaining to age nevertheless remain difficult to handle in the African context. For this very reason, we had instructed our interviewers to be very cautious in this respect and to disregard all answers which were not precise enough. This caution led us to lose much information about the real or presumed age of the respondents, which is the reason that we have not used age per se as a variable. On an ex post facto basis, we feel sorry for our cautiousness; indeed, although we have no way of deciding whether the relevant responses of the persons interviewed are real or confabulated, the census of Abidjan for 1963 still shows that there are relations between variations in age and participation in economic, educational and familial structures. We can infer that we could probably have obtained some significant associations between age and the organization of the familial groups investigated here. Yet the fact that we did lose information on the age of a large majority of the rural respondents of our sample has reduced the validity of the responses of those few persons who did give their age.

On the other hand, an early marriage limits the initiative that a female individual can take, and it increases her subservience toward the older segments of both the population into which she marries and that of her origin. It is this factor which leads many African males to adopt an ambivalent attitude toward the formal schooling of girls; they are aware that education delays marriage and that such a delay tends to decrease the flexibility of their potential brides.

These are the two competing hypotheses that we must analyze. The influence on their familial relations of the respondents' age at marriage is summarized in Table 41. Since the norms pertaining to age at marriage vary with urbanization, we have analyzed here only the responses of rural women, for whom the relevant norms are certainly more clearly defined.

First of all, it should be noted that early marriage tends to be more characteristic of the Abouré than of the Bété women. No less than 84 per cent of the Abouré were married before they were 16 years old, as against a little over two-thirds of the Bété. In addition, there are no significant differences in this respect between women entering into monogamous families and those entering into polygynous households. This suggests that there are no differences in the respective attractiveness of monogamous wives and of senior spouses.

The effects of variations in age at marriage on the organization of monogamous and polygynous families are limited.

CONJUGAL RELATIONS. A late marriage tends to be associated with a lower absorption of Abouré women in their affinal group. They enjoy greater financial freedom and are more often able to oblige their husbands to yield in domestic quarrels. However, a late marriage also modifies the contrasts between monogamous and polygynous families. Senior cowives who married late tend to be more dependent than single spouses upon the financial resources of their husbands. They gain a proportionately smaller amount of domestic power; moreover, they are more inclined to stress the value of female

Table 41

Relationship between Age of Wife at Marriage and Family Life (Percentages)

	Abouré				Bété			
	Monogamous		Polygynous		Monogamous		Polygynous	
	Early Marriage	Late Marriage	Early Marriage	Late Marriage	Early Marriage	Late Marriage	Early Marriage	Late Marriage
Conjugal Relations Incidence of women reporting:								
1. Exclusive control of family budget by husband	11.8	10.0	5.7	10.3	44.4	46.7	56.3	47.1
2. Exclusive control of clothing expenditures by husband	33.3	26.0	25.9	17.2	69.4	65.2	77.3	55.3
3. Domestic quarrels mainly caused by adultery	53.5	58.0	63.8	62.1	18.5	18.4	21.7	15.7
4. Exclusive dominance of husband in domestic quarrels	24.8	12.0	24.7	17.2	64.3	57.6	69.2	73.7
5. Single standard on conjugal morality	71.5	70.0	73.0	58.6	27.4	36.9	23.7	38.1
6. High concern with upward mobility of their husbands	7.7	4.0	9.2	24.1	8.3	8.4	10.1	9.2
7. Patterned segregation at mealtime	90.2	86.0	89.1	96.5	94.2	93.4	94.0	89.4
Relations between Wives and their Families Incidence of women reporting:								
8. Preeminent status of their mothers	13.4	6.0	15.5	17.2	15.5	17.2	10.1	22.3

Table 41—(Continued)

	Abouré				Bété			
	Monogamous		Polygynous		Monogamous		Polygynous	
	Early Marriage	Late Marriage	Early Marriage	Late Marriage	Early Marriage	Late Marriage	Early Marriage	Late Marriage
9. Their mother's residence as the place where they delivered their first child	56.5	42.0	55.2	37.9	5.1	6.5	1.0	5.3
10. Post-partum leaves from their husbands	56.1	56.0	57.1	58.6	49.7	36.9	42.5	46.3
Relations among Co-wives								
Incidence of women reporting:								
11. Cooperative practices in raising children	—	—	60.3	75.9	—	—	37.5	30.2
12. "Frequent" quarrels among co-wives	—	—	46.5	61.5	—	—	50.9	47.3
13. Quarrels mainly caused by jealousy toward husband	—	—	27.6	0.0	—	—	50.9	47.5
Relations between Women and Children								
Incidence of women reporting:								
14. Nursing period of last-born child less than two years	44.7	48.0	49.4	55.2	30.0	41.3	29.8	39.4

15. Initial indulgence period ceasing with talking	69.5	76.0	78.2	79.3	54.8	55.4	57.1	50.0
16. Exclusive control of father over schooling of children	65.9	68.0	63.8	75.9	59.9	58.6	65.2	43.4
17. Exclusive control of father over academic behavior of children	30.1	30.0	29.3	31.0	45.2	47.8	47.0	48.6
18. Exclusive use of physical punishment	16.3	24.1	21.3	20.7	35.7	41.3	32.3	39.6
19. Academic achievement as the most important parental demand	35.4	30.0	37.9	44.8	49.0	54.3	53.0	54.5
20. Socialization of children carried out exclusively by the nuclear family	51.2	46.0	53.4	48.3	45.9	34.7	38.9	35.5
21. Preferences for joint parental control over children	75.6	72.0	77.6	75.9	77.6	75.9	61.1	65.8
N	246	53	174	29	157	92	198	76

NOTE: Early marriage refers to marriage contracted before the bride was 16 years old.

loyalties in marriage.[16] Finally, they are more frequently obliged to acknowledge the preeminent position of their husbands and are therefore more likely to follow rules of meal-time etiquette.

Among the Bété, the effects of a late marriage are similarly most apparent with respect to the status of senior co-wives. Indeed, a late marriage is associated with a decline of their financial dependence. At the same time, however, they are more frequently obliged than are single spouses to yield in quarrels with their husbands.

Finally, an early marriage maximizes the cleavages between the financial authority structure of Abouré and Bété polygynous families. It is conversely associated with a decline of the differences between other aspects of the conjugal style of interaction of these two types of households.

RELATIONS BETWEEN WIVES AND THEIR FAMILIES OF ORIGIN. A late marriage accentuates differences between single spouses and senior co-wives. Single spouses are less often in a position to express their affection toward their mothers. Among the Bété, they are also less likely to take post-partum leaves.

RELATIONS AMONG CO-WIVES. Variations in age at marriage affect the relations between Abouré senior co-wives and the other spouses of their husbands, whereas they do not exert similar influences on the climate of Bété polygynous households. Thus, the late marriage of Abouré senior co-wives reduces not only the incidence of quarrels between them and their co-wives but also the incidence of conflicts resulting from the differential treatment accorded to each one of them by the head of the household. Correspondingly, these women are more likely to cooperate with one another in the upbringing of their children.

16. Thus, 70 per cent of single spouses who married late oblige their husbands to yield most frequently in domestic quarrels, as against less than one-half of their counterparts who married early. The corresponding figures for senior co-wives are 62 and 56 per cent, respectively.

In short, a late marriage accentuates differences along these lines between Abouré and Bété polygynous families; it exaggerates the traits characteristic of the Abouré familial organization, but not those of the second.

CHILD-REARING PRACTICES. It should first be noted that late marriage is associated with a uniform decline in the importance that respondents attach to the social placement of their first child. Table 41 shows that the older the age at marriage of Abouré women, the less frequently they return to their mother's homes for the birth of their first child. Among the Bété, similarly, no less than 53 per cent of all women who married early have given birth to their first child at their husband's residence. This characterizes only 44 per cent of the women who married late.

Second, variations in age at marriage do not markedly affect differences between the child-rearing practices of single spouses and those of senior co-wives. On the whole, responses of these women to a late marriage are parallel. Thus, among the Abouré, late marriage induces all respondents to wean their children at an earlier age. It is also accompanied by a uniform decline in the significance of the socializing functions performed by the nuclear family. There are two exceptions to this general principle: (1) In the case of late unions, the authority allocated to polygynist males over the formal schooling of their children seems to be greater than that made available to their monogamous counterparts. (2) As a result, senior co-wives attach greater importance to the academic achievement of their children than do single spouses.

Among the Bété, the effects of variations in age at marriage on child-rearing practices are also independent of the matrimonial status of the women interviewed. However, senior co-wives who married late are able, more often than are single spouses, to participate in the decision to send their children to school.

Finally, a late marriage accentuates differences in the disciplinary functions of Abouré and Bété polygynous husbands. It tends also to accentuate contrasts in the types of controls used by their wives. Abouré senior co-wives who married late are less likely than their Bété counterparts to use physical sanctions.

In summary, it is relatively easy to demonstrate how the consequences of a late union vary with the matrimonial status of the women interviewed here. Having failed to demonstrate that the consequences of a late marriage are more evident among the Bété than among the Abouré, we have still suggested that a late marriage tends to maximize many of the contrasts between the organizations of these two examples of polygyny.

Brideprice

The relative social value of the women compared here may also be measured by the amount of brideprice that their families received at the time of marriage. Initially, the brideprice represents a compensation for all the losses incurred by the bride's family because of her marriage. Indeed, this group is losing a source of labor, a source of wealth (through her offspring), and a part of its social integrity. However, the estimation of such losses is likely to depend upon the position that the bride occupies in the field of eligibles. The more valuable she is, the more her family will be likely to ask for a high compensation.

According to our general hypothesis, we could expect variations in the amount of brideprice to have more significant effects on the functioning of polygynous families. Further, these effects should be most apparent among the Bété, since the distribution of brideprice has a greater variance there than among the Abouré.

The diversity of the forms of matrimonial compensation has unfortunately prevented both the assessment of their real value and their consequences on styles of familial interaction. Thus our comparison is limited to whether the women answering the questions did or did not receive a brideprice, without reference to what form it may have taken.

Our results are summarized in Table 42. On the whole, the payment of a brideprice does not markedly affect the contrasts in the organization of monogamous and polygynous families.

CONJUGAL RELATIONS. The payment of a brideprice is, nevertheless, associated with an accentuation of the differences in the types of conjugal relations prevailing among Abouré monogamous and polygynous families. When their marriage has been accompanied by a brideprice, Abouré senior co-wives are less often subjected to the financial control of their husbands than are their monogamous counterparts; in other words, they have a greater financial autonomy and are more prone to take initiatives with regard to the purchase of clothes. They are also more likely to quarrel with their husband about their respective sexual behaviors. At the same time, however, they enjoy a more limited amount of domestic power.

In contrast, the payment of a brideprice does not affect the contrasts between the styles of conjugal interaction prevailing among Bété monogamous and polygynous families. It seems possible, however, to suggest that the absence of a brideprice tends to modify the differential degree of social absorption of senior co-wives and single spouses. For example, senior co-wives are more subordinate to the domestic power of their husbands.

RELATIONS BETWEEN WIVES AND THEIR FAMILIES OF ORIGIN. The payment of a brideprice is more rewarding for Abouré senior co-wives than for single spouses from the same ethnic background. They are more willing to give priority to their mothers in the context of the dilemma story used in the questionnaire. They are more often able to take post-partum leaves, and these leaves last longer. Finally, they are more

Table 42

Relationship between Payment of Brideprice and Family Life (Percentages)

Conjugal Relations	Abouré Monogamous		Abouré Polygynous		Bété Monogamous		Bété Polygynous	
	Bride-price	None	Bride-price	None	Bride-price	None	Bride-price	None
Incidence of women reporting:								
1. Exclusive control of family budget by husband	26.7	19.8	11.5	11.8	50.7	50.0	58.7	59.1
2. Exclusive control of clothing expenditures by husband	34.8	34.7	23.1	26.9	56.5	55.8	64.5	64.9
3. Domestic quarrels mainly caused by adultery	44.4	54.9	60.0	59.7	21.9	20.8	21.1	21.9
4. Exclusive dominance of husband in domestic quarrels	22.8	26.0	26.3	19.4	59.1	52.5	64.5	61.3
5. Single standard on conjugal morality	64.6	61.5	66.3	66.3	30.3	40.0	24.6	39.1
6. High concern with upward mobility of their husbands	10.3	10.7	9.3	12.3	21.7	21.8	13.7	15.3
7. Patterned segregation at mealtime	80.2	85.4	86.4	90.4	85.7	85.3	92.2	90.5

Relations between Wives and their Families

Incidence of women reporting:

8. Preeminent status of their mothers	13.3	22.2	24.2	19.9	28.4	35.1	24.4	22.9
9. Their mother's residence as the place where they delivered their first child	38.3	45.8	50.5	42.5	5.9	8.3	3.6	3.8
10. Post-partum leaves from their husbands	55.1	61.2	61.0	57.5	51.3	51.7	49.0	57.3

Relations among Co-wives

Incidence of women reporting:

11. Cooperative practices in raising children	—	—	58.4	56.5	—	—	21.4	15.0
12. "Frequent" quarrels among co-wives	—	—	20.7	13.4	—	—	30.6	31.1
13. Quarrels mainly caused by jealousy toward husband	—	—	44.3	23.9	—	—	45.8	43.8

Relations between Women and Children

Incidence of women reporting:

14. Nursing period of last-born child less than two years	53.1	53.4	48.4	52.2	43.4	30.9	34.2	36.2

Table 42—(Continued)

	Abouré				Bété			
	Monogamous		Polygynous		Monogamous		Polygynous	
	Bride-price	None	Bride-price	None	Bride-price	None	Bride-price	None
15. Initial indulgence period ceasing with talking	68.1	69.2	72.1	78.6	59.5	54.2	56.6	52.2
16. Exclusive control of father over schooling of children	62.8	65.3	62.1	67.8	53.5	55.0	63.9	59.1
17. Exclusive control of father over academic behavior of children	32.4	35.8	42.1	27.4	42.7	28.1	45.1	47.6
18. Exclusive use of physical punishment	31.3	27.4	31.2	24.8	42.5	39.8	40.7	30.5
19. Academic achievement as the most important parental demand	45.7	43.8	41.1	45.2	50.4	50.8	49.8	61.9
20. Socialization of children carried out exclusively by the nuclear family	51.7	54.5	62.1	50.0	40.9	42.5	35.3	40.4
21. Preferences for joint parental control over children	74.9	79.9	68.4	77.4	65.3	59.2	56.6	69.5
N	175	288	95	186	438	120	373	105

prone to return to their mother's residence to give birth to their child.

Results tend to be symmetric among the Bété. A senior co-wife whose family has not received any brideprice cannot express her loyalties toward her mother as often as a single spouse in the same situation can.

RELATIONS AMONG CO-WIVES. The presence or absence of a brideprice does not affect the relations that Bété senior co-wives establish with the junior spouses of their husbands. On the other hand, the payment of a brideprice accentuates competition between Abouré co-wives, which increasingly tends to result from the differential treatment accorded to the women by their husbands. In other words, the payment of a brideprice induces competitive feelings which are alien to the Abouré traditional forms of polygyny.

CHILD-REARING PRACTICES. The payment of a brideprice does not markedly affect the child-rearing practices of Abouré families. It presents more implications for the Bété, because it is closely associated with the social placement of children.

The absence of matrimonial compensation also introduces significant cleavages between the socializing roles of Bété monogamous and polygynous actors. First, senior co-wives for whom no brideprice was paid cooperate with their husbands in these matters more often than their monogamous counterparts do. In turn, variations in cooperation between parents modify the nature of the socializing role held by each of them. The absence of a brideprice is associated with late weaning among monogamous families but not among polygynous households. It is similarly accompanied by a decline in the visibility of the disciplinary structure of monogamous families, and single spouses tend in this case to participate more frequently than do senior co-wives in the disciplining of their children who do not meet academic standards. Conversely, the better cooperation between Bété polygynous parents enables senior co-wives to use physical sanctions less frequently. These same senior co-wives are also more inclined to attach great significance to the academic achievement of their offspring.

Among the Abouré, conversely, the payment of a brideprice markedly reinforces the importance of the socialization functions performed by polygynous families, but such payment has little effect in this regard on monogamous households. Accordingly, the disciplinary structure of the first type of familial group has a greater visibility.

Finally, the absence of a brideprice tends to maximize differences in the child-rearing practices of Abouré and Bété polygynous families. In this case reactions of senior co-wives to young children are highly distinctive. There are also sharper contrasts in the importance of the socialization functions carried out by their respective husbands, and there are correspondingly substantial differences as to the relative importance that these women attach to academic achievement.

SUMMARY AND CONCLUSIONS. Three conclusions may be derived from the present analysis. First, the presence or absence of a brideprice does not exert similar consequences on the status of single spouses and senior co-wives. The direction and intensity of the reactions of the women to the payment of a matrimonial compensation vary with their matrimonial status. This results from the fact that the presence of more than a single wife-mother calls for implicit and explicit comparisons between the relative positions achieved by each woman.

Second, we have seen that the payment of a brideprice is more common among the Bété than among the Abouré. As a result, the effects of this payment are symmetric: Contrasts between Bété monogamous and polygynous families tend to increase when there has been no brideprice; contrasts between monogamous and polygynous Abouré households tend to be greater when a brideprice has been paid. The payment of a brideprice leads to greater rewards for Abouré senior co-wives than for single spouses.

Third, as already indicated, matrimonial compensations serve a greater number of purposes among the Bété than among the Abouré. The definition of uxorial obligations is more extensive in the first than in the second case; hence the presence or absence of such compensations is more likely to affect contrasts in the child-rearing practices of Bété monogamous and polygynous families.

The Influence of Presents
Offered by the Bridegroom

Differences in the absorption of Abouré and Bété women into their affinal groups are accompanied by contrasts in the attitudes and behaviors of their partners at the time of the marriage itself. Bété husbands, who are more prone to offer personal gifts to their brides, are more demanding. This leads us to speculate about the extent to which the offering of such gifts presents universal implications.[17] Thus, these gifts may enable Abouré husbands to expect at least as much from their wives as do their Bété counterparts. They may also reflect the advantageous position held by Abouré women in the field of eligibles, in which case their presence will probably be associated with an accentuation of the demands that Abouré married women are able to impose upon their partners.

Single spouses and senior co-wives have the same chances of obtaining such rewards from their partners. The problem remains, however, to determine whether the effects of gifts vary with the matrimonial status of the women interviewed. We will compare the answers of rural respondents, for it is likely that the significance of such gifts depends upon the environment of the families. (See Table 43.)

17. The nature of such presents is variable, and includes money, cosmetics, clothing, and pots and pans; this diversity has prevented us from introducing more refined distinctions in our analysis.

257

Table 43

Relationship between the Offering of Gifts to the Bride by the Groom and Family Life (Percentages)

Conjugal Relations	Abouré				Bété			
	Monogamous		Polygynous		Monogamous		Polygynous	
	Gift	None	Gift	None	Gift	None	Gift	None
Incidence of women reporting:								
1. Exclusive control of family budget by husband	15.4	9.4	11.1	2.6	43.0	43.9	54.7	50.9
2. Exclusive control of clothing expenditures by husband	33.2	25.1	35.6	15.6	68.3	64.9	71.2	75.0
3. Domestic quarrels mainly caused by adultery	45.5	59.6	63.3	63.8	22.8	18.4	17.9	24.2
4. Exclusive dominance of husband in domestic quarrels	23.1	22.4	28.9	19.0	60.2	66.7	68.9	65.2
5. Single standard on conjugal morality	61.1	72.7	68.9	71.6	29.6	36.8	25.9	29.5
6. High concern with upward mobility of their husbands	5.7	8.7	8.9	12.9	10.6	7.1	16.4	13.4
7. Patterned segregation at mealtime	86.0	92.0	83.4	95.7	93.0	91.3	95.3	88.4

Relations between Wives and their Families

Incidence of women reporting:

8. Preeminent status of their mothers	10.5	13.0	19.0	22.0	23.0	19.4
9. Their mother's residence as the place where they delivered their first child	46.2	60.2	52.5	4.3	5.4	2.7
10. Post-partum leaves from their husbands	55.9	55.9	56.3	45.2	41.2	50.0

Relations among Co-wives

Incidence of women reporting:

11. Cooperative practices in raising children	—	63.4	61.2	—	—	11.7
12. "Frequent" quarrels among co-wives	—	61.7	39.0	—	—	38.6
13. Quarrels mainly caused by jealousy toward husband	—	25.8	21.9	—	—	34.9

Relations between Women and Children

Incidence of women reporting:

14. Nursing period of last-born child less than two years	45.4	44.7	46.6	36.5	29.0	26.4

Table 43—(Continued)

	Abouré				Bété			
	Monogamous		Polygynous		Monogamous		Polygynous	
	Gift	None	Gift	None	Gift	None	Gift	None
15. Initial indulgence period ceasing with talking	69.9	70.8	74.4	81.9	53.8	54.4	53.3	51.8
16. Exclusive control of father over schooling of children	74.1	59.0	75.6	56.9	54.8	61.4	61.8	66.7
17. Exclusive control of father over academic behavior of children	26.6	31.7	26.7	31.9	42.5	41.2	47.6	44.6
18. Exclusive use of physical punishment	20.3	16.8	24.4	18.1	37.6	43.9	37.3	31.3
19. Academic achievement as the most important parental demand	32.9	36.6	34.4	41.4	55.4	43.9	57.5	46.4
20. Socialization of children carried out exclusively by the nuclear family	52.4	47.7	55.6	51.7	41.4	34.2	36.8	33.0
21. Preferences for joint parental control over children	79.0	71.4	74.4	80.2	69.9	67.5	62.3	58.9
N	143	161	90	116	186	114	212	112

Among the Abouré, the presence of such gifts is uniformly associated with an increased integration of married women into their affinal group. They are more financially dependent upon the resources of their husband, they are more subject to his domestic power, and they are more prone to stress the preeminent value of female domestic loyalties. In this sense, the presence of gifts appears to have universal effects: differences in the relative integration of Abouré and Bété married women decline in size. Yet, the presence of such gifts does not have similar implications for the status of Abouré single spouses and senior co-wives. Differences between the financial authority and domestic power structures of monogamous and polygynous families decline, because the gains of polygynous husbands are proportionately greater than those of their monogamous counterparts. At the same time, senior co-wives are also more often in a position to obtain an equalitarian treatment as far as mealtime etiquette is concerned, and their gains in this respect are greater than those acquired by single spouses. Conversely, gifts facilitate the emotional integration of single spouses who become less likely than do senior co-wives to quarrel about sexual matters, but who are also more prone to stress the importance of female domestic loyalties.

The offering of gifts has few effects on the differential status of Bété single spouses and senior co-wives. In the absence of such presents, senior co-wives are more dependent upon the financial initiatives of their husbands, and they are also more prone to have quarrels of a sexual nature.

The offering of gifts by the bridegroom limits the relations that all married women maintain with their family of origin. Such limitations tend to be independent of the matrimonial status of Abouré respondents. Among the Bété, single spouses who received gifts remain more able to take post-partum leaves, to express their solidarity with their mothers, and to return to their place of origin for giving birth to their first child than do corresponding senior co-wives.

The offering of these gifts does not exert similar influences

261

on the relations that Abouré and Bété co-wives establish with their husbands' other spouses. Among the first people there is a sharp decline in the general incidence of tensions between co-wives. Among the Bété this offering leads senior co-wives to be more sensitive about the treatment accorded by their husbands to his other spouses. In brief, these gifts, which do not enhance the level of competition between Bété spouses, focus more sharply the object of their competitive feelings. They accentuate certain latent traits present in patrilineal organizations, and the actualization of such tensions probably accounts for the fact that the presence of gifts is associated with a greater institutionalization of the domestic relations of Bété polygynous households. Senior co-wives of this people do follow rules of mealtime etiquette more frequently than do the corresponding Abouré respondents.

The effects of gifts on the child-rearing practices of senior co-wives and single spouses are even more limited. Among the Abouré they are associated with a decline in the warmth that all women manifest toward their young children. This decline tends to be most apparent among senior co-wives. In contrast, Bété senior co-wives who did not receive such gifts are more indulgent than single spouses; more specifically, they are less likely to use physical sanctions. Finally, the offering of gifts is accompanied by slightly increased contrasts in the socializing roles of Abouré and Bété polygynous fathers. The latter are more often able to control the academic behavior of their children, and their spouses are more likely to emphasize the importance of academic achievement.

In brief, we can see that the presence or absence of gifts does not greatly affect contrasts between monogamous and polygynous families. The changes that do occur vary with ethnic background. Among the Abouré it is the presence of such gifts that seems to modify the differences observed between monogamous and polygynous families; among the Bété it is the absence of these presents that most affects such contrasts.

Previous Matrimonial Experience

The previous matrimonial experience of the respondents constitutes the last indicator of their social attractiveness.[18] As noted in Chapter 3, a previous marriage should be associated with: (1) a decline in the amount of power and authority ascribed to women in their affinal group, (2) an increase in the competition opposing co-wives to the other spouses of their husbands, and (3) an increase of their dependence upon their children.

The incidence of divorce is higher among the Abouré than among the Bété, which leads us to speculate about the degree to which the status allocated to divorced women varies along ethnic lines. The incidence of previous matrimonial experiences is the same among single spouses and senior co-wives, but this similarity has not necessarily uniform implications on their respective domestic statuses.

Our results are presented in Table 44. On the whole, previous matrimonial experience seems to maximize differences between single spouses and senior co-wives. Thus, among the Abouré a single spouse who has already been married tends to be more subordinate to her husband than does a previously married senior co-wife. She is less likely to have an autonomous budget, she has less initiative with regard to the purchase of her own clothes, and she has less domestic power. Conversely, Bété senior co-wives who have already been married exert less control over familial resources than do their monogamous counterparts. They are less often able to make personal purchases, and they are ultimately obliged to yield more frequently to their husbands. In addition, they are more fearful of expressing their loyalties toward their mother.

Among both Abouré and Bété, a previous marriage accentuates the tendency of co-wives to quarrel with each other. In both cases the nature of these quarrels is somewhat more

18. Again, we should be aware that there is a potential relationship between the age of the respondents and their previous matrimonial status.

Table 44

Relationship between Previous Matrimonial Experience of the Wife and Family Life (Percentages)

Previous Marriage:	Abouré				Bété			
	Monogamous		Polygynous		Monogamous		Polygynous	
	No	Yes	No	Yes	No	Yes	No	Yes
Conjugal Relations								
Incidence of women reporting:								
1. Exclusive control of family budget by husband	21.9	22.8	17.1	7.3	51.1	49.3	57.3	62.9
2. Exclusive control of clothing expenditures by husband	36.4	33.3	27.1	23.3	57.2	55.3	65.8	63.6
3. Domestic quarrels mainly caused by adultery	50.0	51.6	59.7	59.3	20.5	25.3	20.2	25.0
4. Exclusive dominance of husband in domestic quarrels	22.3	28.3	21.7	22.0	58.7	56.7	63.7	62.9
5. Single standard on conjugal morality	58.3	67.1	66.7	68.0	33.7	30.0	25.4	33.3
6. High concern with upward mobility of their husbands	10.0	11.4	14.0	9.3	21.6	20.7	14.3	13.6
7. Patterned segregation at mealtime	82.2	85.4	90.9	88.0	84.1	87.4	91.5	92.4

Relations between Wives and their Families

Incidence of women reporting:

8. Preeminent status of their mothers	17.8	20.1	21.7	20.0	27.3	38.0	23.7	25.0
9. Their mother's residence as the place where they delivered their first child	43.0	42.9	40.3	50.0	7.8	3.3	4.4	0.8
10. Post-partum leaves from their husbands	59.1	59.3	60.5	56.6	50.8	44.0	50.0	44.0

Relations among Co-wives

Incidence of women reporting:

11. Cooperative practices in raising children	—	—	63.6	52.0	—	—	19.3	21.3
12. "Frequent" quarrels among co-wives	—	—	7.1	22.6	—	—	27.7	40.0
13. Quarrels mainly caused by jealousy toward husband	—	—	26.1	32.1	—	—	42.5	51.3

Relations between Women and Children

Incidence of women reporting:

14. Nursing period of last-born child less than two years	57.4	48.4	57.4	46.7	43.3	33.4	36.2	30.9

Table 44—(Continued)

Previous Marriage:	Abouré				Bété			
	Monogamous		Polygynous		Monogamous		Polygynous	
	No	Yes	No	Yes	No	Yes	No	Yes
15. Initial indulgence period ceasing with talking	66.1	71.2	78.3	74.7	59.2	56.7	55.8	57.6
16. Exclusive control of father over schooling of children	63.6	64.4	68.2	63.1	54.7	52.0	61.7	65.2
17. Exclusive control of father over academic behavior of children	36.0	33.8	31.8	32.7	41.5	34.7	46.8	43.2
18. Exclusive use of physical punishment	26.0	26.0	28.7	24.7	41.0	42.7	42.4	31.1
19. Academic achievement as the most important parental demand	43.0	46.1	48.1	39.3	51.6	52.0	53.2	51.5
20. Socialization of children carried out exclusively by the nuclear family	51.7	55.7	51.9	56.0	42.8	36.7	38.6	31.8
21. Preferences for joint parental control over children	80.2	74.9	78.3	70.7	65.8	63.3	59.1	60.0
N	242	219	129	150	395	150	342	132

likely to relate to the dependence that these women experience vis-à-vis the heads of their households.

Finally, the fact of having been previously married hardly influences the women's child-rearing practices at all. Among the Abouré there is a decline in the differences in length of the period of initial indulgence observed by all respondents. In addition, senior co-wives without prior matrimonial experience attach greater importance than do single spouses with similar characteristics to the academic achievement of their children, while the reverse is true for the subsample of women with previous matrimonial experience. Among the Bété, previously married senior co-wives are more indulgent than single spouses and hence use physical sanctions less frequently. By contrast, a previous marriage gives more responsibility to their monogamous counterparts, who participate more frequently in the decision to send their children to school and are accordingly expected to play a more significant role with regard to the control of academic behavior.

In brief, our hypotheses are not totally upheld. As predicted, the previous marriages of all senior co-wives accentuate their competition with their co-wives. At the same time, however, this does not uniformly change the style of interaction that these women maintain with their partners. In fact, previous matrimonial experiences accentuate both contrasts between single spouses and senior co-wives of the same ethnic background and contrasts among the co-wives of the two peoples. Thus the implications of divorce on the organization of monogamous and polygynous families vary along ethnic lines. We have, finally, failed to demonstrate that previous matrimonial experiences reinforce the significance of the relations between mothers and children or that they especially affect child-rearing practices.

Some Concluding Remarks

Our purpose in this chapter has been to examine the degree to which differences in conjugal relations, child-rearing practices, and general organizational characteristics of monogamous and polygynous families are stable, or whether they vary with the past and present positions of their actors.

We have demonstrated that such contrasts are not stable. Variations in the direction and the size of these contrasts may result from differences in the *intensity* of the responses of single spouses and senior co-wives to changes in the domestic roles which are allocated to them. Thus, the effects of additional children on the financial status of Abouré single spouses and senior co-wives are similar in direction, but do not have the same intensity. These variations may also result from differences in the *direction* of the responses of monogamous and polygynous families to changes in the roles actually allocated to married women. For example, a decline in the functionality of their role leads Abouré senior co-wives to nurse their children for a longer period of time, but to start disciplining them at an earlier age. Among the single spouses of this people, this decline is associated with later weaning and no change in the length of the initial indulgence period.

More important, variations both in the current forms of participation of married women in familial and larger structures and in the position that they initially occupied in the field of eligibles do not have the same impact on the multifaceted contrast between monogamous and polygynous families. On the whole, current experiences are more significant than elements from the past. They affect a larger number of behaviors and attitudes, and the extent of their influence is also greater. This suggests that cleavages between monogamy and polygyny result less from differences in the recruitment of wives than from inequalities in the constraints to which they are currently exposed. The effects of present and past positions of married

women also vary along ethnic lines, and the differential consequences attached, for example, to the fertility or the previous
matrimonial experiences of single spouses and senior co-wives
depend upon cultural factors.

In addition, variations in the past and present status of
married women may modify the contrasts in the conjugal relations of monogamous and polygynous families but leave differences in their respective child-rearing practices unchanged.
Thus the distinctive components of the organization of monogamous and polygynous families are not equally vulnerable to
the influence of such variations and are, in fact, more autonomous than we had anticipated earlier. Finally, the relative
vulnerability of these components is not the same for the
Abouré and the Bété, which indicates once more the importance of cultural factors.

In short, we have demonstrated that variations in current
forms of social participation do not have universal implications. It is not so much the variations in the number of children
a woman bears or in the number of domestic functions that she
performs which count here; rather, it is the interpretations
that members of a particular culture attach to them. These
variations therefore have a social meaning only as they are
internalized by the actors of a particular group and reinforce
or threaten the cultural system of the group. Hence the influence of variations in the past and present forms of participation of married women on the contrasts between monogamous
and polygynous families can be measured only by reference to
the relevant perceptions of each people. The significance of
these variations cannot be isolated from the preexisting network of interdependencies between familial actors or familial
groups, and these networks have a shape and an intensity
which vary along ethnic lines.

We are now in a better position to define the conditions
under which comparisons between monogamous and polygynous families are most significant. The institution of plural
marriage has functions which vary along ethnic lines. It is

primarily a mechanism designed to facilitate the operation of familial groups and their adjustment to the restraints imposed upon them by cultural norms. As a consequence, contrasts in the organization of monogamous and polygynous families are necessarily affected by discrepancies between (1) the actual and the normative size of the familial groups investigated, and (2) the actual and the normative definition of the positions allocated to married women. The effects of these discrepancies on the resources, rewards, and strains experienced by each familial actor vary with the number of people in each of the roles of the familial system.

Among the Bété it is quite obvious that the effectiveness of familial institutions is perceived as being determined by their size. Indeed, the relative authority and power of the main familial actors depend upon the number of persons that they can control. Additional wives reinforce the rewards that a male actor can claim but also give a more preeminent position to his senior co-wife. The size of familial groups does not only depend, however, on the number of wives but also on the number of children borne by these wives. As a result, the marked contrasts between monogamous and polygynous families with a limited number of children decline when large-sized families are taken into consideration. The addition of a wife or a child does exert homologous influences.

The purpose of plural marriage in this particular group is to enhance the productivity of the activities traditionally imposed upon married women. Maximal functionality introduces, accordingly, significant differences in the relative integration of single spouses and senior co-wives into their affinal group.

Low functionality constitutes a *negative* deviance from traditional norms. It does not, indeed, correspond to the expectations surrounding the role allocated to married women. It could be anticipated that the effects of this negative deviance vary with the number of wives in the family. Low functionality should introduce fewer changes in the status of single spouse than in that of senior co-wife.[19] In fact, this low functionality hardly alters the contrasts between the styles of conjugal interaction of monogamous and polygynous families. Single spouses and senior co-wives respond in a parallel manner to a decline in the demands imposed upon them.

Alternatively, the entry of Bété women into the labor market constitutes a case of *positive* deviance from the norms underlying the traditional definition of domestic roles. The effects of this entry vary noticeably with the matrimonial status of the respondents. It is associated with a sharp decline in the integration of single spouses in their affinal group; however, it modifies even more drastically the relations that senior co-wives maintain with their family of origin and with their children. Given the particular functions which plural marriage serves among the Bété, the rewards and strains associated with female participation in the labor force cannot be alike for single spouses and senior co-wives.

Among the Abouré, the main function of plural marriage is to alleviate some of the tensions associated with the low degree of social absorption of married women into their affinal group. Given the low functionality of female domestic roles, fertility is a particularly significant determinant of the position assigned to single spouses or senior co-wives, and variations in the number of children alter the contrasts between monogamous and polygynous families. At the lower end of the continuum, sterile single spouses are more deeply integrated in their affinal group than are senior co-wives with no children. At the upper end of the continuum we have seen that the addition of new children also tends to reinforce contrasts between the positions allocated to Abouré women with differing matrimonial statuses. At this level, plural marriage is somewhat dysfunctional, since it increases the number of persons able to challenge the power and authority of the husband. In other

19. Namely, we have argued that plural marriage serves as a mechanism reinforcing the *relative* functionality of each co-wife.

words, a large number of children leads to a realization of the strains which are latent in the organization of polygynous matrilineal families.

The disappearance of the Abouré woman's economic independence accentuates differences between the organization of monogamous and polygynous families. Inactive single spouses are more vulnerable than are senior co-wives to the authority and power of their husbands. Furthermore, in both cases the decline of this independence modifies in divergent directions the kinds of relations that women maintain with their own kin group and with their children.

If the decline of this independence constitutes a *negative* deviance from traditional norms, an increase in the functionality of the domestic role of Abouré women represents a *positive* deviance from such norms. This deviance changes the contrasts between the organizations of monogamous and polygynous families. The conjugal status and the child-rearing practices of single spouses and of senior co-wives vary in diverging directions and to differing extents. On the whole, senior co-wives are more affected by high functionality, because this is at complete variance with the functions traditionally assigned to plural marriage.

Traditional norms, however, are not only concerned with the definition of the domestic role allocated to women but also with the definition of ideal patterns of marriage. Such norms —which define the image of "ideal partners" in terms of age, experience, and position in the field of eligibles—may have a uniformly high salience, as seems to be the case with age at marriage, but their relative importance may vary along ethnic lines. For example, it is quite clear that the payment of a brideprice or the giving of gifts to the bride by the bridegroom is more normative among the Bété than among the Abouré. Our analysis indicates that the relative salience of such norms is an important determinant of variations in the contrasts between differing types of marriages. The higher the salience of a norm, the more negative deviances from it will be associated with an accentuation of the contrasts between monogamy and polygyny. Conversely, the lower the salience of such a norm, the more conformity to that norm or positive deviances from it will be accompanied by increased cleavages in the status of single spouse and of senior co-wife. Thus, the absence of brideprice tends to maximize the differences between Bété monogamous and polygynous households, whereas the presence of such compensation has similar effects among the Abouré.

To conclude, contrasts between monogamous and polygynous families may be maximal in the following circumstances:

1. The actual and theoretical definition of plural marriage coincide. In this case, any deviation from the traditional functions of plural marriage tends to obliterate the significance of the contrast between monogamy and polygyny, and there are then increased similarities in the status of single spouse and senior co-wife.

2. Patterns of marriage and concrete definitions of the position occupied by married women differ *positively* from prevailing norms. Thus, economic independence for the Bété, and high functionality, payment of a brideprice and giving of gifts to the bride among the Abouré—both modify the distinctions between monogamy and polygyny.

3. Patterns of marriage and concrete definitions of the position occupied by all married women differ *negatively* from traditional norms. Lack of economic independence and sterility among the Abouré, absence of a brideprice among the Bété, and late marriage and previous matrimonial experiences among both peoples also alter the differences between the organization of monogamous and polygynous families.

This suggests that the visibility of single spouses and of senior co-wives are not comparable, and that for this reason

273

they may be differentially rewarded for conforming with traditional prescriptions or, alternatively, differentially rewarded or sanctioned for deviating positively or negatively from the cultural requirements accompanying their role. These differences in visibility are to be appreciated by reference to two types of factors:

1. Incidence of plural marriage within each people investigated. The lower this incidence, the more sensitive is the distinction between monogamy and polygyny, both to variations in the recruitment patterns of conjugal partners and to variations in the role actually performed by married women. Thus there are more fluctuations in conjugal relations and in child-rearing practices among Abouré single spouses and senior co-wives than among the Bété.

2. Salience and nature of each norm investigated. In certain cases variations in the definition of the role ascribed to women are diluted because of the presence of more than one incumbent in the uxorial and maternal roles, and changes in the contrast between monogamy and polygyny reflect the higher sensitivity of monogamous families to the deviations from relevant norms. Alternatively, the presence of more than one wife-mother may enhance the relative effects of such variations, and changes in the distinction between monogamy and polygyny will result from the higher visibility of senior co-wives.

CHAPTER 8

Social Change and Domestic Power Structures

In our comparative analysis of monogamous and polygynous families, we have disregarded so far the potential influence of the environment in which they live. Yet the colonial and post-colonial periods in the Ivory Coast have been characterized by an increased differentiation in both the residential and occupational distributions of the overall population. New urban centers have been created; the capital city, Abidjan, has grown in size; and a part of the active population has joined the modern sector of the economy.

In Chapter 4, we examined how these two forms of differentiation affect the incidence and the intensity of polygyny among the two peoples compared. We also speculated about the consequences that changes in the distribution of plural marriage could have on the functioning of monogamous and polygynous families. Our concern now is to test the validity of those speculations.

Initially, such testing requires an assessment of the over-all influence exerted by urbanization and economic development on the functions and structures of familial groups. In general, social change is conducive to an increased differentiation of forms of social relations. For example, familial functions and structures vary markedly with educational and occupational characteristics.[1] Accordingly, one would expect that the organization of polygynous families from different residential or occupational sections of a given country will be quite different; similarly, one would anticipate the size and the direction of the contrasts between monogamous and polygynous families to vary markedly along educational or occupational lines. During the early stages of urbanization, ethnicity and migratory experience remain, nevertheless, important determinants of the social position occupied by individuals. Indeed, during such stages determinants of social participation are hardly independent of one another.[2] Thus, the purpose of the present chapter is also to evaluate the converging and diverging nature of the influences exerted by ethnicity on the one hand and socioeconomic differentiation on the other on the contrast between monogamous and polygynous families.

The Effects of Social Change
on Familial Relations:
A Theoretical Framework

In this chapter we will not treat urbanization and industrialization as "melting pots" which assimilate all forms of familial relations into one single type. To be sure, both the degree of exposure of individual actors to modernizing forces and the rewards that they derive from such an exposure should uniformly condition the extent and the direction of the changes affecting monogamous and polygynous families. At the same time, however, these changes are also determined by an anticipation of the new demands and new rewards to come and by

1. For a full discussion, see L. Wirth, "Urbanism as a Way of Life," *American Journal of Sociology*, XXIV (1938), 1–24.

2. The whole problem of the effect of increase in scale on the independence of these various forms of social differentiation is discussed in D. McElrath, "The Social Areas of Rome," *American Sociological Review*, XXVII (1962), 376–90; and in Remi Clignet and J. Sween, "Abidjan and Accra: A Comparative Analysis of the Notion of Increase in Scale," *Urban Affairs Quarterly*, IV (1969), 297–324.

an assimilation of the new situations into past experiences. To be sure, the extent to which individuals are either future-oriented or past-oriented probably varies with type of marriage. Yet these orientations also influence the nature of the responses of distinctive familial groups to environmental change. These responses reflect two distinct processes: assimilation and accommodation.[3]

The first of these is inward and involves a partial or total dissociation of the elements which constitute the new reality, followed by their internalization into the untouched traditional frame of reference used by the individual actors or social groups involved. In this particular context, participation in modern structures can be used by polygynist males to reaffirm their status, authority, and power, as these are defined by traditional norms. There are, accordingly, changes in the tactics used by such actors, but their strategies remain stable. In brief, these actors may use new symbols in their personal dealings, but the core of their style of familial interaction does not change. There is a modernization of *means,* but this is channeled into the framework of traditional *ends.*

The second process, accommodation, is outward and involves a partial or total disintegration of the elements of traditional models, followed by their integration into the stereotypes accompanying the new social reality. Participation of individuals in new structures is accompanied by changes in the values to which they aspire. For example, access of women to new social and economic rewards can be conducive to a new definition of the principles underlying familial relations. The role of achievement in the placement of individuals within familial structures may become as important as that of ascription.

We will suggest that the responses of the two peoples compared to the various manifestations of social change can effec-

3. See the following by J. Piaget: "Cours de psychologie de l'enfant," *Bulletin de psychologie,* VI (1953–54), 143–44; *Le Langage et la penseé chez l'enfant* (Geneva: Delachaux et Niestle, 1923); and *Epistemologie genetique* (Paris: Presses Universitaires de France, 1949).

tively be described in terms of the two processes described here. Since the traditional organization, and hence the past experience, of Bété and Abouré families are quite distinctive, we may expect variations in the degree to which their respective adjustments to modernizing forces result from assimilation or accommodation. We may also, however, expect that the nature of such adjustment processes depends on the type of marriage of the familial groups investigated. Thus, the main purpose of our analysis will be to examine whether accommodation and assimilation are equally characteristic of monogamous and polygynous families.

Urbanization and Marginality

We have argued that in new environments nuclear families should act as agencies of tension management. The fulfillment of this role requires a synchronized specialization of individual familial roles. There must be a perfect complementarity in the changes affecting the economic instrumentality of the role allocated to husbands and in the changes affecting the social-expressive nature of the position occupied by their wives. In fact, these two forms of change are not necessarily synchronized, and the differential exposure of the two sexes to modernizing forces may be associated with divergences in the intensity and the direction of changes affecting their respective roles.

As a result, there may be an increase in the social and emotional distance separating conjugal partners from one another, and this increase is often described as marginality.[4]

The marginality of the position occupied by African husbands depends both on the degree to which they are deprived of the gains resulting from participation in modern and traditional structures and on the degree to which their spouses are unable to alleviate the strains and tensions associated with this type of situation.

In a colonial context, achievement and ascription are equally

4. For examples of a theoretical discussion of this concept, see R. Park, *Race and Culture* (Glencoe, Ill.: Free Press, 1950).

important mechanisms of placement in the occupational structure.[5] Even though there is a certain amount of social mobility in the intermediate rungs of the occupational ladder, there is little fluidity at the two ends of the continuum. Certain ethnic groups are doomed to occupy the positions of underdogs, whereas others are granted an almost automatic access to the rewards of the industrial order.[6] At the same time, personalization of land tenure prevents many African males from maintaining their claims on traditional holdings. Thus, these individuals may be simultaneously deprived of the gains resulting from participation in both modern and traditional structures. Under such conditions, familial ties cease to be assets and become liabilities with which African males cannot always cope effectively.

Furthermore, their spouses are not necessarily able to alleviate the emotional strains and tensions accompanying such deprivations. There are marked contrasts in the relative participation of the two sexes in educational enterprises and in the modern sector of the economy. Their aspirations and expectations are not alike, either.[7] These two phenomena probably account, at least in part, for the multiplication of voluntary associations and informal networks, which are highly segregated along sex lines. This suggests that peers, rather than conjugal partners, provide the form of emotional support needed by urbanized persons.

Unable to respond positively to the new pressures experienced by their husbands, African wives can no longer provide

5. See, for example, R. T. Smith, *The Negro Family in British Guiana* (London: Routledge and Kegan Paul, 1956).

6. For example, the Malinké and Voltaic are significantly overrepresented in the lower ranks of manual occupations, whereas the peoples of the Lagoon areas tend to be over-represented in the highest echelons of the white-collar professions. See *Étude socio economique de la zone urbaine d'Abidjan* (Paris: Societe d'Études et de Mathematiques Appliquees, 1965), report no. 3.

7. For a full description, see Remi Clignet and Philip Foster, *The Fortunate Few* (Evanston, Ill.: Northwestern University Press, 1966), chaps. 3, 4, and 6.

their partners with traditional, legitimate satisfactions. Thus, fertility is a liability wherever the formal schooling of children is both costly and not necessarily followed by entry into remunerative and prestigeful positions. Similarly, the rewards accompanying plural marriage have become narrower and more specific. Additional wives are no longer additional assets, and plural marriage has ceased to be an institution facilitating the growth of resources allocated to a particular individual.

The marginality of the domestic position of African women is a function of the inconsistencies and contradictions between the normative and actual definitions of their participation in familial structures. As suggested in Chapter 4, traditional models define the domestic position of married women in terms of uxorial rights and rights in *genetricem*. Little individualization enters into definitions which use criteria such as number of children and size of land to be cultivated as standards against which the past, present, and future roles of a wife are evaluated. Plural marriage itself appears to minimize the significance of the personal aesthetic, intellectual, expressive qualities of a woman as adequate measures of her social value as a wife.

Urbanization makes such criteria obsolete, but it is not necessarily associated with the emergence of new and consistent norms. As a result, the marginality of the domestic position of urbanized married women depends, first, on their scarcity. This scarcity conditions the bargaining power available to them, both in the field of eligibles and in the familial group into which they ultimately enter. Their gains in this respect vary along ethnic lines. For example, the domestic position of a senior co-wife should be optimal whenever: (1) there is a uniform scarcity of women among all age groups, (2) aspirations toward plural marriage remain uniformly high among all males, and (3) the importing of new potential brides is costly.

Second, the marginality of women's positions is also determined by the extent of their participation in the labor force. Such a participation obliges them to meet requirements which are set up independently of those traditionally imposed by their husbands. It also lessens the control that these husbands can exert on domestic resources. In brief, access of women into the labor market not only limits the relative importance of familial norms but also introduces potential discrepancies in the *de jure* and *de facto* definitions of female domestic roles.

Finally, the marginality of the position occupied by urbanized married women results from the diffusion of Western ideologies, which stress the significance of individual mobility and hence of equality between sexes. The acceptance of such an ideology is highly selective and varies along sex, ethnic, and socioeconomic lines.

In summary, the marginality of the domestic status held by urban women varies as a direct function of the contradictions between the demographic, economic, and ideological circumstances of their participation in urban structures and the dominant features of the familial role ascribed to them by their traditional culture. At the same time, this marginality also results from the differential gains obtained by the two sexes through their participation in urban structures. The size of such differences affects the extent and the direction of the divergences between the traditional and the new expectations that conjugal partners entertain vis-à-vis one another.

Our comparative analysis of the domestic power structure of monogamous and polygynous families must therefore not only take into account the degree to which social change leads the various types of women interviewed to occupy marginal positions in their affinal group; it must also isolate the distinctive mechanisms which can reduce such marginality. There are at least five of these mechanisms:[8]

1. African women can retire completely in the status in which they are most strongly identified by either society at large or its most significant components. True enough, they can be pushed in this direction by the attitudes of many Afri-

---

8. All this section is derived from the theoretical framework suggested by E. Hughes, *Where People Meet* (Glencoe, Ill.: Free Press, 1952), pp. 188–99.

can males, who argue that a greater exposure of women to modernizing forces is associated with an unfortunate decline in the amount of brideprice obtainable from the husbands of their sisters, their daughters, or other female relatives. "Educated and urban girls are spoiled and disobedient" is a leitmotiv frequently found in letters to African popular magazines.[9] Male secondary school students themselves are not necessarily eager to innovate in the field of familial relations.[10] Under such conditions, the full participation of married women in modern structures may cause them to lose the approval of significant segments of the male population. Unable to gain full economic support from their husbands and unable or unwilling to establish or maintain satisfactory emotional and social ties with them, these women may be tempted to repeat patterns of behavior which have been the most rewarding to them in the past and hence to reaffirm certain selected aspects of their traditional roles as mothers, daughters, or sisters.[11] The partial or total restoration of such unequivocal forms of traditional solidarity may indeed alleviate the tensions accompanying their participation in urban structures. Thus, urbanization may lead to the reemergence of ancient forms of matrifocality and matrilinearity. Married women become the central figures of the nuclear family insofar as their husbands lack the proper resources or motivations. These women use the additional power and authority that they have acquired to reinforce their loyalties as well as those of their own offspring toward their family of origin.[12]

9. See, for example, Bingo, *L'Illustré Africain* (Dakar).

10. See, for example, P. T. Omari, "Changing Attitudes of Students in West African Society Toward Marriage and Family Relationships," *British Journal of Sociology*, XI (1960), 197–210. See also P. T. Omari, "Role Expectation on Courtship in Ghana," *Social Forces*, XLII (1963), 147–56.

11. This illustrates the first proposition of G. Homans about human exchanges in *Social Behavior, Its Elementary Forms* (New York: Harcourt Brace, 1961), p. 53.

12. There are two alternative interpretations to this finding. On the one hand it can be argued that as the functions of familial institutions are increasingly social and expressive in nature, the task of maintaining expressive rela-

2. Either the traditional or the urban norms, or both, disappear as meaningful categories. Thus the new civil laws promulgated by the Ivory Coast government tend to impose the image of a European-like nuclear type of family. Polygyny and brideprice are illegal, and there are no differences in the circumstances under which men and women can introduce procedures of divorce. It is not impossible that the male and female members of certain restricted social segments of the Ivory Coast will adopt the new model proposed to them and will free themselves from the influences of their traditional background.

Alternatively, other segments of the population may disregard as inconsequential both the traditional and modern definitions of the rights and obligations attached to the domestic position of women. They perceive conjugal ties as transitory and invest a minimal amount of personal, economic, social, and emotional resources in their marriage. Wives view themselves as concubines rather than as real partners.[13] A possible outcome of this decline in the significance and intensity of conjugal ties is the development of strong, close-knit networks within the urbanized female population itself.[14]

---

tions between the nuclear and the extended family becomes increasingly a female attribute. (See, for example, W. Goode, *World Revolution and Family Patterns* [New York: Free Press, 1963], p. 76.) On the other hand, one can argue that the emergence of strong relations between a married woman and her family of origin primarily reflects the marginality both of her role and that of her husband in urban environments.

13. This mechanism is illustrated by the reactions of many urbanized peoples in South Africa. See for example P. Mayer, *Tribesmen or Townsmen* (Capetown: Oxford University Press, 1961), or Laura Longmore, *The Dispossessed* (London: New English Library, 1962).

14. The fact that this particular strategy is usually accompanied by the development of strong solidarities among urbanized females is illustrated by some of the residential patterns evident in Abidjan. See *Structures et transformations des groupements domestiques d'Abidjan* (Paris: Societe d'Études et de Mathematiques Appliquees, 1965). Out of the households including singles, 21 per cent are comprised of only women. In addition, certain familial households are headed by women and are made up of a majority of female members. We are then in the presence of close-knit networks, as they

3. African women may individually resign from the status which interferes with the aims characteristic of their other status. Accordingly, they do not recognize any longer the validity of the obligations imposed upon them by their community of origin and either contract interethnic marriage (which necessarily changes the terms of their domestic status) or remain single (which suggests that marriage ceases to be the sole determinant of their social position).[15]

4. There may be a broadening and a redefinition of the status involved, with a subsequent decline in the dilemmas internally experienced by individual subjects and in the outward contradictions which separate them from the other segments of the social system. Urbanization may be ultimately accompanied by the emergence of a new style of familial relations, reconciling the diverging demands of European and African models.

5. A last possible solution is the inclusion of the marginal group as an additional category of persons with their own identity and defined position. In the same way that colonial authorities and the various segments of African social systems have established meaningful distinctions between the status of "evolué" and that of "colonial subject," it is not impossible to predict that African societies will recognize the specific properties of the roles performed by African women in an urban environment and will accord them rights and duties different from those of their rural equivalents.

---

have been defined by E. Bott in *Family and Social Network* (London: Tavistock Institute, 1957), pp. 192–215. However, the effects of close-knit networks probably vary with the characteristics of the environment in which they are found. We should distinguish between cases where these networks have the same orientations among both the male and the female populations. We should also distinguish between cases where they characterize only the male or the female members of the population.

15. For a discussion of this phenomenon, see D. Desanti, "Quand l'africain revient d'Europe," in *Le Dossier Afrique* (Verviers: Marabout Universite, 1962); and, more recently, an interview with the president of the Union des Femmes Africaines et Malgaches, Mrs. Kuoh Moukouri, in *Elle*, May 20, 1967, pp. 155ff.

In summary, the variety of mechanisms reviewed here implies the use of both assimilation and accommodation, and it is quite obvious, for example, that the partial restoration of a traditional female status (as it results from the first one of the mechanisms summarized here) rests heavily upon the principle of assimilation.

Our concern here is, accordingly, to determine the degree to which variations in the marginality of respondents and in the mechanisms that they use to reduce this marginality depend on the matrimonial and ethnic status of the populations investigated.

Social change takes at least three forms: (a) residential differentiation (we will compare the responses of urban and rural families); (b) occupational differentiation (we will examine the extent to which contrasts in the organization of monogamous and polygynous families are conditioned by the occupational status of the head of the household); and (c) differentiation in type of employment (we will investigate the degree to which differences between the answers of single spouses and of senior co-wives vary with the characteristics of the type of employment in which their husbands are currently participating).

The Urban-Rural Contrast

The size of the communities in which respondents live constitutes the simplest and most frequently used indicator of exposure to social change. Since almost all the urban centers of the Ivory Coast are the products of colonial influence, their relative size can be treated as a variable reflecting the relative intensity of the modernizing forces exerted on traditional organizations and individual persons. Although we could have compared here the responses of rural women with those of individuals presently living in Gagnoa and Grand Bassam, middle-sized cities located in the heart of the Bété and the Abouré countries, and with those of the individuals who immigrated to Abidjan, the significance of our data would have been limited by the small size of the resulting subsamples. We have therefore grouped into a single category all respondents living in urban centers. In so doing, we probably limit the range of differences characterizing the responses of individuals exposed to modernizing forces of an increasing intensity.

Our results are summarized in Table 45. Our approach will be similar to that used in the previous chapter, and we will examine by turns the differential influence of urban-rural contrasts on the relations that senior co-wives and single spouses maintain with their husbands, their family of origin, their co-wives, and their children.

Conjugal Relations

Among the Abouré, urbanization is obviously associated with a greater integration of married women into their affinal group. This integration is economic, social, and emotional. Indeed, married women are more frequently financially dependent upon their husbands. They tend more often to yield first in domestic quarrels and are increasingly aware of the fragility of their domestic status. Thus, they adopt double standard with regard to conjugal morality and are more demanding of themselves than they are of their husbands. This increased integration in their affinal group is, however, associated with a decline in the extent to which they must observe institutionalized forms of deference toward their husbands. Traditional mealtime etiquette is increasingly abandoned.

Urbanization is accompanied by an accentuation of the differences between the conjugal status of Abouré single spouses and senior co-wives. Integration into affinal groups is obviously easier in the first than in the second case. The pressures which accompany such an integration are not uniformly exerted on monogamous and polygynous families. Thus, although there are limited contrasts in the distribution of domestic quarrels between urban and rural monogamous partners, there are sharp differences in the sources of the conflicts which

Table 45

Relationship between Urbanization and Family Life (Percentages)

| | Abouré | | | | Bété | | | |
| | Rural | | Urban | | Rural | | Urban | |
	Mo-noga-mous	Po-lygy-nous	Mo-noga-mous	Po-lygy-nous	Mo-noga-mous	Po-lygy-nous	Mo-noga-mous	Po-lygy-nous
Conjugal Relations								
Incidence of women reporting:								
1. Exclusive control of family budget by husband	12.5	6.3	41.5	27.0	43.3	53.2	59.5	70.7
2. Exclusive control of clothing expenditures by husband	32.1	24.2	40.3	29.7	67.0	72.4	44.1	48.7
3. Domestic quarrels mainly caused by adultery	52.8	63.1	47.2	48.1	21.0	20.1	22.7	24.0
4. Exclusive dominance of husband in domestic quarrels	22.6	23.3	29.6	17.4	62.7	67.7	52.6	54.5
5. Single standard on conjugal morality	70.2	70.4	47.8	59.4	32.3	26.6	32.8	29.8
6. High concern with upward mobility of their husbands	7.3	11.1	17.6	12.1	9.3	11.5	36.0	19.5
7. Patterned segregation at mealtime	89.2	90.3	71.6	85.1	92.3	92.8	75.3	89.6

Table 45—(Continued)

| | Abouré | | | | Bété | | | |
| | Rural | | Urban | | Rural | | Urban | |
	Mo-noga-mous	Po-lygy-nous	Mo-noga-mous	Po-lygy-nous	Mo-noga-mous	Po-lygy-nous	Mo-noga-mous	Po-lygy-nous
Relations between Wives and their Families								
Incidence of women reporting:								
8. Preeminent status of their mothers	11.8	15.5	32.1	37.8	22.7	14.8	39.7	42.8
9. Their mother's residence as the place where they delivered their first child	53.4	51.9	22.6	25.9	4.7	2.3	8.9	5.9
10. Post-partum leaves from their husbands	55.7	54.8	65.4	68.7	43.6	42.7	56.3	60.3
Relations among Co-wives								
Incidence of women reporting:								
11. Cooperative practices in raising children	—	62.1	—	43.3	—	15.4	—	29.8
12. "Frequent" quarrels among co-wives	—	48.6	—	38.5	—	40.8	—	54.5
13. Quarrels mainly caused by jealousy toward husband	—	23.6	—	50.0	—	45.4	—	44.7

Relations between Women and Children

Incidence of women reporting:

14. Nursing period of last-born child less than two years	44.9	50.0	68.6	55.4	33.7	28.7	39.3	46.7
15. Initial indulgence period ceasing with talking	70.5	78.6	65.4	71.6	54.0	52.9	64.4	64.2
16. Exclusive control of father over schooling of children	66.2	65.3	60.4	64.8	57.3	61.3	49.8	64.3
17. Exclusive control of father over academic behavior of children	29.2	29.6	46.5	39.2	42.0	46.7	36.8	44.8
18. Exclusive use of physical punishment	18.1	20.8	41.5	42.0	40.0	35.2	43.3	47.4
19. Academic achievement as the most important parental demand	34.8	37.8	62.9	59.5	51.0	53.5	52.0	50.0
20. Socialization of children carried out exclusively by the nuclear family	49.5	53.3	61.0	55.4	38.7	35.6	44.1	38.3
21. Preferences for joint parental control over children	75.1	77.6	83.0	64.8	69.0	60.9	60.7	62.4
N	305	206	159	74	300	323	247	154

oppose rural and urban senior co-wives to their husbands. Among urban polygynous families one can note a decline in the tensions due to adultery but an increase in the incidence of strains associated with financial matters and child-rearing practices. Only 7 per cent of rural senior co-wives perceive child-rearing practices as the main determinant of domestic conflicts, compared to 18 per cent of their urban counterparts. In brief, urbanization seems to exacerbate the centrifugal forces exerted by plural marriage upon matrilineal organizations. Alternatively, urbanization modifies more sharply the attitudes of single spouses toward conjugal morality. The fluidity of social interactions in an urban setting represents more serious threats for them than for co-wives. No less than one-third of urban single spouses argue, accordingly, that female adultery is a more serious offense than male adultery; this view is shared by only 17 per cent of rural respondents. Changes in the attitudes of senior co-wives in this respect are more limited, and the proportions of them holding such a view rise only from 15 per cent in rural areas to 19 per cent in urban centers.

Among the Bété, urbanization is accompanied by a decline in the patriarchal orientations of familial groups. To be sure, urbanized Bété husbands are more likely to exert an absolute control on familial resources, and their wives are correspondingly more concerned with problems of upward mobility. At the same time, however, Bété married women have more initiatives with regard to expenses and enjoy a greater share of domestic power. In addition, like their Abouré counterparts, they are less frequently obliged to observe acts of deference toward their partners, and they are not obliged to take their meals after their spouses.

On the whole, effects of urbanization on the status of Bété single spouses and of senior co-wives are parallel. The equalitarian tendencies accompanying urbanization are nevertheless slightly more evident among monogamous families.

Finally, urbanization tends to be accompanied by a decline in the cleavages between the conjugal relations prevailing among Abouré and Bété polygynous families. Exposure to an urban milieu tends to be associated with the emergence of a uniform type of polygynous arrangement. This uniformity reflects, however, the divergent responses of Abouré and Bété senior co-wives to environmental changes.

Relations between Wives and their Families of Origin

The effects of the interdependence between partners that urbanization generates should not be exaggerated. Regardless of ethnicity and type of marriage, urban women are more prone to affirm their solidarity toward their family of origin. They choose to save their mothers rather than their husbands in the context of the dilemma story used in the present study. They are more prone to take post-partum leaves from their husbands after the birth of their last child and to return to their village of origin. In fact, differences along these lines between urbanized Abouré and Bété families are smaller than among their rural counterparts, in spite of both the unequal distances separating Abidjan from the natural habitat of these peoples and their differing rules of descent and residence. In both cases, urbanization reinforces the expressive nature of the ties maintained by the respondents with their family of origin.[16] Emphasizing the significance of their role as daughters or as sisters, these women thereby tend to reduce the marginality of the position that they occupy in the urban environment.

Relations among Co-wives

Urbanization diminishes the economic opportunities offered to Abouré women and increases accordingly their dependence upon their husbands. In turn, this accentuated dependence in-

16. Since these findings are somewhat parallel to the observations made on the Negro family in British Guiana or in the United States, it is possible to speculate about the degree to which this type of familial organization reflects a legacy of the traditional African heritage or, conversely, results from the differential exposure of underprivileged ethnic groups to changing residential and economic conditions.

creases competition between co-wives (particularly with regard to the favors distributed by the head of the household) and reduces their cohesiveness proportionately. These women are not as prone as are their rural counterparts to raise their children jointly, and almost one-fourth of the Abouré senior co-wives living in urban centers report that each co-wife raises her children independently of the other women in the household, as against only 8 per cent of their rural counterparts.

In contrast, urbanization enables Bété women to participate in larger numbers in the labor force and to be accordingly less subject to the absolute control of their husbands. In turn, this decline is accompanied by a decrease in the incidence of quarrels among co-wives. In fact, Bété women in an urban environment are more likely than their rural counterparts to cooperate with one another in the upbringing of their respective children.

Thus, urbanization is associated with the emergence of uniform patterns of interaction between co-wives. Yet, this emergence reflects processes which vary markedly along ethnic lines.

Child-Rearing Practices

Among the Abouré, urbanization enhances the significance of the socialization functions performed by the immediate parents. This trend is most visible among monogamous households. Further, this trend is paralleled by marked changes in the attitudes that respondents hold about division of roles along sex lines. In fact, Abouré urban single spouses are not only more integrated into their affinal group than both urban senior co-wives and the entire rural population but they are also more willing to cooperate with their husbands in the socialization of their common offspring. Alternatively, we have seen that Abouré urban senior co-wives are more likely to quarrel with their partners about child-rearing practices. We have also noted that urbanization accentuates competition between co-wives and that this increased competition is most likely to reflect the differential treatment meted out to them by their husbands. Correspondingly, urbanization is associated with a decline in the degree to which Abouré senior co-wives and their husbands cooperate with one another in the rearing of their children.

Changes in the significance of the socialization functions performed by nuclear families lead to changes in the nature of the maternal and paternal roles. First, the disciplinary structure of the familial group becomes more visible, and Abouré urban spouses are most able to determine which actor should punish a child who fails to meet the requirements of the academic system. Second, there is a decline in the intensity of the emotional ties that all mothers establish with their children. They tend to: (1) wean their offspring at an earlier age, (2) shorten their period of initial indulgence, and (3) use physical rather than emotional punishments. More importantly, their exposure to an urban environment enhances the instrumental aspect of their role as socialization agents, and they attach a greater importance than do rural respondents to the academic achievement of their children. All these changes are more evident among monogamous than polygynous families.

The effects of urbanization on the child-rearing practices of Bété single spouses and senior co-wives are more limited and less differentiated. Thus, urbanization hardly modifies the significance of the socializing role of the nuclear family and has no effect on the attitudes that partners hold in this respect.

Interestingly enough, however, urbanization is associated with increased contrasts in the nursing practices of Bété single spouses and senior co-wives. In an urban environment early weaning becomes more characteristic of polygynous than of monogamous families. To this increased coldness of Bété senior co-wives correspond marked changes in their techniques of punishment. They are more likely than their rural counterparts to use physical sanctions. We have seen that, alternatively, urbanization is conducive to the emergence of equalitarian tendencies among Bété monogamous families. These tendencies are equally apparent with regard to child-rearing practices.

Single spouses are more often in a position to share with their husbands the burden of the decisions pertaining to the formal education of their children.

In summary, differences in the child-rearing practices of Abouré and Bété senior co-wives are more limited in an urban than in a rural environment. As noted earlier, however, the emergence of uniform techniques in this respect involves distinct processes which vary along ethnic lines.

Conclusions

In Chapter 4, we hypothesized that: (1) participation of Abouré and Bété familial actors in distinctive educational, occupational, and residential structures would be associated with the emergence of significant contrasts in their familial organizations; (2) urban polygyny would present a large number of new features among the Abouré both because the co-wives of this background are drawn in proportionately large numbers from an urban environment and because plural marriage is on the wane; and (3) the relative domestic power and authority of Bété married women—more specifically, of Bété senior co-wives—should be enhanced because of both their scarcity in an urban environment and their increased participation in the labor force.

We have verified the first and second assumptions. There are substantial changes in the organization of monogamous and polygynous families, which reflect variations in the strains imposed upon these familial groups as well as variations in the value systems to which they subscribe. Urban-rural contrasts are more visible among the Abouré, because their exposure to modernizing forces has been more prolonged and more intense. Urbanization is also associated with accentuated cleavages in the organization of urban monogamous and polygynous families, and these effects are clearer among the Abouré. We have seen that, among this particular people, urbanization leads to marked differences in the recruitment patterns of single spouses and of co-wives. We have noted here that differences in recruitment are paralleled by differences in style of interaction.

Our third assumption is only partially validated. To be sure, the domestic authority and power of Bété married women is more manifest in urban than in rural areas, yet the gains of single spouses are greater than those of senior co-wives. One thing remains sure, however: the competition which prevails among rural Bété polygynous families declines in urban areas.

Urbanization leads to the emergence of certain similarities in the organization of polygynous families, for example, in the extent to which relations among Abouré and Bété co-wives depend on the favors accorded each of them by their husbands, or in the degree to which these women are able to cooperate with one another in the socialization of their offspring. Similarly, urbanization leads all senior co-wives to nurse their children for a similar amount of time, to be equally dependent upon their husbands for the decision to give a formal education to their children, and to adopt analogous views on the merits of the segregation of parental functions along sex lines.

Urbanization, however, also erodes the differentiating power of both ethnicity and type of marriage. In urban areas all married women attach similar importance to the academic achievement of their offspring.[17] All of them use the same

17. This finding is particularly important in view of the negative effects that plural marriage is supposed to have on the development of needs for achievement, and we have tried to obtain a confirmation of the results analyzed here by examining the interviews of male students of the long and short academic system of the Ivory Coast. (For a definition of these types of schools, see Clignet and Foster, *The Fortunate Few*, chap. 1.) Such a population included 221 Bété individuals from a rural origin and 40 from an urban background. The number of Abouré being too small, we have regrouped them with all the peoples of the Lagoon cluster. This represents 228 persons of rural origin and 74 persons from an urban background. First, we have asked these students to rank-order certain demands imposed upon them by their fathers. No less than 35 per cent of the students derived from Lagoon rural monogamous families see educational achievement as the most important demand imposed upon them by their fathers, as against 27 per cent of their counterparts derived from polygynous families. Alternatively, 38 per cent of Bété students born of rural polygynous families take this view, compared with 26

socialization techniques. More importantly, both senior co-wives and monogamous spouses tend to maintain or restore certain types of emotional ties with their family of origin.

In conclusion, convergences and divergences in the responses of various kinds of urban families illustrate the nature of the strains associated with urbanization. The majority of these strains vary with both ethnicity and type of marriage. This suggests, as we have indicated, that an examination of patterns of interaction prevailing among urbanized familial actors requires an analysis of both their place of origin and their current urban environment. Their marginality is in effect a function of the conflicts between these two circumstances. Such conflicts are not necessarily global; therefore, the strategies used by Abouré and Bété polygynous and monogamous respondents to reduce their marginality are not necessarily alike. Though all married women tend to use the first type of strategy described, that is, reinforce their ties with their family of

per cent of students from monogamous families. Urbanization is associated with a decline of ethnic contrasts but with an accentuation of differences between monogamous and polygynous families: only 39 per cent of the Lagoon students from polygynous families view educational achievement as the most important paternal demand, as compared with 52 per cent of their counterparts from urban monogamous families. The corresponding figures among the Bété are 32 and 53 per cent, respectively. In short, the competitive climate of Bété traditional families seems to enhance the educational aspirations of polygynous rural fathers. However, urbanization introduces significant differentiations in the demands of monogamous and polygynous fathers, and regardless of their ethnic origin, the former are more concerned with the schooling of their sons than are the latter. Interestingly enough, an examination of the emphasis placed on academic achievement by the mothers of these students yields somewhat divergent results. Such emphasis is more characteristic of Bété mothers from rural polygynous families than of their counterparts of the Lagoon area. Alternatively, it prevails more frequently among the monogamous rural mothers of the Lagoon area than among Bété women with similar characteristics. Urbanization increases the concern of all Abouré mothers with the formal education of their male children (but this increase is more apparent among those who live in polygynous families). At the same time, however, only 12 per cent of the Bété urban co-wives take such a view as against 40 per cent of the single spouses. In summary, there are some inconsistencies between the results of our survey and these derived from an analysis of the secondary school populations.

296

origin, monogamous partners seem more prone than their polygynous counterparts to establish certain types of equalitarian
patterns of interaction.

Occupational Differentiation

An examination of the differential effects exerted by urban and
rural residence on the organization of families characterized
by differing types of marriage and differing cultural origins is,
however, certainly insufficient. Urbanization refers not only to
variations in the patterns of settlement of distinct social
groups but also to the differentiation of their respective styles
of life. In other words, the meaning of urbanization is not only
geographic but sociological as well.

Thus, urbanization is also accompanied by an increased
division of labor and hence by a redistribution of the active
population in a variety of occupations which present distinctive
features.[18] For example, it is possible to distinguish between
manual and white-collar types of employment. In a country
such as the Ivory Coast, where industrial division of labor
remains quite low, the tasks to be performed by white-collar
individuals are more codified and clearly defined than are
those demanded of blue-collar persons. Indeed, a manual
laborer is expected to be a "jack of all trades," and the definition of these "trades" varies from firm to firm. Second, the
rewards associated with the exercise of these two types of
occupations are distinctive. The prestige attached to white-collar employment is higher and more universal than that accompanying manual labor.[19] In addition, the wage structure of
these two categories differs. Salaries are higher among white-
collar workers, and their chances for upward mobility are

18. See L. Wirth, "Urbanism as a Way of Life."
19. On the universality of prestige hierarchies, see R. Hodge, D. Treiman,
and P. Rossi, "A Comparative Study of Occupational Prestige," in *Class, Status,
and Power: A Reader in Social Stratification*, ed. R. Bendix and S. Lipset
(New York: Free Press, 1967).

better. Lastly, differences in both the demands and the rewards of these two segments of the labor force are accompanied by contrasts in the patterns underlying the recruitment of their respective members. Access to white-collar employment depends primarily upon education, whereas there is a certain amount of ascriptive selectivity in the recruitment of manual laborers.[20]

In turn, these two occupational categories can be contrasted with farming activities, which represent a lower degree of involvement in a cash economy and do not require as complex principles of division of labor. Furthermore, the social and economic rewards derived from farming are less significant than those gained from a participation in the more modern sectors of the economy. Last, for the time being, the selectivity underlying access into agricultural activities tends to be negative.[21]

Our purpose here is to examine the impact of this occupational differentiation on the functioning of the various types of families compared. Yet we are confronted with two competing hypotheses in this regard.

On the one hand, one can assume that patterns of familial interaction are directly influenced by (1) the nature of the professional demands imposed upon the heads of the households investigated, (2) the rewards that they gain from the exercise of their profession, and (3) the selectivity which characterizes access into their present occupational category. Thus, the maximal exposure of white-collar workers to European educational, occupational, and religious values should enable these individuals to anticipate first the challenges of an industrial style of life and to adopt patterns of familial rela-

20. On this point, see M. J. Bowman and Remi Clignet, "Occupational Success in the Ivory Coast: An Examination of the Salaried Labor Force" (forthcoming).

21. Hence the difficulties of implementing plans for agricultural developments. On this question, see, for example, Guy Hunter, *Manpower, Employment and Education in the Rural Economy of Tanzania* (Paris: International Institute for Educational Planning, 1967).

tions characteristic of a European-like nuclear family before any other group. By the same token, the families of blue-collar workers should have characteristics intermediate between those of white-collar individuals and those of farmers.

The maximal exposure of white-collar individuals to European norms and practices also enables them to enjoy high and stable incomes, derived from the exercise of socially valued occupations and to take constant advantage of the new opportunities provided by their environment. They should accordingly have few incentives to change their internal organization and power structures, for the frustrations that they endure in a new environment are minimal. Correspondingly, it could be assumed that changes will be maximal among those families whose participation in new structures is the most frustrating. They should change primarily because they have nothing to lose in abandoning a form of familial organization which is apparently inadequate to meet the demands of industrialization, urbanization, and modernization. In this context, one would expect the families of manual workers to differ from both those of white collar individuals and of farmers. Their insufficient exposure to both traditional and European norms and values should prevent them from gaining access to any kind of reward. Of course, it will also be our concern in this particular section to determine whether the influence of occupational differentiation is uniform or varies both with ethnicity and with type of marriage. Our results are summarized in Table 46.

Conjugal Relations

The size of contrasts between certain aspects of the conjugal status of Abouré single spouses and senior co-wives seems to increase as one moves up in the occupational ladder. Thus, the financial autonomy of Abouré married women declines with a rise in the occupational level achieved by their husbands, and is most manifest among single spouses. Correspondingly, the aspirations toward upward mobility of single spouses increase

Table 46

Relationship between Occupational Status of Husband and Family Life (Percentages)

Abouré

	Monogamous			Polygynous		
	Farmers	Manual Workers	Clerical Workers	Farmers	Manual Workers	Clerical Workers
Conjugal Relations						
Incidence of women reporting:						
1. Exclusive control of family budget by husband	15.3	28.8	52.9	7.6	27.8	29.7
2. Exclusive control of clothing expenditures by husband	33.3	40.7	38.2	24.1	27.8	32.4
3. Domestic quarrels mainly caused by adultery	52.6	47.5	47.1	59.8	50.0	62.2
4. Exclusive dominance of husband in domestic quarrels	23.4	32.2	25.0	24.1	5.6	16.2
5. Single standard on conjugal morality	69.1	40.7	48.5	70.5	50.0	59.5
6. High concern with upward mobility of their husbands	7.8	15.3	20.6	10.7	16.7	13.5
7. Patterned segregation at mealtime	88.9	76.2	64.7	90.7	88.9	78.4

Relations between Wives and their Families

Incidence of women reporting:

8. Preeminent status of their mothers	14.4	39.0	23.5	18.8	27.8	35.1
9. Their mother's residence as the place where they delivered their first child	50.8	22.0	19.1	51.3	33.3	16.2
10. Post-partum leaves from their husbands	57.7	50.9	76.5	56.7	66.7	67.6

Relations among Co-wives

Incidence of women reporting:

11. Cooperative practices in raising children	—	—	—	60.7	44.5	43.2
12. "Frequent" quarrels among co-wives	—	—	—	48.1	33.5	36.3
13. Quarrels mainly caused by jealousy toward husband	—	—	—	24.1	83.3	45.4

Table 46—(Continued)

| | Abouré | | | | | |
| | Monogamous | | | Polygynous | | |
	Farmers	Manual Workers	Clerical Workers	Farmers	Manual Workers	Clerical Workers
Relations between Women and Children						
Incidence of women reporting:						
14. Nursing period of last-born child less than two years	47.8	66.7	64.8	45.8	67.8	72.5
15. Initial indulgence period ceasing with talking	70.3	69.5	60.3	78.1	77.8	67.5
16. Exclusive control of father over schooling of children	66.4	52.5	64.7	67.3	61.1	56.8
17. Exclusive control of father over academic behavior of children	31.8	32.2	52.9	29.5	33.3	48.6
18. Exclusive use of physical punishment	23.1	28.8	39.7	25.9	16.7	37.8
19. Academic achievement as the most important parental demand	38.7	61.0	58.8	38.8	66.7	59.5
20. Socialization of children carried out exclusively by the nuclear family	50.5	55.9	67.6	52.7	50.0	64.9
21. Preferences for joint parental control over children	75.4	84.7	82.4	75.9	72.2	64.9
N	333	59	68	224	18	37

Bété

	Monogamous			Polygynous		
	Farmers	Manual Workers	Clerical Workers	Farmers	Manual Workers	Clerical Workers
Conjugal Relations						
Incidence of women reporting:						
1. Exclusive control of family budget by husband	46.7	51.2	58.3	54.0	58.5	73.7
2. Exclusive control of clothing expenditures by husband	66.3	50.4	40.2	70.6	53.8	52.5
3. Domestic quarrels mainly caused by adultery	19.6	26.4	22.0	20.8	21.5	23.2
4. Exclusive dominance of husband in domestic quarrels	61.9	52.7	54.3	67.1	58.5	55.6
5. Single standard on conjugal morality	29.9	34.1	37.0	26.5	33.8	28.3
6. High concern with upward mobility of their husbands	11.3	30.2	36.2	10.9	23.0	18.2
7. Patterned segregation at mealtime	92.4	76.8	74.0	94.3	86.1	87.8

Table 46—(Continued)

	Bété					
	Monogamous			Polygynous		
	Farmers	Manual Workers	Clerical Workers	Farmers	Manual Workers	Clerical Workers
Relations between Wives and their Families						
Incidence of women reporting:						
8. Preeminent status of their mothers	25.4	35.7	36.2	16.9	41.5	35.4
9. Their mother's residence as the place where they delivered their first child	5.5	11.6	3.9	3.8	4.6	2.0
10. Post-partum leaves from their husbands	44.7	55.1	54.4	43.3	55.4	60.6
Relations among Co-wives						
Incidence of women reporting:						
11. Cooperative practices in raising children	—	—	—	16.3	29.3	26.3
12. "Frequent" quarrels among co-wives	—	—	—	42.4	53.5	49.1
13. Quarrels mainly caused by jealousy toward husband	—	—	—	43.5	48.8	47.2

Relations between Women and Children

Incidence of women reporting:

14. Nursing period of last-born child less than two years	30.0	40.0	45.5	35.0	45.8	48.1
15. Initial indulgence period ceasing with talking	53.3	60.5	69.3	53.7	63.1	61.6
16. Exclusive control of father over schooling of children	57.0	51.9	48.8	63.6	61.5	58.6
17. Exclusive control of father over academic behavior of children	43.6	32.6	37.8	48.9	30.8	47.6
18. Exclusive use of physical punishment	41.2	45.0	37.8	36.1	47.7	42.4
19. Academic achievement as the most important parental demand	51.5	52.7	50.4	54.3	50.8	47.5
20. Socialization of children carried out exclusively by the nuclear family	36.8	48.1	43.3	36.1	35.4	39.4
21. Preferences for joint parental control over children	69.4	55.8	65.4	60.4	55.4	58.6
N	291	129	127	313	65	99

regularly as a direct function of the position achieved by their husbands, but this increase is not evident among senior co-wives. Lastly, single spouses are systematically less often obliged than are senior co-wives to observe ritual acts of deference toward their partners, and differences between them along these lines are maximal when they have married white-collar workers.

To increased differences in the relative insertion of single spouses and senior co-wives in their affinal group correspond accentuated cleavages in the authority structure of the corresponding types of families. Thus, as one moves up in the occupational ladder, the subordination of single spouses becomes less evident. Only 20 per cent of the single spouses of Abouré farmers claim to have the exclusive privilege of buying their personal clothes, and the corresponding proportions are one-fourth among those married to manual workers and 41 per cent among the spouses of white-collar employees. This trend is reversed among polygynous households, where the subordination of senior co-wives in this respect increases as a function of the occupational status achieved by their husbands.

At the same time, however occupational differentiation does not modify the power structure of monogamous families, but affects sharply that of polygynous households. The amount of domestic power enjoyed by the senior co-wives of manual workers is markedly higher than that claimed by their counterparts married to farmers, while traditional Abouré domestic power structures tend to be partially restored among families of white-collar workers. It may very well be that participation in manual labor minimizes the resources of Abouré male individuals and accentuates accordingly the centrifugal pressures exerted on their wives. The fact that the polygynous families of manual workers are likely to lack adequate resources is also reflected in the distribution of domestic quarrels. Whereas the incidence of tensions due to sexual matters is comparable among the polygynous families of white-collar employees and farmers, such tensions decline sharply in number among the polygnous families of manual workers. In this particular sub-population, domestic quarrels are more likely to result from disagreements about financial resources, division of labor, and child-rearing. In short, a lack of adequate resources obliges these polygynous families to face new problems. Their innovation in this respect reflects the original character of the discrepancies between familial norms and resources.

Thus the extent to which polygyny accentuates the strains and inconsistencies of matrilineal organizations is an inverse function of the resources allocated to individual actors.

Similarly, we can see that all wives of Abouré blue-collar workers consider their matrimonial status as particularly fragile. They are accordingly more likely to stress their own obligations in the context of conjugal relations. Only 18 per cent of the single spouses of farmers view female adultery as a more serious offense than male unfaithfulness; this rises to 38 per cent among the spouses of manual workers and to 33 per cent among those married to clerical employees. The figures are 15, 22, and 18 per cent, respectively, among the corresponding subcategories of senior co-wives. The emotional marginality of married women is maximal among monogamous families.

Among the Bété, changes are more clearly patterned but are slightly less differentiated. First, upward mobility accentuates the dependence of all married women upon the resources of their husbands. At the same time, urbanization is also associated with the emergence of equalitarian orientations, particularly manifest among monogamous families. Single spouses of white-collar workers are less frequently obliged to show deference to their husbands. They enjoy a larger share of domestic power, have more initiatives with regard to the purchases that they want to make, and are more inclined to perceive problems of conjugal fidelity in universalistic terms. Their gains are, on the whole, more substantial than those of senior co-wives, who more frequently retain a traditional style of conjugal interaction.

Relations between Wives
and their Families of Origin

Regardless of ethnic and matrimonial status, upward mobility enables married women to maintain closer informal relations with their family of origin. All married women seem to use the additional resources gained from the higher position of their husbands to reinforce the kind of relations which have been most rewarding to them in the past. However, contrasts between the single spouses and senior co-wives of Abouré manual workers along these lines are somewhat inconsistent. Single spouses are less fearful than senior co-wives of expressing their loyalty toward their mothers, but they are also less often in a position to take post-partum leaves from their husbands after the birth of their last child. An intermediate level of exposure to modernizing forces apparently creates sharp conflicts between aspirations and available patterns of behavior. Such conflicts reflect the marginality of the domestic status allocated to the wives of the corresponding occupational subgroup.

Relations among Co-wives

The effects of occupational differentiation on the relations that senior co-wives maintain with the junior spouses of their husbands are more evident among the Abouré than among the Bété. Among the first people, upward mobility is associated with an increase in the incidence of quarrels opposing co-wives to one another, and a corresponding decline in their propensity to raise their children jointly. Their increased competition results mainly from their sensitivity to the differential treatment meted out to each of them by the head of their households. This sensitivity is maximal among the families of manual workers, where inconsistencies between family resources and the implications of polygynous arrangements are greatest.

Alternatively, the incidence of quarrels between Bété co-wives varies as an inverse function of the occupational level achieved by their husbands. The higher this level, the more stable is the internal order of familial groups and the more co-wives are able to raise their children jointly.

In summary, contrasts between Abouré and Bété polygynous families decline as one moves up in the occupational hierarchy. However, this decline reflects the influence of opposite processes.

Child-Rearing Practices

Among the Abouré, occupational mobility is accompanied by an increase in the significance of the socialization functions of the immediate family group. This increase, however, has distinctive implications on monogamous and polygynous actors. The more important the role of monogamous parents as agents of socialization, the more they are eager to cooperate with one another along these lines. The trend is reversed among polygynous families, where senior co-wives of white-collar workers are more likely to accept a segregation of socialization functions along sex lines than are their counterparts married to farmers.

Correspondingy, the effects of occupational differentiation on the definition of Abouré parental roles vary with type of marriage. To be sure, the visibility of the disciplinary power structure increases uniformly as one moves up in the occupational structure. Yet, changes in the maternal attitudes of single spouses and senior co-wives do not entirely coincide. Upward mobility is accompanied by a decline in the warmth which all Abouré women display toward their young children, and this is most evident among polygynous households. Upward mobility is also associated with a decrease in the significance of social-emotional techniques of punishments used by Abouré mothers. Only 18 per cent of the single spouses of clerical workers use this type of sanction as opposed to almost one-half of those married to farmers. Among senior co-wives, the corresponding figures are 27 and 58 per cent, respectively.

309

Yet 44 per cent of the senior co-wives of Abouré blue-collar workers remain attached to social-emotional control, which is retained by only one-fourth of the corresponding subgroup of single spouses. Thus, socialization techniques of monogamous families appear to respond more promptly to social change than do those of polygynous households.

To changes in the type of social control used by mothers there correspond changes in the division of parental authority along sex lines. Upward mobility is accompanied by a restoration of the privileges accorded to monogamous husbands in this respect; among polygynous households, however, there are corresponding reversals in the relative amount of authority exerted by monogamous and polygynous fathers when one passes from blue-collar to white-collar type of employment.

Among the Bété, occupational differentiation exerts little influence on the relative significance of the socialization functions performed by the immediate familial group. Further, contrasts between monogamy and polygyny in this regard are greatest for the families of manual workers. Single spouses are less likely to send their children to their village of origin, probably because of the limited amount of resources available to them. This lack of resources in turn impedes parental cooperation, and the attitudes of the single spouses of manual workers differ in this regard from both those of farmers and those of white-collar employees.

On the whole, however, effects of occupational differentiation on the socialization techniques of Bété monogamous and polygynous families tend to be parallel. Access to the top echelons of the hierarchy is associated in both cases with a partial restoration of traditional types of sanctions and of controls. Thus, the disciplinary structure of Bété familial groups tends to be least visible among blue-collar workers, and it is in this occupational category that mothers are the most likely to use physical sanctions. At the same time, access to the top echelons of the occupational ladder is also associated with innovations. Senior co-wives and single spouses of Bété white-collar workers wean their children earlier than do the wives of any other group but remain initially indulgent for a longer period of time. They are also more often in a position to participate in the decisions pertaining to the formal schooling of their children.

Some Concluding Remarks

First, occupational differentiation induces more drastic changes in the organization of Abouré families than in the functioning of Bété households. The over-all exposure of the first group to modernizing forces has been more intense and of longer duration. In addition, there are more cleavages in the responses of Abouré monogamous and polygynous families to upward mobility, and this suggests once more that distinctions between styles of familial interaction prevailing among a particular ethnic group depend on the extent of its overall social differentiation. In other words, polygyny remains more uniformly normative among the Bété than among the Abouré. As a result, social change induces parallel strains and pressures on families of the first people, whereas there are marked divergences in both the intensity and the direction of the tensions experienced by monogamous and polygynous Abouré families.

Second, this analysis has enabled us to determine how occupational differentiation modifies the contrasts between monogamous and polygynous families. These contrasts may increase regularly as one moves up on the occupational ladder. Thus, differences in the conjugal relations of Bété single spouses and senior co-wives are maximal at the top of this structure. However, such contrasts may follow a curve and be maximal or minimal for blue-collar workers. This pattern characterizes many aspects of the conjugal interaction of Abouré families. *Maximal* differences between monogamous and polygynous blue-collar families suggest that both types of households have the same value system but are not exposed to similar pressures. Indeed, additional resources will enable them to restore uniform traditional patterns of behavior. Conversely, *minimal* differences between monogamous and polygynous families of blue-collar workers suggest that a limited amount of resources prevents the emergence and development of new orientations.

We can follow the same kind of reasoning in comparing the organization of Bété and Abouré polygynous families. The senior co-wives of Abouré and Bété blue-collar workers simultaneously present both highly similar and highly dissimilar features. Differences between their attitudes toward conjugal morality or between the factors which lead them to quarrel with their husbands are more limited than those observed among other occupational subgroups. At the same time, differences in the relative power of these wives and in the relations that they maintain with their family of origin or with their co-wives are greater than corresponding contrasts observed in any other occupational group.

Blue-collar employment maximizes the strains to which urban families must respond. They are exposed to a new environment without having access to the resources that such an environment can provide. In certain cases such strains are structural, and all families are obliged to respond uniformly. The corresponding decline in the differences between Abouré and Bété polygynous families involves processes of accommodation. Other strains are culturally specific, and the resulting accentuation of ethnic contrasts reflects the intervention of assimilative patterns of adaptation.

In conclusion, occupational differentiation affects the size and direction of the contrasts between monogamous and polygynous families. Variations in these contrasts depend on the extent to which occupational mobility leads to these changes: (1) A decrease or an increase in the total resources allocated to familial groups. The implications of these decreases and increases cannot be alike on households of different sizes. (2) Changes in the value systems of individual actors. Such changes cannot operate uniformly upon the two types of families.

Increase in Scale of Employment

The professional status held by an individual is, however, not the only indicator of the occupational differentiation which has taken place in the Ivory Coast. Economic and political developments have also been accompanied by an increase in the scale of the social and economic enterprises. The notion of scale used here has a variety of meanings. First, it refers to the sheer size of the firms and organizations investigated. Indeed, social change is usually conducive to a decline in the number of economic concerns, but to an increase in the size of their respective labor forces.[22] Second, the concept also refers to the territoriality of such organizations. In this context, the small scale of agricultural or artisanal enterprises may be meaningfully contrasted with the large-sized networks of governmental agencies which cover the entire territory of the country but are also in close contact with foreign agencies and governments. Third, the concept also refers to the type of activity undertaken by the organization analyzed. The higher the scale of an enterprise, the larger the parts of its activities which are devoted to coordination and control. As a result, the proportion of skilled white-collar workers varies as a direct function of the scale of the organizations studied.[23] Finally, participation in enterprises with different scalar characteristics is associated with differing rewards. The higher these characteristics, the higher is the pay, the prestige, and the more stable is the employment of individual workers, a feature particularly important in view of the high value attached by Africans to security.[24]

Our purpose in this section is twofold. On the one hand, we

22. See E. Shevky and W. Bell, *Social Area Analysis* (Stanford: Stanford University Press, 1955).
23. See Bowman and Clignet, "Occupational Success in the Ivory Coast."
24. See Clignet and Foster, *The Fortunate Few*, chap. 7.

will investigate the effects of variations in scale on the contrast between different monogamous and polygynous families. In this context we will have to evaluate once more the validity of the two competing hypotheses formulated at the beginning of the previous section. On the other hand we will have to determine whether the relevant effects of variations in scale are more powerful than those resulting from variations in the occupational status of individual persons.

The problem remains, of course, to operationalize the concept of scale as defined above. We could have used the now classic distinction between entrepreneurial and bureaucratic organizations and compared firms which have less and more than two levels of supervision,[25] but we were not able to obtain the relevant information from our respondents. We have therefore grouped our interviewees in three categories: those whose husbands are self-employed; those whose husbands work for the private sector of the economy; and those whose partners are employed by governmental agencies. It is quite apparent that the patterns of recruitment into public bureaucracies and into self-employed activities are different, just as the organization and the rewards of these two types of employment are different. It seems possible to argue, as we do here, that the private sector of the economy represents an intermediate between these two extremes. We are aware, of course, that the concept of private enterprise is less polarized than the other two. In certain cases private organizations can have an organization as complex as that of a government, exert as large networks of influence, follow the same principles of recruitment, and distribute the same kind of rewards. We have not, unfortunately, been able to make distinctions between large-scale and small-scale private enterprises.

Our findings are summarized in Table 47. The effects of variations in scale are more powerful than those resulting

25. See D. Miller and G. Swanson, *The Changing American Parents* (New York: Wiley, 1958), pp. 43–58.

Table 47

Relationship between Scale of Employment of Husband and Family Life (Percentages)

Abouré

	Monogamous			Polygynous		
	Self-Employ-ment	Private Employ-ment	Public Employ-ment	Self-Employ-ment	Private Employ-ment	Public Employ-ment
Conjugal Relations						
Incidence of women reporting:						
1. Exclusive control of family budget by husband	46.9	48.2	(77.8)	7.6	25.8	41.6
2. Exclusive control of clothing expenditures by husband	33.1	41.0	(55.6)	24.3	29.0	30.0
3. Domestic quarrels mainly caused by adultery	52.0	48.2	(44.4)	60.2	54.8	66.7
4. Exclusive dominance of husband in domestic quarrels	24.3	25.3	(44.4)	23.0	19.3	8.3
5. Single standard on conjugal morality	69.7	38.7	(55.6)	69.6	54.8	66.7
6. High concern with upward mobility of their husbands	7.7	19.3	(22.2)	11.5	12.9	8.3
7. Patterned segregation at mealtime	89.2	56.1	(66.7)	90.9	70.9	100.0

Table 47—(Continued)

	Aboure					
	Monogamous			Polygynous		
	Self-Employment	Private Employment	Public Employment	Self-Employment	Private Employment	Public Employment
Relations between Wives and their Families						
Incidence of women reporting:						
8. Preeminent status of their mothers	16.0	30.1	(11.1)	18.5	38.7	25.0
9. Their mother's residence as the place where they delivered their first child	50.9	15.7	(33.3)	50.9	16.4	25.0
10. Post-partum leaves from their husbands	56.9	68.7	(88.9)	56.4	77.4	58.3
Relations among Co-wives						
Incidence of women reporting:						
11. Cooperative practices in raising children	—	—	—	60.7	38.3	41.7
12. "Frequent" quarrels among co-wives	—	—	—	47.5	25.0	xxx [a]
13. Quarrels mainly caused by jealousy toward husband	—	—	—	26.8	58.3	xxx [a]

[a] All the answers of Aboure senior co-wives were in the "No Answer" category.

Relations between Women and Children

Incidence of women reporting:

14. Nursing period of last-born child less than two years	46.9	72.3	(77.7)	48.7	83.9	50.0
15. Initial indulgence period ceasing with talking	69.1	62.7	(55.6)	77.3	74.1	66.7
16. Exclusive control of father over schooling of children	66.3	56.6	(88.9)	67.2	51.6	58.3
17. Exclusive control of father over academic behavior of children	31.7	50.6	(44.4)	30.7	51.6	25.0
18. Exclusive use of physical punishment	23.7	30.1	(77.8)	25.6	38.7	25.0
19. Academic achievement as the most important parental demand	39.1	62.1	(55.6)	40.1	77.4	25.0
20. Socialization of children carried out exclusively by the nuclear family	49.7	62.7	(77.8)	53.9	61.2	83.3
21. Preferences for joint parental control over children	76.0	79.5	(88.9)	76.0	64.5	75.0
N	350	83	9	234	31	12

Table 47—(Continued)

Bété

	Monogamous			Polygynous		
	Self-Employ-ment	Private Employ-ment	Public Employ-ment	Self-Employ-ment	Private Employ-ment	Public Employ-ment
Conjugal Relations						
Incidence of women reporting:						
1. Exclusive control of family budget by husband	45.2	57.1	72.2	53.8	68.1	79.3
2. Exclusive control of clothing expenditures by husband	62.8	48.8	55.6	71.8	53.6	41.3
3. Domestic quarrels mainly caused by adultery	19.2	26.9	33.3	21.3	18.1	37.9
4. Exclusive dominance of husband in domestic quarrels	62.2	50.9	66.7	67.4	56.3	55.1
5. Single standard on conjugal morality	30.1	38.9	38.9	27.2	23.6	44.8
6. High concern with upward mobility of their husbands	13.4	29.7	11.2	10.5	22.7	13.8
7. Patterned segregation at mealtime	90.7	74.7	77.8	93.7	86.3	89.7

Relations between Wives and their Families

Incidence of women reporting:

8. Preeminent status of their mothers	24.7	36.6	27.8	17.3	38.1	34.5
9. Their mother's residence as the place where they delivered their first child	6.1	8.0	0.0	3.4	4.5	0.0
10. Post-partem leaves from their husbands	45.9	53.7	50.0	42.7	54.5	62.0

Relations among Co-wives

Incidence of women reporting:

11. Cooperative practices in raising children	—	—	—	16.4	24.5	31.0
12. "Frequent" quarrels among co-wives	—	—	—	43.5	53.4	42.1
13. Quarrels mainly caused by jealousy toward husband	—	—	—	47.3	50.0	42.1

Table 47—(Continued)

	Bété					
	Monogamous			Polygynous		
	Self-Employ-ment	Private Employ-ment	Public Employ-ment	Self-Employ-ment	Private Employ-ment	Public Employ-ment
Relations between Women and Children						
Incidence of women reporting:						
14. Nursing period of last-born child less than two years	35.9	48.5	28.5	29.7	51.8	41.3
15. Initial indulgence period ceasing with talking	53.2	64.0	77.8	52.6	65.4	58.6
16. Exclusive control of father over schooling of children	56.4	50.3	33.3	63.4	62.7	51.7
17. Exclusive control of father over academic behavior of children	42.3	37.1	38.9	48.8	41.8	48.3
18. Exclusive use of physical punishment	40.7	41.7	33.3	36.8	43.6	48.3
19. Academic achievement as the most important parental demand	52.2	50.9	33.3	54.1	50.9	48.3
20. Socialization of children carried out exclusively by the nuclear family	37.2	43.4	61.1	35.6	35.6	41.3
21. Preferences for joint parental control over children	68.6	59.4	72.2	60.3	60.6	62.0
N	312	175	18	323	110	29

from the differentiation of individual occupations. They are also accompanied by a greater dissociation in the patterns of behavior and of attitudes of monogamous and polygynous respondents.

Conjugal Relations

Among the Bété, the extent to which both monogamous and polygynous husbands exert an exclusive control on familial resources varies as a positive function of the scale of the enterprises in which they participate. This phenomenon has, however, a differential impact on the conjugal relations prevailing among monogamous and polygynous families. Indeed, as the scale of the enterprise in which their husbands work increases, Bété senior co-wives tend more frequently than do monogamous spouses to make by themselves the decision to buy their own clothes. Similarly, they are more rarely under the obligation of yielding in quarrels with their husbands. Further, although increase in scale modifies the over-all distribution of Bété domestic quarrels, corresponding changes are more manifest among polygynous households. The increase in the incidence of quarrels pertaining to conjugal infidelity reflects the decline of the functionality of the domestic role allocated to married women. This decline varies with type of marriage and is most extreme for senior co-wives. As a result, increase in scale modifies the views that senior co-wives hold about conjugal obligations, and makes them more prone to adopt equalitarian orientations. Such changes are not evident among single spouses.

In brief, type of employment seems to condition the degree of integration of Bété married women into their affinal group. The higher the scalar characteristics of the organization for which a Bété man works, the more equalitarian the relations that he establishes with his wife or wives. Yet the gains obtained along these lines by senior co-wives seem to be both more numerous and more significant than those acquired by single spouses.

The effects of employment variations on the conjugal relations of monogamous and polygynous Abouré families are not alike. Increase in scale accentuates the integration of single spouses into their affinal group. Their functionality becomes more apparent, and there is a decline in the incidence of domestic quarrels pertaining to adultery. Further, their financial dependence upon their husbands' resources is enhanced, and they have a more limited amount of domestic power.

By contrast, participation of Abouré polygynist males in public administration is accompanied by a partial restoration of traditional styles of conjugal interaction. This type of employment is not associated with an increase in the amount of financial authority invested in polygynous husbands. It is, however, accompanied by a decline in their domestic power by a restoration of mealtime etiquette and of the forces which traditionally separate these men and their wives.

Thus access to the top echelons of the occupational hierarchy enhances the resources of familial groups and accordingly increases the number of choices that they can make with regard to style of life; however the use of these additional resources and potential choices differs with marriage type. Abouré monogamous families are increasingly oriented toward innovation, whereas polygynous groups remain more definitely attached to traditional norms and values.

On the whole, differences in the organization of Abouré and Bété polygynous families tend to be inversely related to the scalar characteristics of the employment of the head of the household. The similarities observable at the top of the occupational structure, however, involve quite different processes. The degree of social absorption of Bété senior co-wives declines markedly, whereas there is no change in that of their Abouré counterparts.

Relations between Wives
and their Families of Origin

Since an increase in scale is associated with a decrease in the
subordination of Bété women toward their husbands, it should
be correspondingly accompanied by an increase in the extent to
which these women are able to maintain strong loyalties toward their family of origin. This tends to be the case. Senior
co-wives of Bété public servants are more likely than monogamous spouses to take post-partum leaves and to remain at their
village of origin for a long period of time. They are also less
afraid of expressing their affection and loyalty toward their
mothers.

Trends are far less clear among the Abouré. To be sure,
public employment is associated with a restoration of the traditional limitations imposed by Abouré polygynist husbands
upon their spouses. Senior co-wives of public servants are less
often able to return to their mother's residence after the birth
of a child than those married to individuals working in the
private sector of the economy. In addition, they are also more
fearful of expressing their loyalty toward their mothers. Such
a fear is equally characteristic of single spouses who are nevertheless more likely to take post-partum leaves from their husbands.

Interestingly enough, as one moves up in the scale of employment there is a reversal in the contrast between the relative amount of loyalty displayed by Abouré and Bété senior
co-wives vis-à-vis their family of origin. At the lower end of
the continuum Abouré senior co-wives are better off than their
Bété counterparts. The reverse is true at the upper end of the
scale.

Relations among Co-wives

Participation of Bété males in economic activities with high
scalar characteristics enables their senior co-wives to enjoy a
more rewarding domestic position. We can expect these co-

wives to feel less competitive and less threatened by their husbands' junior spouses. Although the extent to which married co-wives cooperate with one another in the upbringing of their children increases regularly as their husbands move up the employment ladder, the incidence of quarrels between these women follows a different pattern. Such quarrels are minimal among the wives of individuals working for private interests and quite frequent among the spouses of males working for government agencies.

In contrast, the incidence of quarrels between Abouré co-wives seems to be positively associated with the type of employment of their husbands. Also, such quarrels are most likely to result from the differential treatment accorded to each co-wife by the head of the household. Correspondingly, these women tend to abandon their traditional habits of jointly raising their respective children. In short, the social distance between them seems to increase as the husband moves up on the occupational ladder.

Thus, while access to the most rewarding types of employment is accompanied by the partial restoration of traditional patterns of conjugal interaction among Abouré polygynous households, there is an emergence of new patterns of interaction between co-wives. Changes in patterns of conjugal relations are dominated by principles of assimilation, but changes in patterns of interaction between co-wives seem to be conditioned by principles of accommodation. Once more we can verify that the pressures exerted on each aspect of familial organizations are probably not equal in intensity and, accordingly, do not induce comparable types of responses.

Child-Rearing Practices

Differentiation in type of employment tends to exert parallel effects on the child-rearing practices of Bété monogamous and polygynous families, but these effects are more visible in the first than in the second case. Thus, participation in public service increases the significance of parental roles, but the increase is most evident among monogamous households. This increased significance induces partners to cooperate with one another, but single spouses take a more pronounced position in this respect than do senior co-wives. Single spouses of Bété civil servants are warmer toward young children than are those of any other occupational category. Changes in the maternal roles of senior co-wives are less clear and less marked; these women remain much colder toward their young children than do their monogamous counterparts. Similarly, public employment is associated with a redistribution of the parental authority and control exerted over children. Monogamous wives acquire larger responsibilities in this respect than do senior co-wives. Changes in the definition of maternal roles are accompanied by changes in the demands imposed upon children. As we move up the employment ladder, we observe that the relative importance attached to academic achievement declines, and families become increasingly concerned about the respect and deference that children should display toward the older members of the group. Such changes are most conspicuous in monogamous families. Finally, access to public employment is accompanied by marked divergence in the techniques of control used by monogamous and polygynous families. We have observed that, as we move up in the occupational structure, senior co-wives tend to make more use of physical sanctions, while the reverse is true of single spouses.

Among the Abouré, differentiation in type of employment is also associated with changes in the functionality of the socializing role of the immediate family, and these changes affect monogamous and polygynous households equally. Maximal at the upper end of the scale, this functionality induces positive attitudes toward conjugal cooperation among single spouses. The senior co-wives of civil servants, however, do not differ in this respect from those married to self-employed males.

Variations in the functionality of the socializing role allocated to Abouré single spouses influence their child-rearing practices. As one moves up the ladder of employment, these

325

women become colder toward their children, wean and discipline them at an earlier age, and are less emotional in their sanctions. At the same time, the disciplinary structure of their familial group is more visible, and there is an accentuation of the disciplinary role played by their husbands. In turn, these changes modify the nature of the demands imposed upon children, and monogamous families attach more significance to the academic success of their children as we move up in the occupational structure.

All these trends are not evident among Abouré polygynous households. On the whole, senior co-wives are able to restore partially or totally the socializing values and techniques defined as ideals by relevant cultural norms.

Conclusions

Our data have enabled us to measure the different influences exerted by increase in scale on the contrasts between the organizations of Abouré and Bété monogamous and polygynous families. Among the Abouré, occupational differentiation is associated not only with variations in the relative amount of resources allocated to family members but also with an increased differentiation of the value systems of monogamous and polygynous families. On the whole, a maximal amount of resources leads monogamous families to adopt new patterns of interaction. Conversely, senior co-wives in this situation are more likely to restore traditional norms. In brief, changes affecting the first type of household are based on *accommodation,* and Abouré single spouses acquire a status which differs both from that traditionally allocated to them and from the ideal defined by modern norms. Correspondingly, changes affecting the second type of family are based upon *assimilation,* and the marginality of the position occupied by urban senior co-wives tends to be reduced by a reinforcement of traditional values.

Among the Bété the effects of social change on familial

organization are of smaller magnitude. Moreover, the responses of monogamous and polygynous families tend to have parallel directions but different intensities. Senior co-wives are able to innovate more often than single spouses with regard to conjugal relations. In contrast, the effects of social differentiation on child-rearing practices are more visible among monogamous than among polygynous families.

The effects of increase in scale on the contrasts between Abouré and Bété polygynous families are not necessarily alike. Access to the most rewarding positions of the occupational structure may be associated with the emergence of uniform responses on the part of Abouré and Bété senior co-wives; it may also be accompanied by a reinforcement of ethnic cleavages. For example, the techniques of control and the types of demands that the co-wives of civil servants impose upon their children vary along ethnic lines. The observed dissimilarities occur in part because additional resources induce changes in only one of the two ethnic groups studied. They also occur because one group assimilates the new elements of the urban scene into traditional norms, whereas the second people accommodate themselves to the new situation.

In addition, this chapter has enabled us to compare the relative influence exerted by two main forms of occupational differentiation on patterns of familial interaction. Theoretically, socio-economic status should be a better predictor than scale of employment of the changes affecting familial relations. There are fewer variations in the demands and the rewards associated with each occupational category than in the corresponding characteristics of each type of employment. Participation in governmental agencies may involve a manual or a clerical type of job. At the lower end of the continuum, among self-employed individuals, traders have to face problems which are significantly different from those met by farmers.

Our data show nevertheless that among the Abouré variations in both occupational status and type of employment are uniformly associated with a partial restoration of traditional styles of both conjugal interaction and child-rearing practices prevailing in polygynous households. Conversely, although occupational status has little effect on the organization of monogamous families, these families still react quite strongly to variations in the type of employment.

Among the Bété, the two forms of differentiation exert parallel influences on the functioning of monogamous and polygynous families. On the whole, occupational status seems to exert stronger effects on the status of single spouses than on the status of senior co-wives. Variations in type of employment affect the conjugal relations of polygynous families more than those of monogamous households, but the more significant variations in child-rearing practices occur in monogamous families.

It would have been appropriate to combine the two forms of differentiation and to test their effects on familial organization. The small size of the corresponding subsamples tends, however, to limit the significance of this approach.

We are now in a better position to summarize how social change affects the contrasts between monogamy and polygyny:

1. Changes may be uniform, but they will be more visible among single spouses because the presence of more than one wife dilutes the effects of modernizing forces.

2. Either an intermediate or a maximal level of exposure to modernizing forces may change the terms of the contrasts between monogamy and polygyny. In this sense, the two competing hypotheses presented earlier in this chapter are both valid. Attitudes and behaviors of individual actors and familial groups are subjected to new restraints and new choices. The pressures accompanying these restraints and the aspirations associated with these choices are necessarily dependent on the number of wives in the family.

3. The specific responses of monogamous and polygynous families to the limitations and opportunities of an urban environment vary along ethnic lines. First, they depend upon the

328

incidence of plural marriage among the urbanized segments of each people investigated. The higher this incidence, the more parallel are the changes in monogamous and polygynous families. Second, these responses depend upon the over-all occupational level achieved by the male population of each group. The greater the occupational differentiation, the more variations there will be in the reference groups used by individual actors, and the more contrasts there will be in their adaptation to the urban scene. In some cases, modernization of the *means* accessible to these individuals will be reinforced by a modernization of their *ends,* whereas these two factors will vary independently in other cases. In short, there are parallels in the amount of occupational differentiation present in a particular ethnic group and in the range of possible variations characterizing the repertoire of responses that familial groups can give to the challenges of their environment. Correspondingly, this differentiation affects both the intensity of the marginality experienced by family members and the nature of the mechanisms that they use to reduce this marginality.

Finally, these responses vary with the dominant traits of the traditional organization of the people. In this context, the increased marginality of urban senior co-wives accentuates some of the characteristics attached to matrilineal plural marriage. Thus the direction of the influence of social change on the contrast between monogamy and polygyny depends on the degree to which the strains and opportunities produced by urbanization reinforce the demands imposed upon the individual actors of the monogamous and polygynous households.

In conclusion, we have isolated here three distinct patterns in the responses of familial groups to the strains and pressures which accompany various forms of occupational differentiation.[25] These patterns are:

1. *Linear.* For example, the control of husbands over famil-

25. See D. Miller and G. Swanson, *The Changing American Parents* (New York: Wiley, 1958), pp. 43–58.

329

ial resources increases regularly as they occupy more rewarding positions.

2. *Thresholdlike.* This happens where there is little differentiation in the responses of the families whose participation is medium. For example, the percentages of Bété families whose husbands make by themselves the decision to send their children to school are alike for the groups of self-employed individuals and of individuals working for private employers, but such percentages in turn differ markedly from those observed among civil servants. Similarly, traditional mealtime etiquette prevails as often among families of Abouré manual workers as among those of farmers, whereas the mealtime etiquette of white-collar workers is more equalitarian in nature. Of course, the threshold at which occupational differentiation introduces maximal changes in familial relations does vary. Although this threshold is generally located between manual and white-collar occupations, it can also affect lower rungs of the scale. For example, the proportion of Abouré senior co-wives taking post-partum leaves from their husbands is alike among the polygynous families of both manual and clerical workers, but these proportions are far greater than those observable among families of farmers. Similarly, the amounts of domestic power held by polygynist males engaged in public and private organizations are comparable but tend to be smaller than that exerted by self-employed individuals.

3. *Curvilinear.* The pattern of familial interaction under study increases or decreases up to a certain point after which it moves in the opposite direction. The increase in scale of the collective activities in which Abouré individuals are engaged is often accompanied by a partial restoration of traditional sets of attitudes, beliefs, and behaviors. The emergence of this pattern, as we have noted, illustrates our view that the modernization of ends and of means do not necessarily coincide.

Further, our analysis has enabled us to distinguish between various dimensions of the processes by which Abouré and Bété families characterized by differing types of marriages respond to the strains of social change.[26] These processes may be analyzed in terms of four factors: [27]

1. *Rate of change.* For example, the decline in the power held by Abouré polygynous males working in the public sector of the economy is much more marked than that observable among their Bété counterparts.

2. *Trajectory of change.* Increase in scale is associated with a decline in the control that Bété husbands exert over the purchases of clothing desired by their wives, but it is associated with an increase of this control among the Abouré. Similarly, increase in scale induces cooperation among Bété co-wives but stimulates competition among the Abouré.

3. *Timing of change.* Because our analysis is cross-sectional and is undertaken at one point in time, it does not therefore enable us to correctly analyze the longitudinal dimensions of change; however, we may still observe that there are parallel modifications in the definitions of parental roles and in the significance of the socialization functions performed by Abouré nuclear families, whereas such parallels are not found among the Bété. These differences between the two groups lead us to the tentative conclusion that changes in this particular aspect of the functionality of nuclear families only take place whenever there have been substantial modifications in the roles performed by adult familial actors. This condition is found among the Abouré but not among the Bété.

4. *Sequential order of change.* Among the Bété, we have noted that variations in occupational status are associated with variations in the relations that senior co-wives entertain with their husbands, their family of origin, and their co-wives, but these variations do not affect child-rearing practices. It is

26. See Remi Clignet, "Type of Descent, Environmental Change and Child Rearing Practice," in *The City in Modern Africa,* ed. H. Miner (New York: Praeger, 1967), chap. 10.

27. This framework is derived from A. Feldman and W. Moore, "Industrialization and Industrialism: Convergence and Differentiation," *Transactions of the Fifth World Congress of Sociology* (1962), II, 151–69.

tempting to conclude that changes in such practices occur only after marked changes in conjugal relations.

In brief, the distinction between types of marriages is initially drawn from an examination of traditional societies, yet it becomes most significant in the context of changing environments. Emerging cities and systems of social stratification open up new avenues to individuals and may lead them to challenge traditional choices. The new environment is characterized by different forms of pressure and restraint, which give a new dimension to the contrasts between monogamy and plural marriage.

CHAPTER 9

General Conclusions

Our long journey into the maze of African familial institutions is not yet finished. We have thus far considered all our independent variables separately, but we must also determine how they operate *simultaneously;* in other words, we must compare the relative importance of plural marriage and other social factors as determinants of the behavior patterns examined here. This can be accomplished through a discriminant function analysis.[1]

1. The Stepwise Multiple Discriminant Analysis Program alters the conventional multiple discriminant analysis in the following manner: First, we use Rao's generalization of the Mahalanobis D^2 statistic for measuring intergroup distance, which we term *Rao's V*. We use Rao's V to identify those variables which add significant independent information to the analysis of group differences. We add one variable at a time until the incremental distance which is added between groups by a new variable is not significant. The increment in Rao's V caused by each succeeding variable is chi-square distributed with (number of groups minus one) degrees of freedom. Hence we can test at each step whether any additional variable can significantly add to the intergroup variance explained by the multivariate set of variables already entered at that point. If no additional variables can be found, then the set of all variables entered at that point is used as the input to a multiple discriminant analysis to find a linear function of the variables in that set. We then have an F ratio to test the Wilk's Lambda statistic for the null hypothesis that the means across the groups in the multivariate set are the same. Hence, we can

Results of the Analysis

The *stepwise multiple discriminant function analysis* serves two purposes. First, it enables us to decide whether differences in the characteristics of the respondents who chose one mode of answer as a particular indicator of familial relations could have occurred by chance. In other words, we have identified distinct groups of responses to a particular dependent variable, and we must now determine whether these groups present a cluster of characteristics which enable us to distinguish them in terms of selected independent variables. Are these clusters randomly distributed among the distinct groups of respondents, or are they significantly associated with those groups? The second purpose of the analysis is to evaluate the contribution of each independent variable in accounting for the variance of the dependent variable.

We are therefore interested in three tests of the importance of type of marriage as a determinant of individual behavior. First, we must assess whether type of marriage contributes significantly to the variance of each of our indicators of familial relations. Second, we must determine whether the results obtained by a discriminant function analysis are similar when one takes into consideration the entire population of married women and the limited subsample of co-wives. Should type of marriage be the sole determinant of familial relations, the null hypothesis would be accepted when we analyze the responses of Abouré and Bété senior co-wives solely. Thus subsequent differences between the characteristics of these two groups of respondents should be nonsignificant and attributable to random fluctuations. A third test remains necessary. Although we

---

determine if this reduced set of variables can significantly differentiate between the groups.

For a more detailed discussion, see C. R. Rao, *Advanced Statistical Methods in Biometric Research* (New York: Wiley, 1952), chaps. 7, 8, and 9; W. W. Cooley and P. R. Lohnes, *Multivariate Procedures for the Behavioral Sciences* (New York: Wiley, 1962), chaps. 6 and 7; and R. L. Anderson, *An Introduction to Multivariate Statistical Analysis* (New York: Wiley, 1958), § 6.

may be able to reject the null hypothesis for both the entire population and the subsample of co-wives, the nature and salience of the contributors to the over-all variance of a particular indicator of familial relations may differ as between these two samples, and such differing may suggest that type of marriage acts as an intervening variable by altering the degree to which a particular factor influences conjugal relations or child-rearing practices.

We will not consider here all of our indicators of familial styles of interaction with respect to conjugal relations; we will examine the distribution of (1) the handling of familial resources, (2) the modes of clothes purchases for the respondents, (3) the domestic power structure, (4) the attitudes toward conjugal morality, and (5) the mealtime etiquette of the families investigated.

As far as the relations between the respondents and their own families are concerned, we will examine the distribution of post-partum leaves. We will also analyze the distribution of cooperative practices between co-wives; finally, in terms of child-rearing practices we will investigate the distributions of (1) patterns of weaning, (2) demands imposed upon children, and (3) techniques of control used by mothers.

Two considerations have dictated such choices. First, it would be too costly and time consuming to treat all of the items used in the present survey. Second, it was quite apparent that this treatment would be optimal when the number of possible answers is limited and when the number of no answers does not exceed a certain amount.

Our independent variables are the following: (a) ethnicity, (b) type of marriage, (c) female participation in the labor force, (d) fertility, (e) matrimonial antedecents, (f) age at marriage, (g) urbanization, (h) type of occupation of husbands, and (i) type of employment of husbands.

Obviously, certain independent variables are highly interrelated. Thus male occupation and urbanization are not independent of one another. Farmers are bound to have a rural residence, whereas individuals working for public and private organizations (such as manual or white-collar workers) are most likely to be derived from an urban milieu. Similarly, there are relatively high correlations between ethnicity and female participation in the labor force (.711), matrimonial antecedents (.238), age at marriage (.274), and fertility (.223). High correlations between independent variables make it necessary to exclude some of them from the analysis, and the variables eliminated are those whose contribution has been accounted for by another factor, namely that with which it is highly correlated.

The results of this analysis are presented in Table 48.

Conjugal Relations

The question pertaining to the handling of familial resources includes four possible answers. There may be two separate budgets, one handled by the husband and the other by the wife. Alternatively, there may be one single budget, handled by the husband, by the wife, or by both. As indicated earlier, our analysis enables us to determine whether the groups of persons indicating any one of the four solutions present a cluster of highly distinctive characteristics. The answer to this question is positive. Although taken separately many of our independent variables are positively associated with one of these four answers, the introduction of all of them into one single equation reveals that only ethnicity and, to a minor extent, urbanization contribute significantly to the variance of the distribution. Furthermore, there are no significant differences between the results obtained on the population at large and on the subsample of senior co-wives. In all cases, urbanization and ethnicity *best* enable us to predict which population is more likely to have separate male and female resources. While a substantial majority of Abouré have two budgets the number of Bété families with two budgets is more limited. In brief, financial autonomy is most characteristic of Abouré rural households.

Table 48

Results of Discriminant Function Analysis

	Total Sample	Senior Co-wives only
Handling of Familial Resources		
DF (3 and 1401)		(3 and 635)
Rao's V		
Ethnicity	2847.94	1771.58
Urbanization	23.08	5.55
Scaled Vectors		
Variance explained	2.03 (99.4%)	2.79 (99.6%)
Ethnicity	10.58	6.33
Urbanization	−0.07	−0.46
F (test of H_2)	353.61	304.03
Purchases of Respondents' Clothes		
DF (3 and 1401)		(3 and 635)
Rao's V		
Ethnicity	532.00	216.28
Urbanization	26.37	16.25
Blue-collar employment	0.95	1.70
Public employment	—	2.42
Scaled Vectors		
Variance explained	0.38 (94.8%)	0.36 (95.0%)
Ethnicity	15.84	10.99

Table 48—(Continued)

	Total Sample	Senior Co-wives only
Blue-collar employment	−0.11	0.05
Urbanization	−0.13	−1.71
Public employment		−0.40
F (test of H_2)	57.20	28.22
Domestic Power		
DF (2 and 1402)		(2 and 635)
Rao's V		
Ethnicity	213.53	152.61
Blue-collar employment	2.51	1.00
Urbanization	1.80	1.42
Public employment	1.67	1.57
Scaled Vectors		
Variance explained	0.16 (98.6%)	0.25 (98.7%)
Ethnicity	17.26	10.90
Urbanization	1.64	−0.91
Public employment	−0.70	0.27
Blue-collar employment	0.21	0.20
F (test of H_2)	26.67	18.59
Attitudes toward Adultery		
DF (2 and 1402)		(2 and 635)
Rao's V		
Ethnicity	218.49	115.73
Public employment	5.70	0.57

Blue-collar employment	0.77	2.46
Urbanization	—	0.91
White-collar employment	—	0.85
Scaled Vectors		
Variance explained	0.16 (98.2%)	0.19 (95.3%)
Ethnicity	17.25	11.22
Public employment	−0.71	0.20
Blue-collar employment	−0.03	−0.12
Urbanization	—	0.74
White-collar employment	—	−0.07
F (test of H_2)	36.21	11.80

Mealtime Etiquette

DF (2 and 1402)		(2 and 635)	
Rao's V			
Ethnicity	547.63	207.17	
Urbanization	62.95	27.58	
Polygyny	41.50		
Blue-collar employment	8.88	9.87	
Public employment	—	3.96	
Self-employment	—	0.17	
Scaled Vectors		(1)	(2)
Variance explained	0.43 (95.2%)	0.35 (87.0%)	0.05 (12.9%)
Ethnicity	15.04	10.23	−1.17
Urbanization	−3.11	2.58	4.39

Table 48—(Continued)

	Total Sample	Senior Co-wives only
Polygyny	7.67	— —
Blue-collar employment	−0.18	0.03 2.13
Self-employment	—	0.29 −2.67
Public employment	—	−0.21 −1.04
F (test of H_2)	78.25	24.37

Cooperation between Co-wives [a]

DF		(2 and 544)
Rao's V		
Ethnicity	—	135.88
Urbanization	—	7.94
Blue-collar employment	—	2.43
Scaled Vectors		
Variance explained	—	0.26 (95.2%)
Ethnicity	—	10.22
Urbanization	—	−1.12
Blue-collar employment	—	−0.47
F (test of H_2)		23.19

Post-Partum Leave [a]

DF (2 and 1187)		(2 and 547)
Rao's V		
Ethnicity	23.35	15.77
Residence	19.74	7.62
Previous matrimonial status	7.75	—

		(1)	(2)
Public employment	—		7.87
Age at marriage	4.61		1.37
Polygyny	3.75		—
Blue-collar employment	3.11		4.36
Fertility	0.18		3.34
Self-employment	—		0.51
Scaled Vectors			
Variance explained	0.06 (96.75%)	0.07 (82.1%)	0.02 (17.8%)
Residence	−5.86	−4.10	−0.22
Ethnicity	12.48	6.08	1.85
Public employment	−6.89	−0.99	−1.71
Fertility	−2.49	6.64	−6.15
Previous matrimonial status	−6.55		
Age at marriage	−5.19	−0.79	6.76
Blue-collar employment	0.96	1.28	−0.76
Self-employment		−0.30	−2.43
F (test of H_2)	4.97		3.21
Patterns of Weaning [a]			
DF (2 and 1187)		(2 and 552)	
Rao's V			
Ethnicity	411.02	177.50	
Residence	60.61	30.40	
Private-sector employment	6.27	—	
Polygyny	5.58	—	

Table 48—(Continued)

	Total Sample	Senior Co-wives only
Blue-collar employment	—	0.15
Public employment	—	0.14
Patterns of Weaning (cont.)		
Scaled Vectors		
Variance explained	0.43 (99.7%)	0.36 (93.4%)
Ethnicity	14.08	9.78
Residence	4.07	2.90
Private-sector employment	−1.48	—
Polygyny	3.28	—
Public employment	—	−0.24
Blue-collar employment	—	−0.04
F (test of H_2)	58.59	25.07
Demands Imposed upon Children [a]		
DF (2 and 1187)		(2 and 544)
Rao's V		
Participation in labor force	31.37	13.37
Residence	14.86	3.27
Age at marriage	7.23	8.95
Fertility	2.95	—
Blue-collar employment	1.27	1.96
Polygyny	0.16	—
Public employment	—	0.11

Scaled Vectors	(1)	(2)	(1)	(2)
Variance explained	0.05 (85.9%)	0.008 (14.1%)	0.05 (78.4%)	0.01 (21.7%)
Residence	7.27	3.50	−3.28	3.04
Public employment	—	—	−0.33	0.27
Blue-collar employment	−0.08	2.11	0.10	2.28
Participation in labor force	11.30	7.28	8.92	−2.59
Fertility	7.48	−3.10	—	—
Polygyny	0.89	−5.62	—	—
Age at marriage	−6.66	12.38	6.64	6.09
F (test of H_2)	5.65		3.08	

Punishments [a]

	(1)		(2)
DF (2 and 1187)			(2 and 544)
Rao's V			
Fertility	66.61		5.83
Participation in labor force	43.17		30.52
Residence	26.08		11.76
Polygyny	5.28		—
Blue-collar employment	2.34		1.96
Age at marriage	1.92		—
Previous matrimonial status	0.66		1.61
Public employment	—		0.16

Scaled Vectors	(1)	(2)	(1)	(2)
Variance explained	0.08 (59.0%)	0.05 (40.2%)	0.09 (83.4%)	0.01 (16.1%)

Table 48—(Continued)

	Total Sample		Senior Co-wives only	
Residence	−6.21	−3.79	−3.42	5.67
Public employment	—	—	−0.14	−0.95
Blue-collar employment	0.53	0.87	−0.96	−0.42
Participation in labor force	10.18	−25.07	6.60	−0.08
Polygyny	3.57	−6.40	—	—
Previous matrimonial status	3.00	−.048	−2.82	1.50
Age at marriage	−4.48	−.069		
F (test of H₂)	11.69		5.00	

NOTE: The F ratios indicated are significant at the .0001 level.
ª The N's are smaller than in the previous table because the No Answers have been eliminated. For the last four indicators, the childless respondents have also been eliminated.

An examination of the three modes of clothes purchase for the respondents yields similar results. There are significant differences between the characteristics of the persons who gave each of the three possible answers. Ethnicity, urbanization, and occupational status are the only significant contributors to the general variance of the overall population. The households in which the decision to make such purchases is an exclusively male privilege are most likely to be Bété and least likely to be headed by a blue-collar worker or to live in an urban residence. There are slight divergences in the profile of the subsample of senior co-wives. Public employment is a significant contributor to the variance of the responses given by this particular subpopulation and is, indeed, a negative predictor of the male privileges in this regard. We can see here that polygyny acts as an intervening variable and that there are some variations between the responses of monogamous and polygynous households.

There are three distinctive types of responses to be examined with regard to domestic power structure. The wife may yield in most cases, she may dominate the husband, or there may be a certain equalitarianism in their relations. The equation introducing all of our independent variables shows that there are significant differences between these three groups of answers. Once more the significant contributors to the variance are ethnicity, urbanization, and the two types of occupational status. As in the previous case, blue-collar employment is a better predictor than either farming or white-collar work, and this confirms our view that the additional restraints caused by urbanization are as important determinants of familial behavior as are the additional opportunities accompanying environmental changes. The families in which the domestic power of the wife is maximal are most likely to be Abouré; they are also more likely to be derived from an urban environment, but their heads are least likely to be engaged in public services. There are no differences between the nature and the relative value of the contributors to the variance of the distribution of answers given by the entire population and given by the senior co-wives solely.

Attitudes toward adultery can be divided into three groups. Individuals may choose a single-standard rule; they may alternatively choose a double-standard rule emphasizing the importance of male or female responsibilities. The equation introducing all independent variables shows that there are significant differences in the characteristics of the groups of persons giving one of the three responses. The significant contributors to the general variance are ethnicity, blue-collar employment, and participation in public services. The women in favor of a single-standard rule are most frequently Abouré, with husbands engaged in nonmanual occupations or in the public services. There are, however, certain differences between the overall population and the subsample of senior co-wives. Urbanization and white-collar employment which do not enter in the variance of the distribution of the attitudes characteristic of the entire population become significant contributors when the subsample of polygynous families is taken into consideration. Changes both in the nature of the contributors and in their relative value suggests that polygyny acts as an intervening variable in the question treated here.

As we could have predicted, however, the significance of polygyny as a determinant of conjugal relations is maximal with regard to the institutionalization of male preeminence and hence with regard to mealtime etiquette. First, in this case, type of marriage is a significant contributor to the variance observable on the general population, and segregation is most likely to occur in polygynous families. In addition, the values of the contributions made by various forms of occupational statuses are proportionately higher for the distribution of polygynous families than for that of the overall population.

All of these points confirm most of our previous analyses. Ethnicity is by far the most significant determinant of conjugal relations which are also influenced by social differentiation and urbanization. We know, consequently, that contrasts between families characterized by differing types of marriages depend upon the cultural, ecological, and economic characteristics of the environment in which they live. The distinction between types of marriages is in itself limited in scope and importance. It is obviously an important predictor of mealtime etiquette, and it may also alter (although moderately) the terms of the influence exerted by major determinants of familial organization.

Relations between Co-wives

We have seen that wives may raise their children (1) independently of one another, (2) under the supervision of the senior co-wife, or (3) jointly with a system of rotation. There are significant differences in the characteristics of the subgroups of co-wives who adopt each one of these solutions. Once more ethnicity and occupational status are the most significant contributors to the variance of the populations studied. The authority of senior co-wives along these lines is most characteristic of Bété polygynous families and least characteristic of the households of blue-collar individuals. The predictive value of the first factor is significantly higher than that of the second.

Relations between Wives and their Families of Origin

The subgroups of answers considered here are the following: women who have not taken any post-partum leave, women who have left their husband's residence for less than a month, and women who have done so for more than one month. Although significant, differences between these three groups are by far more limited than those observed earlier. Further, there is both an increase in the number of contributors to the variance of this particular distribution, and a decline in their respective saliences. Thus, ethnicity and social change remain significant predictors of the answers to this particular question, but their differentiating power is less apparent than with regard to conjugal relations. At the same time, this particular pattern of behavior is also influenced both by the position initially occupied by the respondents in the field of eligibles and by the number of children that they have borne. Both an early marriage and previous matrimonial experiences prevent women from taking long post-partum leaves, and an increase in the number of children has the same effect. Most important, the frequency and the duration of such leaves are also determined by matrimonial status and senior co-wives are most unlikely to take advantage of this institution.

The significance of polygyny in this regard is not only evidenced by the fact that it enters in the equation accounting for the variance of the distribution of the entire population but also by the fact that the nature and the value of contributors to the variance differ as between the total sample and the subsample of co-wives.

Child-Rearing Practices

Patterns of weaning appear to be simultaneously determined by cultural norms, urbanization, matrimonial status of respondents, and occupational position of the husband. Late weaning is most characteristic of Bété rural senior co-wives, but least characteristic of women whose husbands are engaged in the private sector of the economy. In addition, it should be noted that the patterns of nursing prevailing among senior co-wives are affected by specific factors. Weaning is most likely to occur early among women married to blue-collar workers and to public servants.

The demands imposed upon children have been divided into three categories: (1) respect for parents, (2) participation in domestic chores, and (3) academic achievement. Differences between the selected characteristics of each group of respondents are significantly lower than those observed earlier. Parental demands are not influenced by cultural norms but rather by structural factors such as family size (both through an increase in the number of wives and children), and female participation in the labor force.

As far as the entire population is concerned, the relative emphasis put upon academic achievement varies as a positive function of urbanization. It is also most typical of economically active women, but least typical of women who married early and whose husbands are manual workers.

Not only does type of marriage enter as a significant contributor to the variance of the overall sample along these lines, but there are differences in the nature and the importance of the contributors for the entire population and for senior co-wives solely. Among the latter, the stress attached to academic achievement is most characteristic of non-active respondents who married early, but least typical of those who are derived from a rural environment and whose husbands are working for the public sector of the economy.

Lastly, we have divided the types of sanctions used by the women interviewed here into three categories: punishments which are expressive in nature, physical sanctions, and others. The significant contributors to the variance of this particular indicator can be entered into three categories: (1) those reflecting the structural organization of the family (fertility, type of marriage, and economic independence of women), (2) those related to social change (urbanization and occupational differentiation), and (3) those related to the position of the respondents in the field of eligibles (age at marriage and matrimonial background). There are marked differences between the contributors to the variance of the answers of the entire population and of the senior co-wives solely. Social-expressive punishments tend to most frequently characterize women who have many children, who have at least another co-wife, who have been previously married, and who have married a man presently engaged in a manual occupation. Alternatively, such sanctions are most typical of non-active senior co-wives and least typical of those who live in rural areas, have many children, have been previously married, and

349

whose husbands participate in governmental and administrative services.

To conclude this section, the discriminant function analysis has shown that:

1. The distributions of conjugal relations and of child-rearing practices are somewhat independent. Conjugal relations are overwhelmingly determined by cultural factors and, to a certain extent, by the various forms of social change. Furthermore, there seems to be a close association between the relations that a woman establishes with her husband and those that she maintains with her co-wives. A high dependence and subordination toward husbands is accompanied by competitive feelings between co-wives. In contrast, the determinants of child-rearing practices are more numerous, less significant, and less culture-bound. Types of social control and demands (as measured here) are affected by the various facets of the matrimonial status of a woman but appear to be independent of the cultural orientations of each people analyzed.

2. The influence of social change is not necessarily cumulative. Conjugal relations and child-rearing practices are affected not only by variations in the level of exposure and the level of opportunities made available to familial actors, but also by variations in the additional restraints that they face as a consequence of environmental change.

3. Type of marriage seems to be a more important determinant of the techniques of socialization used by married women than of the distribution of domestic authority and power among adult actors, and this suggests that further explorations of the contrasts between monogamy and polygyny should be concerned mainly with child-rearing practices.

Final Remarks

In the introduction to this book, we argued that an examination of polygynous arrangements necessarily leads to a reevaluation of the universality of the nuclear family. Does this particular group constitute an invariant basic form of social organization from which further kin and other social elaborations develop or does its emergence depend alternatively on the presence of certain structural arrangements at the level of the society at large?[2]

Given the fact that the nuclear family is defined as a social system consisting of three positions (husband-father, wife-mother, and offspring-sibling), its universality may be evaluated in the context of two distinct theoretical frameworks: functions and role structures.

Universality of the Functions of the Nuclear Family

The nuclear family may be considered universal insofar as it is irreplaceable in the fulfillment of certain basic social functions. There are, however, disagreements as to the nature and the number of these basic prerequisites. For Murdock, there are four societal imperatives: sexual, economic, reproductive, and educational functions are believed to be universally placed in the hands of the nuclear family.[3] Parsons holds more restricted views and argues that this particular unit is universal only in regard to the exclusive role that it plays in the socialization of children and in the socio-psychological integration of adult individuals.[4] Regardless of their differences, such theoreticians treat as abnormalities societies or subpopulations within which basic societal imperatives are fulfilled by institutions other than the nuclear family. Such situations are consid-

2. For a full discussion, see M. Zelditch, "Cross-cultural Analysis of Family Structure," in *Handbook of Marriage and the Family*, ed. Harold Christensen (Chicago: Rand McNally, 1964), pp. 477ff.

3. See P. Murdock, *Social Structure* (New York: Macmillan, 1949), p. 10.

4. See Talcott Parsons, "The American Family: Its Relation to Personality and the Social Structure," in *Family, Socialization and the Interaction Process*, ed. Talcott Parsons and Robert Bales (Glencoe, Ill.: Free Press, 1955), pp. 3–33.

ered both accidental and temporary, and, if they should last, the entire society or subgroup is doomed to disintegration.

To prove that the nuclear family successfully fulfills certain basic social functions is, however, not sufficient to demonstrate its universality. It must be also established that such functions cannot be suitably performed by other institutions. A growing amount of evidence shows that the role of the nuclear family along these lines is not exclusive.[5]

In the present study, we have demonstrated that the forms of economic cooperation between conjugal partners differ markedly between the two peoples compared. Variations in the degree of absorption of married women into their affinal group condition both the significance of the economic contribution of the nuclear family as a whole and the form and extent of the cooperation between conjugal partners along these lines. The preeminence of the nuclear family in the field of economic activities is more marked among the Bété than among the Abouré. Similarly, the extent to which nuclear families exclusively carry out the functions of socialization is not alike for these two ethnic groups, and seems to vary both with residential arrangements and with relative degree of modernization. At the same time our data also suggest that the presence of more than one wife-mother modifies both the economic and educational functions of Abouré and Bété nuclear families. In addition it affects the mechanisms of socio-psychological integration of the individual familial actors. Indeed, variations in type of marriage are accompanied in both cases by corresponding variations in the style of emotional interaction developed between spouses and between each one of them and their relatives. All these observations lead us to reject assumptions concerning the universal nature of the functions performed by the nuclear family.

5. See R. Adams, "An Inquiry in the Nature of the Family," in *Selected Studies in Marriage and the Family*, ed. Robert Winch and L. Goodman (New York: Holt, Rinehart and Winston, 1968), pp. 44–57.

Universality of the Role Structure of Nuclear Families

Hypotheses about the universality of such a unit also imply that the number and the specifications of roles found in the nuclear family remain identical in a variety of cultural contexts. Does this mean then that we should treat both polygynous and matrifocal families as abnormalities because they do not have the proper number of specified familial positions? Or should we take the position, with Adams, that they constitute alternative stable forms of familial organization corresponding to the presence of certain conditions at the community level?[6]

The assumption that there are alternative forms of familial organizations rests, however, upon the postulate that there are more basic elements of social interaction. The only two universal basic elements of interaction are: (1) the sexual dyad, based on the relationship between men and women, which can be institutionalized to become the marital dyad, and (2) the maternal dyad, which concerns the interdependence between a mother and her child. These two dyads are universal in the sense that they are biological as well as social. Yet since both of these are unstable and temporary, the survival of larger human groups requires the combination of such dyads and their integration into larger wholes. The wife-mother being the sole common element to the two basic dyads analyzed here, it is easy enough to see how their combination may lead to the formation of the nuclear family with the corollary emergence of the paternal dyad. The occurrence of such a combination does not, however, imply its perpetuation. Indeed, for certain functions and under certain circumstances, the combination of elemental dyads may lead to other forms of familial organization.

6. Certain authors distinguish polygynous families from nuclear families (for example, see Paul Bohannan, *Social Anthropology* [New York: Holt, Rinehart and Winston, 1963]). Others do not make such distinctions (see Zelditch, "Cross-cultural Analysis of Family Structure," p. 467).

Our first task in this book has been, accordingly, to identify what forms of community and what aspects of the social structure favor particular combinations of the elemental dyads. Thus we have examined how variations in the economic, social, political, and residential organization of African societies are accompanied by corresponding variations in the forms of familial organization and, more specifically, by variations in the incidence of polygynous arrangements. The grouping of more than one marital dyad and more than one maternal dyad within the same familial unit seems, however, to reflect the presence of heterogeneous social factors. Given the variety of functions served by plural marriage, we can expect disparities in both the distribution of this institution among African peoples and the recruitment patterns of the different categories of actors.

These observations lead us to reformulate the problems posed by the universality of the nuclear family. First, this basic form of familial organization may be defined as universal in the sense that the distributions of its major characteristics have limited variances. For example, this universality might be established, when it is demonstrated that marital and parental roles remain uniform in spite of disparities in the combination patterns of elemental dyads. Disregarding the influence of ethnicity, we have suggested that the organization of both monogamous and polygynous families in the Ivory Coast is alike and that there are marked similarities in the patterns of attitudes and behavior of single spouses and senior co-wives. Yet, as we have shown, these similarities are misleading.

Second, we may evaluate the differences in the distributions of the dominant characteristics of the nuclear family and in those of non-nuclear familial organizations. The universality of the nuclear family may be established insofar as the role structures of this group differ significantly from those observed in non-nuclear units and insofar as these differences remain constant across cultures. In this latter context there arises the question of whether we should lump polygynous and matrifocal families together in the same category and hypothesize that all forms of familial organization characterized by the presence of more women than men regardless of the members involved present similar structures. The presence of a different dyad—two co-wives—may modify the effects of the excess of female roles on the socio-psychological distance separating familial actors from one another. Accordingly, this book has been concerned only with variations in type of marriage and with an examination of the degree to which contrasts between monogamy and polygyny are either constant across cultures or vary with (1) the distributional and functional characteristics of plural marriage and, hence, (2) the dominant traits of the peoples analyzed.

The Significance of Contrasts between Monogamy and Polygyny

Universality of role structures implies universality in patterns of division of labor and of authority structures. However, as far as division of labor is concerned, it has been demonstrated that although certain tasks are universally masculine, virtually none is always feminine. Furthermore, there are also significant variations in the number and nature of tasks which are performed jointly by both spouses or indifferently by either.[7] Our problem is to determine the degree to which such variations can be uniformly accounted for by disparities in the number of wives. Indeed, the effects of variations in this number may be universal or may, alternatively, operate only within discontinuous cultural frameworks. Although our study has not been directly concerned with an examination of this question, it seems possible to suggest that in the economic sphere the presence of more than one wife in basic Abouré and Bété familial groups accentuates contrasts in the rules underlying the division of labor in these two peoples. We have suggested that polygyny reinforces the degree of social absorption of Bété wives but minimizes that of their Abouré counterparts.

7. See Zelditch, "Cross-cultural Analysis of Family Structure," p. 481.

In short, variations in type of marriage do not directly modify the existing principles of familial division of labor. Rather, these principles are primarily cultural in nature, and polygyny is just a mechanism to facilitate the realization of cultural expectations.

Our study has been concerned mainly with an examination of economic and educational authority structures as well as with an investigation of the mechanisms of socio-psychological integration of married women. We have demonstrated that contrasts between monogamous and polygynous families with respect to these three dimensions are not stable but are influenced by the factors that we have partially identified.

First, plural marriage serves certain manifest functions in each of the two ethnic groups studied. Contrasts between monogamous and polygynous families are likely to be maximal when both the actual recruitment pattern of senior co-wives and the actual definition of their present role follow normative prescriptions. Conversely, any deviation from these norms tends to minimize and obscure the significance of the distinction between the roles of single spouses and senior co-wives. Yet, the specific demands imposed upon senior co-wives are limited in scope and affect only a limited number of behaviors and attitudes.

Regardless of marriage type, all families are influenced by other common norms and expectations. While families may adopt innovative practices or fail to meet the minimal demands imposed upon them, the effects of such positive and negative deviations from existing norms are not necessarily alike on single spouses and on senior co-wives. In certain instances, the presence of more than one incumbent in the position of wife-mother dilutes the consequences of such deviations, and monogamous families respond more intensely than do their polygynous counterparts to the strains and tensions resulting from discrepancies between cultural expectations and actual patterns of behavior and attitudes. In other instances, the presence of more than one wife enhances the visibility of these discrepancies, and polygynous families react more drastically than do their monogamous counterparts to the ensuing pressures.

Variations in the magnitude and the direction of contrasts between monogamy and polygyny also depend upon variations in the relative salience of norms concerning conjugal roles. Whenever such norms have a low salience, it seems possible to suggest that senior co-wives will be proportionately more *rewarded* than will single spouses for conforming with the demands imposed upon them, particularly when the incidence of polygyny remains limited. Conversely, an increase in the relative salience of conjugal norms should lead senior co-wives to be proportionately more severely *sanctioned* than single spouses would be for failing to meet the expectations attached to their roles, especially whenever the incidence of polygynous arrangements is high. In brief, given the fact that plural marriage enhances the visibility of the senior co-wife and leads various classes of conjugal partners to compare their relative domestic positions, the outcomes of such comparisons are open and may weaken or strengthen the status of senior co-wives.

Having delineated the limits within which the magnitude and direction of the contrasts vary, we must still ascertain the determinants of such limits. Many wives, many powers. Indeed, it is impossible to draw uniform contrasts in the roles and statuses of single spouses and senior co-wives from distinctive ethnic backgrounds. Differences between types of marriages cannot be assessed cross-culturally but only within specific cultures. Thus, marriage enables men of the patriarchal Bété people to acquire both uxorial rights and rights in genetricem to their wives, but the importance of these rights is a direct function of the number of persons effectively controlled by the men. Ideally, polygyny is a mechanism which facilitates the fulfillment of male aspirations. At the same time, however, their senior co-wives are entitled to certain rewards in the

357

form of accentuated authority exerted over the other spouses of their husbands and over the children of the entire household.

In contrast, Abouré women must fulfill only a limited number of obligations toward their husbands, and plural marriage in such a context is an institution designed to alleviate some of the dysfunctions resulting from matrimonial arrangements. Although it facilitates the functioning of familial organizations by reducing the burden imposed on each wife, it also accentuates certain strains typical of matrilineal peoples by multiplying the networks of competition and interdependence between husbands and their wives' brothers.

In brief, plural marriage tends to reinforce the specific cultural orientations which prevail among the two peoples. Accordingly, differences between the responses of Abouré and Bété senior co-wives tend to be greater than differences between the single spouses from these two peoples. At the same time, similarities in the contrasts between Abouré monogamous and polygynous families on the one hand and between the corresponding Bété families on the other are necessarily limited. These similarities may have three separate origins. First, they can reflect uniformities in the level of resources required of men who are able to acquire an additional wife, and we have indeed observed that all senior co-wives adopt similar attitudes toward the occupation—and hence the wealth —of their husbands. Second, they may reflect the fact that plural marriage maximizes distance between familial actors and is a uniform mechanism for facilitating male preeminence (for example, mealtime etiquette in polygynous families seems to be uniform). Third, these similarities may result from discrepancies between actual and ideal patterns of recruitment of individual actors or between the actual and ideal functions performed by plural marriage within each cultural context.

Thus, we hope that we have circumscribed the reasons why neither the nuclear family nor the contrast between this and other forms of basic familial organizations are universal. Variations in community arrangements are accompanied by corresponding variations in the combination patterns of elemental dyads, which in turn are associated with variations both in the recruitment of the incumbents of the dyads and in the styles of interaction that these incumbents develop vis-à-vis one another. Cross-cultural differences in this regard reflect not only disparities in the distribution of certain crucial institutions but also qualitative discontinuities in the models underlying these institutions. It is not only *what* peoples do which counts but also *why* they do it. What is important are the rationalizations that individuals build up in order to stabilize the outcome of their dealings with their peers, their subordinates, and their superordinates.

This type of analysis has nevertheless been static and has not taken into account the variety of influences that social change exerts upon the functioning of familial organizations. Given the complex network of interdependence among community structures, basic forms of familial organization, recruitment patterns of familial actors, and their styles of interaction, the problem remains to determine whether urbanization and social differentiation accentuate or minimize existing strains, whether they create new tensions and lead to a universal rearrangement of familial structures.

In the short term, we have suggested that participation in urban and modern structures is not necessarily associated with an immediate decline in the incidence of polygynous arrangements. It is quite clear, however, that the purposes underlying this institution are changing and that such changes are in turn associated with variations in recruitment patterns.

Because of the increased social differentiation prevailing in urban centers, each familial system is confronted with new tasks, new choices, and new restraints. Our data have suggested that the responses of familial systems to this new situation depend upon: (1) their position in the life cycle, (2) the changes in the relative resources that they can make available to each actor, and (3) their antecedents and the expectations prevailing in their culture of origin. Our task has been to identify the circumstances under which urbanization maximizes or minimizes contrasts in the organization of monogamous and polygynous families and reduces or accentuates the importance of ethnic cleavages along these lines.

There is no doubt that urbanization and industrialization alter the role-bargaining processes within familial organization by modifying the control that elders want and are able to maintain on both existing and new opportunities.[8] There is also no doubt, however, that the effects of such modifications are not unequivocal. The push of the traditional familial underdogs (the women, the junior members of a lineage or of a family, the young, etc.) is not necessarily exerted with the same intensity and in a single direction. We have suggested that the introduction of new ideologies and new opportunities enables certain specific categories of familial actors both to destroy the familial relations which are most costly to them and to restore or strengthen those which are most rewarding. Thus, the increasing equality of women does not necessarily lead them to be closer to their husbands and to move in the direction of a Western nuclear family. Rather it enables them to strengthen their domestic position and to more successfully oppose the traditional limitations of their status.

To conclude, the effects of urbanization and social differentiation on familial relations are two-fold: First, they change the form, the level and the distribution patterns of the resources available to familial groups and actors, and it is quite clear that these changes will first affect groups and individuals who have nothing to lose in abandoning preexisting patterns of attitudes and behaviors.[9] Second, it enhances both the choices that individuals can make and the limitations with which they are confronted regarding their life-style. Their aspirations and expectations are as much conditioned by anticipation of

8. See W. Goode, *World Revolution and Family Patterns* (New York: Free Press, 1963), first and last chapters.

9. *Ibid.*

360

new experiences to come as by attachment to the past. As a result, urbanization and social differentiation conjoin to limit even more seriously the universality of the role of the nuclear family. They create new cleavages in types of familial organization without necessarily minimizing the importance of previous disparities. Indeed, the significance of contrasts between monogamy and polygyny is greater in urban than in rural and traditional areas. Many wives, many powers; this is particularly true in societies touched by rapid social change.

Afterword

It is not sufficient merely to evaluate the positive and negative conclusions that the present study has enabled us to reach. We must also analyze the factors which have limited the validity of our exercise.

First and most important, there is more than one difference in the actual organization of the Abouré and the Bété. To be sure, we can suggest that their distinct types of descent lead them to have different attitudes about divorce, brideprice, fertility, and plural marriage, and that, in turn, these distinct attitudes are associated with marked contrasts in their respective familial organizations. Yet, the political organizations of these peoples are dissimilar, and differences in the form and level of political integration may also affect patterns of familial interaction in ways that we cannot ascertain. Further, the distance separating the natural habitat of each of these two peoples from the focus of modernizing forces is not the same. Accordingly, their respective participation in the modern sector of the economy is uneven, and thus the interaction between the initial organization of these peoples and their present involvement in modern structures remains problematic.

Second, we have analyzed synchronically the effects of social change as if cross sectional and longitudinal analyses are interchangeable. Yet, we cannot be sure that present differences between rural and urban segments of population reflect the changes produced by urbanization at the individual level. In

362

short, we are not sure that contrasts between urban and rural populations are parallel to those of the attitudes of an individual *before* and *after* his participation in urban structures.

Third, we have examined, in the context of polygynous households, only the answers of senior co-wives. A complete assessment of the contrast between monogamy and polygyny also requires an examination of the attitudes of husbands, junior co-wives, and children. Our view of the organization of families characterized by plural marriage is certainly incomplete.

Fourth, we have not really ascertained the exact nature of the relationship between the monogamous and polygynous respondents and their familial environment. Thus, we know that the two ethnic groups compared follow the same rules concerning residential arrangements. We do not know, however, whether there are variations in such arrangements. How many relatives live in the vicinity of the respondents? What is the familial position of such relatives? How many of them belong to the husband's kin group and how many to the wife's descent group? Are there any variations in such distributions between urban and rural populations? What is the frequency and the object of communications between such relatives and our respondents?

Fifth, we are unable to decide whether contrasts between monogamy and polygyny are permanent, or whether they reflect differences in the life cycles of individuals.

In brief, we can see that this study has opened a veritable Pandora's box, and we end our analysis with more questions than when we began.

What Remains to be Done

In trying to resolve these issues, there remains a choice between two strategies. On the one hand, we could return to the places where we conducted this study and start a more ethnographic investigation of monogamous and polygynous families. This would enable us to more clearly understand the relations between the two types of families and their immediate social and physical environment. More important, it would also enable us to explore the real nature of ethnicity and to have a better understanding of the models developed by individuals to rationalize their daily patterns of interaction with their partners, their co-wives, their relatives and affines, and their own children. We should then be in a better position to understand *why* peoples behave in particular ways.

On the other hand, we could duplicate this study in another environment and measure the degree to which we obtain comparable results. We would then be able to isolate the independent variables which are really irrelevant to our examination of familial organizations. This strategy is indeed the logical conclusion of an initial controlled comparison. We must establish not only that the contrast between monogamy and polygyny changes with variations in certain social arrangements but also that this contrast remains constant despite variations in other social arrangements.

Appendix A

Methodology

The exclusive use of an ethnographic approach would be inappropriate for this study of polygyny. Based upon participant observation or upon the interview of selected informants, this approach intends to define the models of social relationships prevailing in the society under study. The use of such techniques rests upon the implicit assumption that the people analyzed are culturally homogenous and that there are no important spatial or temporal variations in the models used to describe their main social forms. The gathering of ethnographic data constitutes a necessary condition for a complete understanding of interpersonal ties within an underdeveloped area, and provides an indispensable historical background. But this procedure does not accurately depict the situation in underdeveloped countries which have been increasingly exposed to foreign norms. The increased degree of social differentiation justifies the use of survey research techniques which will add essential complementary information to the data provided by more traditional approaches.

For the present study, the interviews of 1,771 women are used. Of these, 745 belong to the matrilineal Abouré society and the remaining 1,026 to the patrilineal Bété society.[1] For such sources of data, the reliability of the interview procedure must be considered. The nationality and sex of the researcher constituted insurmountable handicaps in establishing any rapport with many African women. In the rural areas of the Ivory Coast, the immediate reaction

---

1. The discrepancy between the number of interviews used by the author here and in chapter 10 of *The City in Modern Africa*, ed. H. Miner (New York: Prager, 1967), results from variations in the number of farmers used in each case.

of a housewife to the arrival of a European man in the village is often to disappear into her compound.[2] Even when the foreigner has been tentatively accepted by the elders of the village, women are still likely to display attitudes of subtle hostility. Under the circumstances, and since I was teaching sociology and psychology in the Ecole Normale Menagere (Teacher's College of Home Economics) in Abidjan, I asked fifteen female students to help me collect the information I needed. They agreed, and we started a pilot study of child-rearing practices among the mothers of children attending school in the vicinity. After discussing with my students the results of this pretest, the validity of the questions asked, and their translation, we jointly constructed the questionnaire used for the present study. (This questionnaire is reproduced here as Appendix B.)

The ethnic affiliations and the age of the interviewers could have affected the reliability of the data they gathered. Abouré students conducted the majority of the interviews in the Abouré areas with the assistance of girls who belonged to somewhat similar tribes (Agni, Baoulé, and Attié). For the Bété region, I asked Malinké girls who lived in that area to perform the greater part of the work. To be sure, relationships between Bété and Malinké are ambivalent. Nonetheless, these girls mastered the Bété languages quite well, and they were helped by Kru and Abbé girls—members of tribes whose social organization does not differ drastically from that of the Bété. All of the interviewers were over eighteen years old and were approaching adulthood, so they could be looked upon as the age equivalents of the younger sisters of the women interviewed. To clarify the interviewer's role in each village in which the survey was to take place, the goals of the inquiry were explained as thoroughly as possible to the elders, with the help of the local district officer.

Second, one may question the validity of responses to questionnaires in an African context.[3] To be sure, answers to questions constitute verbal behavior

2. The influence of the sex and color of the investigator on the relations that he can develop with the various members of the peoples being studied are eloquently suggested by E. Smith Bowen who shows, in her novel *Return to Laughter* (New York: Doubleday, 1964), that access to African women, even for a European woman, depends upon the good will of the senior elders of the village.

3. Thus far, the theoretical problems associated with the use of questionnaires in Africa have hardly been seriously discussed. There have nevertheless been recent attempts to systematically analyze this problem. See, for example, Robert C. Mitchell, "The Problems and Possibilities of Measuring Social Attitudes in African Social Surveys" (paper presented at the 1966 African Studies Association meetings, Bloomington, Indiana).

366

which may be quite remote from the patterns of social behavior that these answers purport to reflect. It should be noted, however, that neither the interviewers nor the interviewees were aware of the nature of the contrasts which were expected. Under these conditions, I have no reason to believe that any biases introduced by either interviewers or interviewees have contributed to the differences observed in the responses of the various ethnic and residential categories. Should they exist, these biases would tend to reduce the significance of existing contrasts.

The third uncertainty raised by the use of survey research techniques concerns the choice of questions—the vast bulk of which provided fixed-answer alternatives in order to simplify the task of the interviewers. The questions were either taken from survey materials already used elsewhere in Africa or else were based on particularly significant observations made by ethnographers concerning the two tribes. As indicated above, the use of survey research in Africa presupposes the existence of ethnographic data; the use of survey techniques leads only to the measurement of variability with and among patterns reported by ethnographers.

The fourth problem raised by this technique is that of sampling. Interviews were gathered in a large number of villages, in two larger towns (Gagnoa in the Bété area, Grand Bassam in the Abouré area), and in Abidjan, the capital. In constructing the sample, it was assumed that patterns of response would be affected by the type of community being sampled and that responses would be more variable in larger centers than in the smaller villages. It was, therefore, decided to interview a limited number of women in each of a large number of small villages, and, conversely, to increase the size of the sample in a more limited number of larger townships. In each village and in Gagnoa and Grand Bassam, women were randomly selected from the census data sheets. In Abidjan, respondents were drawn from a list of owners and tenants which had been established by the Institut Francais d'Afrique Noire (Table 49).[4]

The fifth and last problem concerns the use of a "one-shot technique," and the difficulties of equating the results of synchronic and diachronic analyses. Indeed, it is not certain that the differences between the patterns of attitudes prevailing among manual and white-collar workers are comparable to the changes experienced by individuals who climb the various rungs of the occupational ladder. More important for our purpose, it can be argued that our

4. I would like to express here my gratitude to E. Bernus of IFAN, who gave me kind and efficient help at the time.

Table 49

Distribution of Women Interviewed
by Residence and Marriage Type

Abouré

	No. of Sample Units	No. of Single Spouses	No. of Senior Co-wives
Rural areas	4	305	206
Semi-urbanized areas	1	57	40
Urbanized areas	1	102	35
Total	6	464	281

Bété

Rural areas	45	300	323
Semi-urbanized areas	1	25	28
Urbanized areas	1	223	127
Total	47	548	478

comparison between polygynous and monogamous families may be spurious in the sense that the contrasts observed may reflect differing positions in the life cycle of familial groups rather than differing types of matrimonial arrangements.

The respondents are in all cases the wives of monogamous men and the senior co-wives of polygynous families. Two caveats must therefore be entered at this point: our analysis rests upon patterns of verbal answers, which do not necessarily reflect accurately the perceptions of senior co-wives, and these perceptions may be distorted in directions which are not controlled in the present analysis.

Appendix B

Questionnaire

1. Place where the interview is being taken.
   a. Is this your usual place of residence?
2. How old are you? (If the respondent does not know, ask her if she knows how old she was when the following events took place: [a] the beginning of the Second World War [1939], [b] the suppression of forced labor [1946], and [c] the opening of the canal between the lagoon and the sea [1951]. Do not try to guess her age.)
3. What is your religion?
4. What is your ethnic group of origin? (What people do you belong to?)
5. Have you attended school?
   a. *If no:* Do you know how to read and write French?
   b. *If yes:* Did you complete your primary education?
      Did you go beyond your primary education?
6. What is the occupation of your husband? (Indicate with precision, [a] the kind of job [the nature of his crop if a farmer], [b] the skill level, if necessary, and [c] the employer.)
7. What is your own occupation? (Note: For peoples living in villages, probe if women cultivate crops different from those grown by their husbands and if the returns of such crops belong to them.)
8. How many children have you had with your present husband?
9. How many wives does your husband have?
   a. *If more than one:* Are you the senior co-wife?
   b. *If answer to 9a is NO:* Can you lead me to the senior co-wife of

your husband? (If answer to 9a is NO, the interview is terminated.)

10. Is this the first time you ever were married?

    a. *If no:* How many times were you married before this present marriage?

11. What is your husband's ethnic group?

12. Was your husband born in the same village or the same neighborhood as you were?

    a. Was your husband raised in the same village or the same neighborhood as you were?

13. How did you meet your present husband for the first time?

    You were introduced—by your parents.

                    —by a paternal uncle or aunt.

                    —by a maternal uncle or aunt.

                    —by a brother or sister.

                    —by a cousin or a friend.

    You met—at school.

             —at the market.

             —at the movies.

             —in the street.

             —at some friend's.

    You (or your families) have always known one another.

    Other. (Describe how the meeting did take place.)

    No answer.

14. How old were you when you married for the first time?

    It was before your first period?

    It was right at the time of your first period?

    It was some time between 14 and 18?

    You were definitely over 18?

15. Do you think it was the proper age?

    It was too early?

    It was too late?

    No answer

16. Do you know how old your husband was when he married for the first time?

17. Do you think that:

    A husband should be much older than his wife?

    Husbands and wives should have the same age?

    This age question is not important?

370

No answer

18. Do you think that husbands and wives:

Should belong to the same ethnic group?

Should not belong to the same ethnic group?

May have the same or a different ethnic origin, it does not matter?

No answer

19. Can you tell us the two most important things that your marriage has brought you?

To be respected by people in your village or your neighborhood.

To have things on your own (house, clothes, garden, etc.).

To have pleasant contacts with your husband.

To have children.

To be free.

I did not gain anything in getting married.

I do not know.

20. Did your present husband have to pay a brideprice to your family?

a. *If yes:* What did the brideprice consist of?

21. To whom was the brideprice payed?

Your parents

Your maternal uncle

Your paternal uncle

Your brother

Some other person (Whom?)

Nobody

22. Did your husband give you personal gifts at the time of your wedding?

a. *If yes:* What were they?

23. Did your own family give you personal things at the time of the wedding?

a. *If yes:* What were they?

24. Does your husband go out at night without you (to go to the movies, to see friends and relatives, to play cards, etc.)?

Often

Once in a while

Never or almost never

25. Do you think it is proper for a husband to go out on his own?

a. *If yes:* Once in a while

Each time that he feels like it

26. What do you think is a worse domestic offense?

For a husband to have an affair with a girl friend?

For a woman to have an affair with a boy friend?

It does not make any difference. Both spouses should be equally faithful.

No answer

27. What do you think of the present occupation of your husband?

I do not care. It is not my business.

It is OK but I would like him to earn more money.

I want him to change jobs. (*If so:* To do what? Why?)

He has a good job and I am happy.

No answer

28. How do you manage with your husband as far as money is concerned?

Each of you has his or her own money.

Your husband is the one who keeps the money and he gives you what you need.

You are the one who keeps the money and you give your husband what he needs.

You have one common "kettle" and everybody takes from it the money he or she needs.

We have another arrangement. (What?)

No answer

29. Who makes the decision to buy new clothes for your husband

Husband

Wife

Husband and wife together

Either one

Somebody else (Who?)

30. Who makes the decision to buy new clothes for yourself?

Husband

Wife

Husband and wife together

Either one

Somebody else (Who?)

No answer

31. Who makes the decision to buy new clothes for your children?

Husband

Wife

Husband and wife together

Either one

Somebody else (Who?)

No answer

32. Who makes the decision to buy new clothes for the other persons living in your household?

    Husband
    Wife
    Husband and wife together
    Either one
    Somebody else (Who?)
    No answer

33. Who makes the decision to buy dishes, pots and pans, etc.?

    Husband
    Wife
    Husband and wife together
    Either one
    Somebody else (Who?)
    No answer

34. When somebody is sick in your family, who makes the decision to call for a doctor or to bring the patient to the hospital?

    Husband
    Wife
    Husband and wife together
    Either one
    Somebody else (Who?)
    No answer

35. Who has made the decision to live where you are now?

    Husband
    Wife
    Husband and wife together
    Either one
    Somebody else (Who?)
    No answer

36. Who makes the decision to visit relatives?

    Husband
    Wife
    Husband and wife together
    Either one
    Somebody else (Who?)
    No answer

37. Who has (will or should) decided whether children will attend school?

Husband

Wife

Husband and wife together

Either one

Somebody else (Who?)

No answer

38. Whom do you receive most often at your home?

Your husband's family (Who?)

Your own family (Who?)

Friends

Nobody

No answer

39. Whom do you visit most often?

Your husband's family (Who?)

Your own family (Who?)

Friends

Nobody

No answer

40. In every family there is always a certain amount of quarrels between spouses. In your own family who gives in most frequently?

Husband

Wife

Both

None

No answer

41. What do you quarrel most frequently about?

42. *For senior co-wives only:* In your household, who is in charge of the children?

43. *For senior co-wives only:* Would you say that your quarrels with other co-wives are very frequent?

Frequent

Once in a while

Rare

Very rare

No answer

44. *For senior co-wives only:* What is the most frequent quarrel among co-wives?

45. How do you ordinarily take your meals in your family?

Everybody sits together.

Your husband is the first one to be served.

Your husband and your sons are the first ones to be served.

You eat with your husband but the children eat after.

Other (What?)

No answer

46. There is a little story which is often discussed in Africa. If you were on a boat with your mother and your husband crossing a river and were the only person able to swim, whom would you save?

Your husband

Your mother

No answer

47. On the whole would you say that your marriage is:

Very satisfactory

Satisfactory

So-so

Unsatisfactory

Very unsatisfactory

No answer

48. Where did you give birth to your first-born child?

49. When did you stop breast-feeding your last-born child?

50. After the birth of your first-born child did you go to or did you stay with your own family?

   a. *If yes:* How long?

       Few days

       Week or so

       About a month

       More than a month

       No answer

51. How old was, will, or would your child be when you start disciplining him when he does not behave the way you expect him to?

52. What is the best solution for raising children?

Fathers should look after their sons and mothers after their daughters.

Fathers should look after all children.

Mothers should look after all children.

Father and mothers should look jointly after their children.

No answer

53. Where do (will, would) your children spend most of the time?

At your place

With your own parents

With your husband's parents

With somebody else (Who?)

No answer

54. Who in your family punishes children when:

They are dirty? (a)

They do not want to help? (b)

They are tardy and have no sense of time? (c)

They do not work well at school? (d)

They fight and quarrel with siblings or friends? (e)

They do not take proper care of things? (f)

	(a)	(b)	(c)	(d)	(e)	(f)
Husband						
Wife						
Together						
Either one						
Somebody else (Who?)						
Nobody						
No answer						

55. Do you punish a child who does not do what you expect him to do?

    a. *If yes:* How?

56. Does your husband punish a child who does not do what he expects him to do?

    a. *If yes:* How?

57. What is it that you consider most important to obtain from your children?

Respect for yourself and elders

Help and assistance in your chores

Adequate academic performance

Cleanliness

Stop fighting and quarrelling when asked

Others

No answer

58. What is it that you consider most difficult to obtain from your children?

Respect for yourself and elders

Help and assistance in your chores

Adequate academic performance

Cleanliness

Stop fighting and quarrelling when asked

Others

No answer

Index